Knowledge Integration

Antonie Jetter · Jeroen Kraaijenbrink
Hans-Horst Schröder · Fons Wijnhoven
(Editors)

Knowledge Integration

The Practice of Knowledge Management in Small and Medium Enterprises

With 53 Figures and 24 Tables

Physica-Verlag

A Springer Company

b 2828203

Dr. Antonie Jetter
Professor Dr. Hans-Horst Schröder
Chair for Business Administration
with Focus on Technology and Innovation Management (TIM)
RWTH Aachen University
Templergraben 64
52056 Aachen
Germany
jetter@tim.rwth-aachen.de
schroeder@tim.rwth-aachen.de

Jeroen Kraaijenbrink
Professor Dr. Fons Wijnhoven
University of Twente
School of Business,
Public Administration and Technology
P.O. Box 217
Drienerlolaan 5
7500 AE Enschede
The Netherlands
j.kraaijenbrink@utwente.nl
a.b.j.m.wijnhoven@utwente.nl

ISBN-10   3-7908-1586-1 Physica-Verlag Heidelberg New York
ISBN-13   978-3-7908-1586-3 Physica-Verlag Heidelberg New York

Cataloging-in-Publication Data applied for
Library of Congress Control Number: 2005934345

Physica is a part of Springer Science+Business Media

springeronline.com

© Physica-Verlag Heidelberg 2006
Printed in Germany

Cover-Design: Erich Kirchner, Heidelberg

SPIN 11423379   43/3153-5 4 3 2 1 0 – Printed on acid-free paper

Preface

Imagine Measure & Co, a two-person company creating optical measurement instruments for the graphical industry. Mark, the owner and founder of Measure & Co has a thorough background in measurement technology and has worked for years on his own. Lately, he has found a partner, Susan, who is experienced in commercial and marketing activities and takes care of customer relations and sales.

Although Mark and Susan together possess much of the knowledge that is needed to run their company, it is by far not sufficient. They need to stay informed about new measurement technologies, changing customer demands, changes in the printing industry, and so on, and so on. Moreover, they have to make sure that this knowledge is kept within their company and that they can apply it as well; a job that is extremely challenging in their dynamic industry. Thus, for Mark and Susan, it is important to manage their knowledge.

As this example shows, knowledge management (KM) is relevant for even an extremely small company like Measure & Co. Equally, or perhaps even more so, KM is relevant for thousands and thousands of other small and medium sized enterprises (SMEs) all around the globe. In particular, SMEs in high-tech areas, characterized by complex and dynamic environments, are affected. However, if we look around us in the literature on KM, we see that most of it has a strong focus on large or even very large multi-national companies. Much has been written on, for example, knowledge strategies, intra- and interdepartmental knowledge sharing, KM information systems, and on KM in dispersed organizations. To what extent does this apply to Measure & Co?

We see the bias towards large firms also in the development of commercial KM solutions. How should Measure & Co make use of, for example, groupware, intranets, data mining, semantic networks, knowledge maps, and content management systems? Yet, for Mark and Susan there remains knowledge to manage.

This book addresses the challenges of managing knowledge in SMEs and in particularly those SMEs that operate in high-tech sectors. As illustrated in the example of Measure & Co, these challenges are different than those for large companies, not the least because SMEs are much more dependent on their environment than many large companies. Therefore, this book introduces the concept of *knowledge integration* (KI), which consists of the identification, acquisition, and utilization of external knowledge. KI is different from KM in that it places much more emphasis on external knowledge than KM does.

As good KM and KI ensure that high-quality knowledge is applied successfully, this book aims to provide knowledge that is both of high quality and applicable. To this end, it provides many examples and cases from practice, but always with a thorough foundation in the literature.

The book is not exclusively written for academics, nor is it exclusively written for practitioners. It rather aims at integrating both views. It is written by academics and practitioners together who attempted to learn from each other. As editors, we have extensively and successfully cooperated with the authors of the chapters in this book during a 3-year project 'Knowledge Integration and Network eXpertise' (KINX). This project was supported by the European Community under the "Competitive and Sustainable Growth" Programme.

In an attempt to impart our experiences to a wider audience we decided to publish our findings in this book. Drawing on a theoretical basis, it presents concepts and instruments that are designed to help SMEs to cope with their problems in identifying, acquiring and using external knowledge. We hope that it contributes to fill the current gap in useful books for KM in SMEs.

The editors
  Antonie Jetter
  Jeroen Kraaijenbrink
  Hans-Horst Schröder
  Fons Wijnhoven

Table of Contents

1 Knowledge Management: More than a Buzzword

Fons Wijnhoven

University of Twente, Enschede, The Netherlands, a.b.j.m.wijnhoven@utwente.nl

1.1 Introduction

Knowledge management (KM) has become a major issue in academia and industry in the last 30 years [16]. KM has at least three roots.

1. Suppliers of information technology and academics in this field have developed opportunities of supporting knowledge reuse and knowledge creation by, for instance, artificial intelligence, knowledge-based systems, and Internet applications [12, 20],
2. Organization and human relations professionals and academics have recognized the need for academically challenging jobs and for using the opportunities of an increasingly highly educated work force in modern societies [2, 31, 32, 36] and
3. Strategic management has recognized that, especially for firms in western societies, competition based on motivating people to work harder will not be effective and, instead, the optimal use of intellectual capabilities may be the best source for sustaining competitiveness in our global economy [2, 13, 28].

Consequently innovations in IT, organization, and organizational strategies jointly realize the development of knowledge management. The aimed-at knowledge leverage [38] mostly cannot be done within a task unit, nor within an organization, but requires inter-organizational collaboration. This is particularly so for high-tech small and medium enterprises (SMEs), which need much advanced knowledge that, because of SMEs limited organization size, must to a far extent be identified and acquired from other organizations, and be finally internally used. These processes of external knowledge identification and acquisition, and internal utilization of external knowledge are what we name knowledge integration (KI) in this book.

SMEs often suffer from a lack of resources - tangible resources, such as physical assets, as well as intangible ones, e.g., databases, property rights, and market power. Scarcity of resources also pertains to knowledge available internally at high-tech SMEs. Therefore, SMEs are under strong pressure to identify, acquire and use knowledge generated externally and, therefore, KI is a specific issue of KM by SMEs. This chapter gives theoretical and practical arguments as to why KM (and KI) are important to SMEs (Sect. 1.2), what we mean by KM (Sect. 1.3), and what we mean by knowledge (Sect. 1.4), particularly in the context of SMEs and KI (Sect. 1.5). It closes with an outline of the book's structure (Sect. 1.6).

1.2 The Relevance of Knowledge Management for High-tech Small and Medium Sized Firms

Knowledge management is particularly important to high-tech SMEs, because high-tech SMEs create most of their value-added by knowledge work, like engineering, research, and new product development (NPD). Unfortunately, however, it is difficult to implement KM in SMEs, because SME-specific KM theories, methods and techniques are rare. Most of the current KM concepts have been developed in the context of large firms. This is illustrated by Table 1.1, which presents a few of the major KM concepts and their organization of origin.

Table 1.1. KM concepts and their organizational roots

KM concept	Authors	Organizational case studied
Knowledge strategy	[16]	Boston Consulting Group, McKinsey, Dell computers
Knowledge valuation	[30]	Skandia
Knowledge creation	[24]	Matsushita
Knowledge acquisition	[15]	Philips Electronics and Sony
Knowledge sharing	[10]	CapGemini
Knowledge information systems	[17]	Ericsson

If KM and KI are so important to high-tech SMEs, two major questions come up for them:

1. Can we move up into the knowledge management swing and be successful by working smart, or will we become the non-knowledge-based firm that has to succeed by working hard?
2. If we want to pick up KM, how can we - as an SME - do this, given our limited resources?

Most SMEs in western countries quickly found out that, with respect to question 1, there is no alternative. An increasing level of production overcapacity and (Internet and telecom-based) globalization resulted in fierce competition that was not sustainable in high-wage countries. Consequently, becoming smart has become the imperative for SMEs as well, and resulted in the occurrence of large numbers of high-tech SMEs in western countries. These high-tech SMEs have high capital investments, the profitability of which can only be achieved by highly educated professionals resulting in high salary costs per employee and the need to invest heavily in personal learning and development.

With respect to question 2, becoming smart has been achieved through business process reengineering, resulting in lean production [11, 43], as well as through superb new product development processes (in high-tech firms), possibly for niche markets [8]. In NPD, SMEs always have to identify, acquire, and incorporate external knowledge. Consequently, for understanding KI by high-tech SMEs, a focus on new product development as the KI context is more fertile than a focus on business process reengineering.

1.3 Knowledge Management – What Is It About?

Answering the question of what KM is about is difficult because 1) KM is often confused with competence management, 2) there are many different perspectives on management, each emphasizing different issues, and 3) KM, like other management areas, is a very broad category of activities ranging from strategic to operational levels.

1.3.1 Knowledge Management versus Competence Management

Knowledge is regarded as the key production factor in the post-industrial society [4, 15, 28]. If knowledge is a unique competitive force, it is a core competence and provides an organisation with sustainable competitive advantage. Core competencies, however, in addition to knowledge, may also include tangibles, e.g., land, money, installations, and buildings, and non-knowledge intangibles, like social networks, legal and infrastructural arrangements, power and influence. Fig. 1.1 shows the conceptual relations between core competencies and knowledge.

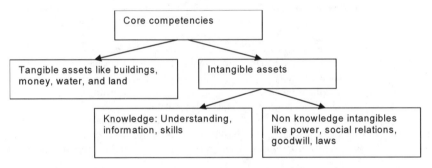

Fig. 1.1. Relations between core competencies and knowledge. Adapted from [41].

1.3.2 Approaches to Knowledge Management

A way to structure perspectives of knowledge management is to relate them to paradigms of knowledge and paradigms of social reality. The two major paradigms of knowledge are subjectivism and objectivism [6, 24]. Subjectivism assumes that knowledge is connected to an individual's mind and has no objective law-like nature. In addition to people's explicit views of the world, it is often even more important to grasp their tacit knowledge while trying to understand their behavior [31]. Alternatively, objectivism is interested in the (scientific) validity of knowledge and the ability of explicating and formalizing it, possibly in manuals and information systems. Thus, the emphasis is on person-independent knowledge, created by making the tacit knowledge explicit and documented.

With respect to the nature of social reality, again, two main paradigms may be distinguished, one based on order and regulation, and a second one based on conflict and radical change. Knowledge management has an obvious role in both of them. In regulation, it can provide or help to define the solution to shared problems and increase organizational integration and efficiency. In radical change, knowledge management may be used as an instrument for outperforming competitors in the market place, as well as a source for internal power.

Table 1.2 describes the four knowledge management perspectives that result from combining the perspectives on knowledge (epistemology) and social reality (ontology). The perspectives differ on the
- basic *definition* of knowledge management (process and purpose),
- basic *requirements* for knowledge management (data, views, etc.),
- definition of *knowledge actors* (a group or an individual, a specific elite, all organization members or the organization), and
- definition of the *knowledge* (that changes under the influence of learning).

Table 1.2. Perspectives for the study of knowledge management. Adapted from [41].

		Ontology	
		Order	Conflict
Epistemology	Objectivism	*Cybernetic perspective.* • Knowledge management is discovering objective reality. • Requires data and models. • Individualistic developing and testing of knowledge. • Knowledge is about the production process (organizational technology).	*Scientific Management.* • Knowledge management is used to change power relations. • Requires detecting sources of conflict, and latent dysfunctions. • Knowledge management is mainly done by the power elite. • Knowledge is the technology of domination.
	Subjectivism	*Soft Systems.* • Knowledge management is about perceptions that motivate behaviour and about organizational change. • Requires feeling with 'reality', by soft modeling. • Individuals interacting in a specific social context (culture). • Knowledge is, e.g., work attitudes, collaboration, leadership, and understanding cause-effect relationships.	*Organization Development.* • Knowledge management is about understanding dysfunctions caused by routine processes and problems of change. • Requires open communications, mutual feelings of trust and willingness to change. • People interacting in a specific social setting (power relations). • Knowledge is about social and political issues influencing organizational processes and thought.

1.3.3 Levels of Knowledge Management

These approaches and issues can be organized by different levels of management. Gulick [14] defined management as the functional elements of the task of the executive. These elements are planning, control, financing, budgeting and reporting, organizing and staffing, coordinating and directing. Additionally, the executive tasks involve responsibility for operational management and information systems [22]. A major question is whether it is feasible to manage knowledge. Because it involves much person-dependent tacit knowledge and information, one may state that KM is the purposeful sum of human resource management and information management. If we group the general management concepts under the headings of strategic, tactical and operational management [3], we find the following workable list of KM activities.

Strategic knowledge management: Knowledge management at this level is the definition of the organization's knowledge architecture [15]. The organization's knowledge architecture is a view on which "functionalities" will be offered to customers over the next decade or so, on what new core competencies will be needed to create those benefits, and on how the customers' interface will have to change to allow customers to access those benefits most effectively [15: 107-108]. More concretely, a knowledge architecture is about the knowledge and information needed in the longer term, how this knowledge and information will be acquired and handled, and how effective use can be made of it. This means that knowledge and information policies and plans must be well in line with the organization's ambitions and environments. Furthermore, within strategic knowledge management, knowledge is evaluated on its strategic relevance, by stating which competencies should be given superior attention and what control policy is needed so that knowledge is defended against fraud and theft. This activity is called knowledge control.

Tactical knowledge management: Tactical management is concerned with the acquisition of resources, determination of plant locations, new product initiation, establishment and monitoring of budgets. At the tactical knowledge management level, general rules should be set for the handling of knowledge in terms of responsibilities, procedures, and means (motivational and financial). This involves organizing, financing and budgeting of knowledge management activities.

Operational knowledge management: Operational management is concerned with the effective and efficient use of existing facilities and resources within given budget constraints. For knowledge management, this implies that concrete ways of developing, storing, disseminating, using (reusing) and adjusting of knowledge and information must be established, in line of course with the strategic and tactical outlines [1, 35].

The activities to be performed at each level are summarized in Fig. 1.2.

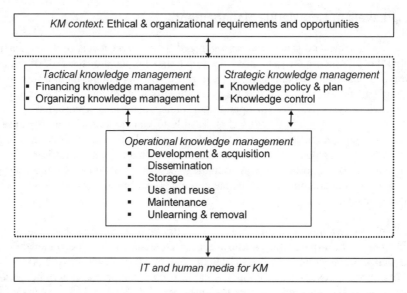

Fig. 1.2. A model of knowledge and information management. Adapted from [41].

Although Fig. 1.2 can easily be transformed to an interesting managerial structure for KM, much of what is presented therein is independent from the substance of knowledge. In addition, the KM model presented focuses upon internal organization and, thus, needs to be extended to include the context of knowledge transfers between organizations. In our efforts to structure the field of KI, we therefore shall improve the KM model in two directions that are discussed in Sects. 1.3 and 1.4:

1. To further specify what we mean by knowledge,
2. To further develop the inter-organizational aspects of KM.

1.4 What Aspects Are Related to Knowledge?

To realize KI, one may approach the knowledge phenomenon from the angles of their identification and acquisition, as well as from the angle of knowledge utilization. The identification and acquisition stages emphasize how knowledge is represented and possibly made explicit and person-independent because, the more knowledge is tacit and person-dependent, the more difficult it is to identify and to acquire the knowledge. This is what we call the content aspect of knowledge. Furthermore, for the utilization of knowledge, its context is important. Company-foreign knowledge - i.e., knowledge that is created at a company other than where it is used - is harder to apply than knowledge that originates from the same context. In addition, knowledge in many ways is related to activities and process flows in and between organizations. This is so because knowledge is far from being a static entity but is under constant improvement or revision, and because knowledge exerts several roles in knowledge intensive business processes. Finally, KM employs human and information technological media for processes like knowledge sharing, storage, and reuse. We shall explain these four aspects of knowledge (content, context, flows and media) step by step.

1.4.1 Content in Knowledge Identification and Acquisition Processes

Knowledge is frequently defined in relation to information and data. Table 1.3 gives an impression of the diversity of interpretations of these three terms in the current literature. It shows that there is no unanimity on either of them, but the distinction between data, information and knowledge seems to be a very popular way of thinking about what it is what we want to identify and acquire in KI contexts. Because this book is on KI and not on information or computer science, the distinction between data and information is not as interesting as the distinction between different types of knowledge is.

Table 1.3. Definitions of data, information, and knowledge (based on [34])

Data	Information	Knowledge	Source
Not yet interpreted symbols	Data with meaning	The ability to assign meaning	[37]
Simple observations	Data with relevance and purpose	Valuable information from the human mind	[9]
A set of discrete facts	A message meant to change the receiver's perception	Experience, values, insights, and contextual information	[10]
Text that does not answer questions to a particular problem	Text that answers the questions who, what, or where	Text that answers the questions why or how	[27]
Facts and messages	Data vested with meaning	Justified, true beliefs	[7]
Signs/carriers	Representations with linguistic meaning	Norms & values, explicit understanding, skills	[41]
Carriers of information and knowledge	Description carried by data	Correlational and causal associations	[18]
-	Facts organized to describe a situation or condition	Truths, beliefs, perspectives, judgments, know-how and methodologies	[40]
-	A flow of meaningful messages	Commitments and beliefs created from these messages	[24]

The purpose of this book is to provide insights into and examples of KI processes, problems, and solutions for SMEs. A typology of knowledge that is useful for this purpose is the distinction between **tacit**, **explicit**, and **latent knowledge**. This typology is useful because these three types of knowledge require very different processes, involve different problems, and demand different solutions (see also Chap. 4 of this book). The distinction between tacit and explicit knowledge has been well described by the philosopher Polanyi who said that "we can know more than we can tell" [26: 4]. In short, the part that we can tell is the explicit part and the part that we cannot tell is the tacit part of knowledge. Polanyi has stressed that knowledge always has both a tacit and an explicit dimension. For example, the knowledge represented in this book is explicit because it can be explained in detail in text, figures, and tables. However, the extent to which you as a reader are able to understand this book is what Polanyi would have called the tacit part of knowledge. It is tacit since you cannot explain exactly why you understand it (or not). Just like Nonaka and Takeuchi did in the early 90s [23, 24], however, we treat these two dimensions as a distinct typology: there is tacit and explicit knowledge.

While Polanyi, Nonaka, and Takeuchi have made the distinction between knowledge that *can* and knowledge that *cannot* be expressed, their distinction is often confused with the distinction between knowledge that *is* and knowledge that *is not* expressed (for example in documents). In this book, we distinguish three levels of explicitness of understanding or prehension in order to reflect this difference. The first type is *tacit* knowledge, which is not and cannot be expressed. The second type is *explicit* knowledge, which is expressed, or could be expressed without attenuation. The third type is *latent* knowledge, which could be expressed, but is not because of inherent difficulties to express it without attenuation. The difficulties to express this knowledge without attenuation usually stem from the fact that this knowledge resides in the subconsciousness.

Often, the distinction between tacit and explicit knowledge is equaled with the distinction between written up and not documented knowledge, or between representation and no representation. This is basically incorrect, because often documentation/representation of explicit knowledge is forgone, due to a lack of motivation or cost effectiveness. People may not convey what they know to others because that would result in a personal value reduction or the costs of knowledge documentation will not outweigh its value. This results in the combinations of understanding/comprehension and representation (or information [33]), with related knowledge types. These are given in Table 1.4:

Table 1.4. Content: knowledge prehension and representation

		Representation	
		Not represented	Represented
Comprehension	Tacit	Person-dependent skills; personal knowledge;	-
	Latent	Shared informal norms and values (paradigms).	Information about people with their personal knowledge (of course the personal knowledge stays personal, but the representations of the people are feasible so that they can be found)
	Explicit	Person-independent, non-documented shared knowledge embracing explanations, predictions and methodologies	Documented knowledge and information, i.e., representations of knowledge or of objects and events in reality that may be used for knowledge creation (potential knowledge)

1.4.2 Utilization of Knowledge in Contexts

Task and firm/industry setting are important contexts for knowledge and information. Following this division, Nordhaug [25] distinguishes background knowledge, industry-based knowledge, intra-organizational knowledge, standard technical knowledge, technical trade knowledge, and unique knowledge, as shown in Table 1.5.

Table 1.5. Knowledge and contexts. Adapted from [25].

		Firm/industry specificity		
		Low	Medium	High
Task specificity	Low	Background knowledge	Industry knowledge	Intra organizational knowledge
	High	Standard technical knowledge	Technical trade knowledge	Unique knowledge

Background knowledge is general knowledge with often a significant tacit component like individual literacy, knowledge of foreign languages and mathematics. Industry-based knowledge is relevant for role-related organizational activities and comprises, for instance, knowledge of the industry structure, its current state of development, the key individuals, networks and alliances. Intra-organizational knowledge is highly firm- and industry-specific, but not specific to organizational tasks or activities. This is firm-specific background knowledge and comprises, e.g., knowledge about organizational culture, communication channels, informal networks, organizational strategy and goals. Standard technical knowledge is task-specific and involves a wide range of operationally-oriented knowledge that is generally available to all actors, like financial and accounting practices, knowledge of computer programming and software packages, knowledge of craft and engineering principles. Technical trade knowledge is task- and industry-specific, i.e., generally available among firms in an industry, like knowledge of automobile construction methods and knowledge of techniques for computer hardware construction. Unique knowledge is specific across all dimensions. It consists, at the individual level, of self-knowledge and skills, and, at the organizational level, of unique organizational routines, production processes, and IT infrastructures.

1.4.3 Knowledge Flows

Many different knowledge flows can be recognized in organizations. Much of the KM literature, e.g., [10 and 18], focuses on the knowledge process, which consists of the development, maintenance, storage, dissemination and removal of knowledge. From a KI perspective, this is too limited because the actual utilization of the knowledge in NPD processes gives the ultimate reason for KM activities. Consequently, important knowledge flows exist between 1) the knowledge processes and the business use processes, and 2) within the business process between the different business activities, like NPD activities and commercial activities. Also, managerial activities occur that guide how the knowledge flows in the knowledge processes and business processes take place and how knowledge flows between knowledge processes and business processes interact. Finally, an important role of management is to facilitate knowledge flows. We discern knowledge facilitation processes, covering the sub-processes of generating, exploiting and maintaining the supportive means, like funding, organization (including HRM policies and leadership), and information technological and human media.

Fig. 1.3 (based on [29, 41]) gives some knowledge flows for knowledge management, knowledge facilitation, knowledge processes, and business processes. It also describes what knowledge flows occur between these knowledge management areas.

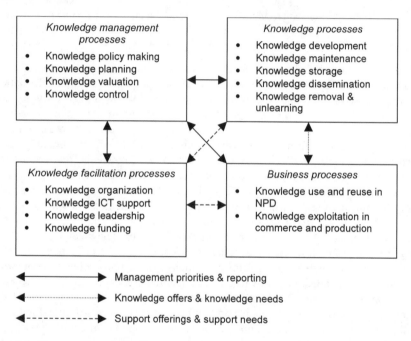

Fig. 1.3. Classes of knowledge flows

1.4.4 Knowledge Media

Basically we distinguish two knowledge media: human and information technological. Human media have been extensively discussed in the past and are summarized in Table 1.6 with typical examples for their content.

Table 1.6. A list of human knowledge media and related content. Adapted from [39].

Human media	Knowledge content
Individual	Professional skills; knowledge about evaluation criteria and results; explanations of procedures and decision rules; personal ethics and beliefs, performance criteria; individual routines
Culture	Schemes; stories; external communications; cultural routines; norms
Business processes	Task experiences; rules, procedures and technology; patents and prescriptions
Structure	Task divisions; hierarchy; social structure; formal structure; communication structure
Internal ecology	Layout of shop floor; building architecture
External ecology	Client and market characteristics; competition profiles; list of knowledgeable people and organizations; technology of competitors

Information technological media have been classified in many ways. One type of classification describes what kind of applications and technologies are supportive of what knowledge processes; another type describes architectures of knowledge information systems. An example for the first is given in [5]. [21] gives an example for the second type. Because [21]'s architecture is more informative, we present it here in Fig. 1.4. The elements of the knowledge management software systems of Fig. 1.4 will not be discussed here in detail, but several of them are discussed further in Chaps. 5-10 of this book.

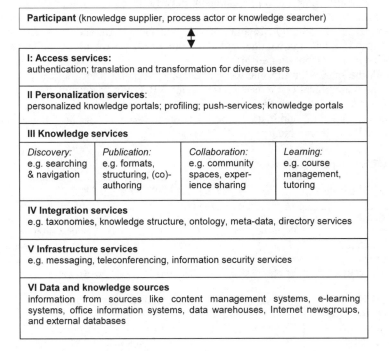

Fig. 1.4. Classes of KM software

1.5 The Knowledge Integration Context

The KM models developed so far by other authors do not explicitly consider the need for activities to go outside the firm and detect knowledge from other organizations. Additionally, much is known in the KM literature on internal (hierarchical context) KM, but not so much is known about identifying, acquiring and using **external** knowledge. Sect. 1.4 explained that at least three types of KI contexts can be distinguished 1) identification, 2) acquisition, and 3) utilization context.

The economic literature has extensively discussed two types of interorganizational exchange mechanisms which have high implications for how KM and KI happen: markets and networks [19, 42]. For market exchanges to work properly, the goods to be exchanged must be very precisely defined (that is, codified), prices act as communication mechanisms, and coordination is realized via the price mechanism. The actors involved must be fully independent and, if the existing exchange mechanism does not work properly (e.g., a buyer cannot find an existing supplier or the costs of negotiating prices are too high), brokers can be useful intermediaries. In the context of KI, this involves the exchange of explicit knowledge, such as knowledge documented in patents and software, or specified commercial services (e.g., accounting and legal and financial consultation).

In the context of network exchanges, economic actors collaborate and, thus, are mutually beneficial to each other. The collaboration is mainly based on mutual trust and respect and, in such a situation, pricing is not needed (and, in addition, is a too expensive coordination mechanism, because it requires a lot of negotiations that obstruct effective collaborations). The network exchange context also enables the exchange of ambiguously and non-codified knowledge and, thus, enables the exchange of latent knowledge and the joint development of explicit and tacit knowledge in collaboration efforts.

Both the market and the network exchange mechanism are radically different from the hierarchical context. Hierarchies for NPD may work sometimes in large firms but are mostly insufficient for SMEs, given the latter's limited knowledge resources. Table 1.7 summarizes the KI context variables and how these behave compared with hierarchical contexts.

Table 1.7. Comparison of exchange models

Context variables	KI governance type		
	Market	*Network*	*Hierarchy*
Knowledge type	Explicit	Tacit, latent, explicit	Tacit, latent, explicit
Coordination	Price mechanism	Collaboration	Supervision
Formalization of exchange process	High	Low	May be bureaucratic or based on authority
Communication means	Prices	Relational	Routines
Network participant dependency	Independent	Interdependent	Dependent
Tone or climate	Suspicion	Mutual benefits	Power
Intermediation	Broker	Network facilitation	Administration and communication offices

1.6 Outline of this Book

This chapter gave a short introduction to the field of KM, and it stated that the identification, acquisition and use of external knowledge, particularly in the contexts of new product development, is a core aspect of KM for high-tech SMEs. We also reviewed the differences - but also the close relations - between knowledge and information, and distinguished three types of knowledge, i.e., tacit knowledge, latent knowledge, and explicit knowledge. The types of knowledge were related to their relevant contexts, flows, and media. These considerations resulted in a list of KM tasks at the strategic, tactical and operational level. Since all these tasks are probably too many for a single SME to organize in-house, SMEs have to gain most of their knowledge from the market or from their business networks, a KM field which this book terms knowledge integration (KI). There are various strategies for SMEs to actively pursue knowledge management, in particular business and NPD process reengineering. Due to the importance of NPD for high-tech SMEs, this book has opted for the latter. Some core questions of KI from each of its knowledge aspects will be accentuated in the rest of this book:

1. With respect to knowledge identification: How do you know what knowledge you need?
2. With respect to knowledge acquisition: If you know what you need, how do you get it?
3. With respect to knowledge utilization: How can you get the externally acquired knowledge to be used internally?
4. With respect to the support of KI processes: What tools and techniques are available to help you identify, acquire and utilize external knowledge?

This book will discuss all these questions with an emphasis on the last one, because the tools and techniques for KI will simultaneously help SMEs in answering the other ones. Before we are able to answer the last question, however, we need a firm understanding of the concept of knowledge integration and of the problems that occur in practice. Whereas the former is supplied in Chap. 2, the latter will be presented in Chap. 3 by reporting the results of an empirical investigation of KI in 317 European SMEs. Chap. 4 analyzes what methods and techniques for KI are relevant, given different content, context, flows and media. From the onset of the KINX project that formed the basis for this book, the KINX consortium was aware of the fact that any "once and for all" answer to the question of what KI tools and techniques are appropriate for solving KI problems of SMEs would be inapt, because new problems will come up constantly and new KI solutions will be produced by software firms, consultants, researchers or who ever more. Consequently, Chap. 4 is designed as a theoretical foundation for a portal, the KINX portal, that has the ability to integrate new problems and solutions, and to match them. This portal is further described in Chap. 11. The KINX consortium was also aware of the fact that, for successful KI, more is needed than knowledge alone; tangibles, such as financial support and supportive policies for SMEs also have to be addressed. This is done in Chap. 12. Chaps. 5-10 present the techniques and tools available for KI in high-tech SMEs. Their organization follows the structure of KI activities developed in Chap. 2 and particularly in Chap. 4: Based on a short presentation of the theoretical background of each activity and an overview of the techniques and tools available for each activity, some new KI tools and techniques are described that have been developed and tested in real high-tech SMEs within the KINX project. Chap. 5 studies how latent knowledge can be elicited, and how representations of this knowledge type can be created that improve the possibilities of knowledge application and knowledge transfer in the practical context of the German high-tech SME Cerobear. Chap. 6 describes a technique for reuse of elicited (explicit) knowledge, called knowledge mapping, in the context of another German high-tech SME, Aixtron. Chap. 7 describes how knowledge can be detected from electronic sources on the Internet and what use a high-tech SME can make of knowledge retrieval tools in this connection. This chapter again is grounded on experiences of the high-tech SME Cerobear. Chap 8. analyses KI in a strategic context and describes a method to identify and acquire knowledge from the external context of an SME. This chapter builds on high-tech Israeli SME Optibase's experiences with a method for external knowledge collection to verify a company's strategy by a method called Decision Validity Tracking. Chaps. 9 and 10 focus on the human means for KI. Chap. 9 describes inter-organizational knowledge transfer in networks. That chapter specifically identifies the needs for multiple interactions in KI as a consequence of the cognitive distance between the actors that aim to integrate each other's knowledge. Chap. 10 describes incentive systems and their implementation to improve KI. It presents a new methodology to motivate employees to provide external knowledge that has been developed and tested in the German high-tech SME HEAD Acoustics.Chap. 13 completes the book by a review of what has been learned and a discussion of where KI for high-tech SMEs may go. The structure of this book is summarized in Fig. 1.5.

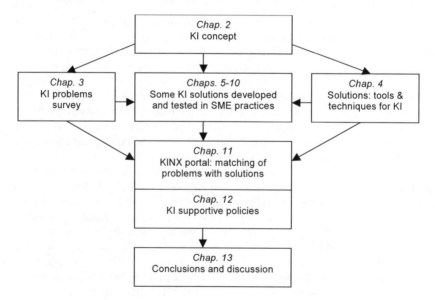

Fig. 1.5. Structure of this book.

References

1. Ackerman MS (1994) Augmenting the Organizational Memory: A Field Study of Answer Garden. In: CSCW'94, pp. 243-252. ACM Press, Chappel Hill (NC).
2. Allee V (2003) Evolving business forms for the knowledge economy. In: C.W. Holsapple (ed.), Handbook on knowledge management, vol. 2, pp. 605-622.
3. Anthony RN (1965) Planning and Control Systems: A Framework for Analysis. Harvard University Press, Cambridge (MA).
4. Bell D (1979) Communications technology for better or for worse, Harvard Business Review, 57 (3): 20-42.
5. Binney D (2001) The knowledge management spectrum: Understanding the KM landscape. Journal of Knowledge Management, 5 (1): 33-42.
6. Burrell G, Morgan, G (1979) Sociological Paradigms and Organizational Analysis: Elements of the Sociology of Corporate Life. Heinemann Educational, London:
7. Choo CW, Detlor B, Turnbull D (2000) Web Work: Information Seeking and Knowledge Work on the World Wide Web. Kluwer Academic Publishers, Dordrecht, The Netherlands
8. Clark K, Wheelwright, S (eds.) (1994) The product development challenge: Competing through speed, quality and creativity. Harvard Business School Press, Boston (MA).
9. Davenport TH (1997) Information Ecology. Oxford University Press, New York.
10. Davenport ThA, Prusak L (1997) Working Knowledge: How Organizations Manage What They Know. Harvard Business School Press, Cambridge (MA).
11. Davenport Th, Short JE (1990) The New Industrial Engineering: Information Technology and Business Process Redesign. Sloan Management Review, 31 (4): 11-27.
12. Gaines BR (2003) Organizational knowledge acquisition. In: C.W. Holsapple (ed.), Handbook on knowledge management, vol. 1: 317-348
13. Grant RM (1991) The Resource-Based Theory of Competitive Advantage: Implications for Strategy Formulation, California Management Review, Spring 1991: 114-135.
14. Gulick L. (1937) Notes on the Theory of Organization. In: Gulick, L. and L. Urwick (eds.), Papers on the Science of Administration: 3-45. Institute of Public Administration, Columbia University, New York.
15. Hamel G, Prahalad, CK (1994) Competing for the future. Harvard Business School Press, Boston (MA).
16. Hansen MT, Nohria N, Tierney, Th (1999) What's Your Strategy for Managing Knowledge, Harvard Business Review, 77 (2): 106-116.
17. Hellström T, Kemlin P, Malmquist U (2000) Knowledge and Competence Management at Ericsson: Decentralization and Organizational Fit. Journal of Knowledge Management. 4 (2): 99-110.
18. Kock N, Murphy F (2001) Redesigning Acquisition Processes: A New Methodology Based on the Flow of Knowledge and Information. Defense Acquisition University Press, Defense Systems Management College, Fort Belvoir, Virginia
19. Liebeskind JP, Lumerman Oliver A, Zucker L, Brewer M (1996), Social Networks, Learning, and Flexibility: Sourcing Scientific Knowledge in New Biotechnology Firms, Organization Science, 7 (4): 428-443.
20. Lucas HC (1996) The T-Form Organization: Using Information Technology to Design Organizations for the 21st Century. Jossey Bass, San Francisco.
21. Maier R (2004) Knowledge management systems: Information and communication technologies for knowledge management. Springer, Berlin.

22. Mintzberg H (1983) Structures in Fives: Designing Effective Organizations. Prentice-Hall, Englewood Cliffs (NJ).
23. Nonaka I (1994) A Dynamic Theory of Organizational Knowledge Creation, Organizational Science, 5 (1): 14-37.
24. Nonaka I, Takeuchi H (1995) The Knowledge-Creating Company: How Japanese Companies Create the Dynamics of Innovation. Oxford University Press, New York.
25. Nordhaug O (1994) Human capital in organizations: Competence, training and learning. Oxford University Press, New York.
26. Polanyi M (1966) The Tacit Dimension. Anchor Books, Garden City (NY).
27. Quigley EJ, Debons A (1999) Interrogative Theory of Information and Knowledge. ACM Press, New Orleans, LA, pp 4-10
28. Quinn JB (1992) Intelligent Enterprise: A Knowledge and Service Based Paradigm for Industry. The Free Press, New York.
29. Remus U, Schub S (2003) A blueprint for the implementation of process-oriented knowledge management. Knowledge and Process Management, 10 (4): 237-253.
30. Roos G, Roos J (1997) Measuring your company's intellectual performance. Long Range Planning, 30 (3): 413-426
31. Senge P (1990a) The Fifth Discipline: The Art and Practice of The Learning Organization. Doubleday Currency, New York.
32. Senge P (1990b) The Leader's New Work: Building Learning Organizations, Sloan Management Review, 32 (1): 7-23.
33. Stamper RK (1973) Information in Business and Administrative Systems. John Wiley, New York.
34. Stenmark D (2001) The Relationship Between Information and Knowledge. In: IRIS 24, Ulvik, Norway
35. Stein EW, Zwass V (1995) Actualizing Organizational Memory with Information Systems, Information Systems Research, 6 (2): 85-117.
36. Swan J, Newell S, Robertson M (2000) Knowledge management: when will people enter the debate? Proceedings of the 33rd Hawaii International Conference on Systems Sciences, file DDOML07.pfd. http://www.sigmod.org/sigmod/dblp/db/conf/hicss/.
37. Van der Spek R, Spijkervet A (1997) Knowledge Management: Dealing Intelligently with Knowledge. CIBIT, Utrecht
38. Venkatrama N, Henderson J (1998), Real strategies for virtual organizing. Sloan Management Review, 40 (1): 33-48.
39. Walsh JP, Rivera Ungson G (1991) Organizational Memory, Academy of Management Review, 16 (1): 57-91.
40. Wiig KM (1993) Knowledge Management Foundations: Thinking About Thinking: How People and Organizations Create, Represent, and Use Knowledge. Schema Press, Arlington, TX
41. Wijnhoven F (1999) Development Scenarios for Organizational Memory Information Systems. Journal of Management Information Systems, 16 (1) 121-146.
42. Williamson OE (1991) Comparative economic organization: The analysis of discrete structural alternatives. Administrative Science Quarterly, 36: 269-196.
43. Womack JP, Jones DT, Roos D (1990) The Machine That Changed the World. The Story of Lean Production. Harper Perennial, New York.

2 Knowledge Integration by SMEs – Framework

Jeroen Kraaijenbrink[1], Doron Faran[2], Aharon Hauptman[3]

[1]University of Twente, Enschede, The Netherlands, j.kraaijenbrink@utwente.nl

[2]Net Knowledge Ltd., Karmiel, Israel, dfaran@yahoo.com

[3]Interdisciplinary Center for Technology Analysis and Forecasting (ICTAF) at Tel-Aviv University, Israel, haupt@post.tau.ac.il

2.1 Introduction

As indicated in Chap. 1, for high-tech SMEs, integrating and managing *external* knowledge is a vital aspect of knowledge management (KM). Moreover, it is not only necessary to *manage* knowledge, but there are several operational activities that are also relevant and challenging. To denote this difference with 'normal' KM, we use the term 'Knowledge Integration' (KI) instead of KM throughout this book. This chapter explains this concept of KI, which is summarized in Fig. 2.1. The chapter helps to understand the main concepts and dynamics of KI in high-tech SMEs. As shown in Fig. 2.1, we concentrate on KI in new product development (NPD). As we explain below, this is because this is one of the core processes of high-tech SMEs. While the focus of this whole book is on the middle part of Fig. 2.1, this chapter also explains the left and right parts for a better understanding of the context in which this middle part is taking place.

This chapter is organized as follows: Sect. 2.2 touches upon the specific characteristics of high-tech SMEs. Consequently, Sect. 2.3 discusses the types of knowledge that are used for NPD and the various sources from which this knowledge can be obtained. Sect. 2.4 elaborates on the KI activities that are executed to identify, acquire, and utilize this knowledge for the NPD process. Sect. 2.5 provides a discussion on problems that can occur during KI and types of solutions that exist. Finally, the chapter concludes with a summary and conclusions in Sect. 2.6.

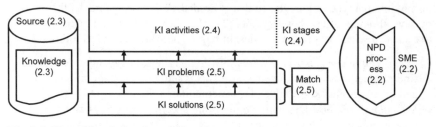

Fig. 2.1. KI model and overview of Chap. 2

2.2 High-tech SMEs: Characteristics and Differences

Although SMEs differ from large size enterprises (LSEs) by their size, it is not size *per se* that makes them different. The main effect of their smaller size is that SMEs have less economies of scale and fewer resources than LSEs. This gives them behavioural advantages (for example, rapid decision-making, flexibility, less strict regulations, governmental support, fast internal communication) rather than material advantages (for example, possessing research facilities, access to external capital, professional management, risk spreading) [22, 23]. These characteristics cause SMEs and LSEs to play different roles in society [14]:

- Generation of new basic technology: LSEs (and universities)
- Daring implementation in new product/market combinations: SMEs
- Large scale, efficient production and distributions: LSEs
- Adaptations for specialized or residual market niches: SMEs

High-tech SMEs distinguish themselves from other SMEs in that they (a) employ more scientific and technically qualified people; (b) face considerably higher rates of product obsolescence; (c) invest larger sums in R&D; (d) focus on developing new products from new technology; and (e) rely more on rapid, efficient new product introductions [2, 7]. Therefore, one of their core processes is new *product* development (NPD), which can account for up to 85 % of the total cost of the product [19]. *Process* development is more likely to take place in LSEs, since it focuses on streamlining processes and cutting down production costs [6].

To understand NPD, it is useful to have a look at a few models of the NPD process. The innovation adoption model of Rogers [21], which consists of six phases, is well known: (1) Identification of needs/problems; (2) research (basic and applied); (3) development; (4) commercialization; (5) diffusion and adoption; and (6) consequences. Since external knowledge for product development is mainly relevant in the first three stages, the latter stages are less relevant for this book. A model that focuses on the earlier stages of product development is Pahl & Beitz's [18] engineering design model that discerns four stages: (1) planning and clarifying the task; (2) conceptual design; (3) embodiment design; and (4) detail design. Cooper's [3] model is also well known. It provides decision gates after each of the five phases of (1) preliminary analysis; (2) business case; (3) development; (4) pilot study; and (5) launch and implementation.

Although these models are very helpful for understanding NPD, they offer little insight into the type of knowledge that is needed. A three-stage model that is used by several others offers these insights [27, 10, 24, 1]. This model discerns a creative stage, a selection stage, and a design stage. These are defined as follows:

- *Creative stage or generation of options:* in this stage, knowledge is collected to find product ideas, requirements, etc. This is a diverging stage in which broad and little specified knowledge plays an important role.
- *Selection of options*: alternative options are specified, priorities and evaluation criteria are set and those options are selected that are most promising. This is a converging stage in which more specified and directed knowledge is needed.

- *Design:* when an option is chosen, design can go into more detail. This is a deepening stage in which detailed and very specific knowledge is crucial.

The ordering of these stages should not imply that NPD is a linear process. In practice, the stages occur simultaneously and in various orders.

Although we have distinguished high-tech SMEs from other organizations, we have to realize that SMEs are very diverse as well. The scope of this diversity becomes clear when we look at the official International Standard Industrial Classification (ISIC) of high-tech and low-tech industries (see Table 2.1).

Table 2.1. Industry classification (source: OECD [16])

High-technology industries	Medium-low-technology industries
Aircraft and spacecraft	Coke, refined petroleum and nuclear fuel
Pharmaceuticals	Rubber and plastic products
Office, accounting, computing machinery	Other non-metallic mineral products
Radio, television, and communications equipment	Fabricated metal products, except machinery and equipment
Medical, precision and optical instruments	Basic metals
	Building and repairing of ships and boats
Medium-high-technology industries	**Low-technology industries**
Electrical machinery and apparatus	Other manufacturing and recycling
Motor vehicles, trailers and semi-trailers	Wood, pulp, paper, paper products, printing and publishing
Chemicals excluding pharmaceuticals	Food products, beverages and tobacco
Railroad and transport equipment, Machinery and equipment	Textiles, leather and footwear

Differences between individual SMEs will be large, for example, in terms of company size, age, and country. However, we are convinced that KI is relevant for all SMEs in the high-tech and medium-high-tech industries of Table 2.1. In Chap. 3 we will see to what degree KI is different – or similar – for these various companies.

2.3 Types and Sources of Knowledge

The defining of knowledge is not trivial because, in the literature, there are as many definitions and typologies of knowledge as there are authors that write about it. It is also not value-free because every definition and typology is made for some reason, that is, it allows you to treat various types of knowledge differently.

In Chap. 1, three types of knowledge were defined: tacit, explicit, and latent knowledge. This typology is useful because these three types of knowledge require very different KI processes, involve different problems, and ask for different solutions – as can be read throughout this book.

In addition to the general definitions and typologies of knowledge that were mentioned in Chap. 1, numerous definitions and typologies of knowledge exist in the NPD domain. We distinguish three main categories that are needed for NPD [17]: customer/market knowledge (requirements; what should the product do?), technological knowledge (design; what should the product features be?), and organizational knowledge (process: how should the product be realized?). These are explained and exemplified in Table 2.2.

Table 2.2. Typology of knowledge needed for NPD [based on 4]

Type of NPD knowledge	Example
Customer / market knowledge	
Design criteria and specifications	Understanding of user requirements, specifications
New product ideas	New product/market combinations
Knowledge about the market	Trends, needs and demands of market segments
Socio-economic knowledge	Economic climate, cultural factors
Governmental knowledge	Legislation, political situations, policy changes
Technological knowledge	
Scientific and engineering theory	'Laws' of nature, theoretical tools
Technical process knowledge	Required steps in specific chemical processes
Properties of materials	Properties of natural and artificial materials
Design concepts	Operating principles, normal configurations
Design instrumentalities	Judgment skills, ways of doing and thinking
Design competence	General and product-specific design competence
Practical experience	Best practices
Experimental and test procedures	Product testing procedures, computer simulation
Research instrumentalities	Ability to use experimental techniques and equipment
Research competence	General and specialized research competence
Experimental and test data	Results of test procedures
Operating performance	Performance of components or materials in pilots
Organizational knowledge	
Knowledge of manufacturing	Ability to manufacture, capacity, logistics
Production competence	Competence in pilot production/scale-up
Knowledge of support processes	Management information, principles of organization
Knowledge of knowledge	Location and availability of particular knowledge

As Table 2.2 shows, there is a lot of variety in the knowledge that is needed for NPD. For example, on the one hand, NPD requires long-term capabilities, such as design and research competences, while on the other hand; it also requires knowledge that might just be collected instantaneously, like new product ideas or properties of a specific material.

When we look at Table 2.2, it may seem that knowledge used in NPD is mainly explicit. However, the contrary is the case [15, 25]. It is even said that one core problem in NPD is the over-reliance on explicit rather than tacit knowledge [19]. We therefore stress that the knowledge inside the different categories of Table 2.2 can be tacit, latent, or explicit and is even more likely to be tacit or latent than explicit.

The various types of knowledge come from a diverse set of sources, ranging from formal expert systems to informal chats with colleagues. These sources are often characterized by dichotomies, that is, by giving two extremes of a dimension. The most important of these dichotomies are listed below.

A first dichotomy is the distinction between *internal* and *external* sources of knowledge. Internal sources are sources within a company's boundaries. Examples are colleagues, personal archives, and intranets. External sources are sources outside a company's boundaries. Mostly these sources belong to other organizations or individuals. Examples are the Internet, public libraries, and customers.

A second dichotomy is the one between *personal* and *impersonal* sources. Personal sources refer to direct human contact and include family, friends, and close business associates. Impersonal sources are typically written and include trade publications, newspapers, and management information systems. This distinction resembles the distinction between oral and written sources of knowledge.

A related but different dichotomy is the distinction between *formal* and *informal* sources of knowledge. Knowledge from formal sources is usually structured according to strict rules. Collecting knowledge from formal sources requires much expertise and is usually costly [13]. Examples of formal sources are conferences, journals, research centres, and universities. Examples of informal sources are conversations, colleagues, and other companies [9].

A final dichotomy is the distinction between *nearby* and *remote* sources. A core difference between the two types is that nearby sources can easily be visited and remote sources cannot. All conditions equal, knowledge transfer is harder from remote sources than from nearby sources. In some cases, knowledge can only be collected by someone being physically present at the source, because it is embedded in the structure and processes of a company, or in the machines that are used [e.g. 26].

With respect to the sources of knowledge that SMEs use for NPD, it has repeatedly been shown that they use mainly knowledge of their close partners, such as customers and suppliers, and that they prefer personal above impersonal sources, informal above formal sources, and internal above external sources [20, 8, 9, 11].

To illustrate the diversity of sources of knowledge that SMEs use for their NPD, Table 2.3 shows a top-10 of sources ranked on their relative importance [9].

Table 2.3. Sources of NPD knowledge [from 9]

Rank	Source
1	Customer
2	Specialized magazines
3	Production employees
4	Staff
5	Suppliers
6	Sellers
7	Brochures and catalogues
8	Industrial fairs
9	Commercial fairs
10	Business magazines

We find it remarkable that some sources fall outside of this top-10 and thus are less important than we might expect. For example, consultants appear at place 18, the board of directors at place 24, and universities even at place 26 in this ranking. Although these sources' main role is to provide the SMEs with knowledge or information, it seems that they do not fulfil this role towards SMEs.

2.4 KI Processes and Activities

There are several processes for managing the various types of knowledge from the various sources described in Sect. 2.3. To understand these processes, it is useful to see their relation with the NPD process. This relation is depicted in Fig. 2.2, which zooms in on the relation between the KI activities, KI stages and the NPD process as they were depicted in Fig. 2.1.

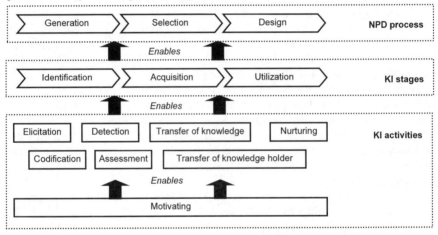

Fig. 2.2. The relation between NPD, KI, and knowledge activities

Fig. 2.2 explains that the NPD process is supported by KI activities in three KI stages that are performed when there is sufficient motivation. We have defined NPD as the generation, selection, and design of new product(idea)s (see Sect. 2.2). In order to execute the three NPD phases, developers need knowledge both from within their firm and from outside their firm in each NPD phase.

The middle part of Fig. 2.2 demonstrates that this knowledge needs to be identified, acquired, and utilized in the NPD process. We have called the internal processes that are the focus of most of the KM literature *utilization*. Because external knowledge needs to be acquired before it can be utilized, a stage of *acquisition* (not necessarily commercial acquisition), that precedes the utilization stage, is included in the model. Correspondingly, to acquire external knowledge it needs to be identified first. Acquisition is therefore preceded in the model by a stage of *identification.* A KI process can start in two different ways. *Need-driven* KI starts with a need for certain knowledge. Consequently, companies will actively seek to fulfil their need for knowledge. On the contrary, *opportunity-driven* KI does not start from a knowledge need (or gap), but from knowledge that is found accidentally or by scanning the environment.

The lower part of Fig. 2.2 illustrates that the identification, acquisition, and utilization of knowledge can be realized by eight KI activities, of which motivation supports the other seven activities. While Fig. 2.2 was already zooming in on the middle part of Fig. 2.1, we now further zoom in on the KI activities mentioned in Fig 2.2. These activities are explained below in what we have called the 'KI Watermill model' (see Fig. 2.3). Each of the activities is explained in more detail in Chaps. 4-10 of this book.

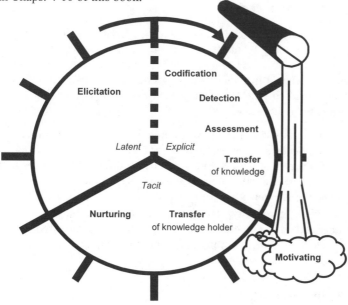

Fig. 2.3. The KI watermill model

We define KI activities as those transactions or manipulations of knowledge where the knowledge is the object, not the result. For instance: finding, studying, and institutionalizing a new production process are all KI activities, but producing accordingly is not.

This division into eight activities is a high-level division. Every activity aggregates a set of sub-activities that uniquely fit other distinct conditions. This is further described in Chap. 4. As depicted in Fig. 2.3, the rationale behind the following categorization is that each knowledge type tolerates a different sort of activity and that people need to be motivated to execute any of them.

Activities for Latent Knowledge

By definition, as long as the knowledge is latent, it can be used by its holder exclusively (others can imitate him, but only blindly). Thus the only pertinent activity is to make it explicit by elicitation. For latent knowledge that remains latent, the KI activities are similar to those for tacit knowledge (see below). Elicitation is depicted by the dotted line in Fig. 2.3 and is defined as:

• Elicitation: Explication of unarticulated *latent* knowledge or engendering new insight(s). If successfully performed, the knowledge in point becomes *explicit*.

Activities for Explicit Knowledge

Explicit knowledge is the type of knowledge that is easiest to manipulate by the "classic" knowledge activities. To make it clear: only explicit knowledge can be acted upon directly. As for tacit or latent knowledge, only their outcomes are discernible. For example: when a firm detects a skilful designer, it is his or her marvellous design that is explicitly detected, not the skill itself. The following activities are defined for explicit knowledge:

• *Codification:* articulation and transit of explicit knowledge from a human source to any kind of media, either straightforward (e.g. plain text or model) or adapted (e.g. embedded in a work procedure). Once codified, the knowledge is detached from its source and independently transferable to others.
• *Detection:* intended or accidental identification of useful explicit knowledge.
• *Assessment:* Attaching credibility, value, significance or meaning to explicit knowledge, either actively or by omission (e.g. ignorance, unawareness).
• *Transfer of knowledge:* addressed transit of *explicit* knowledge from a human source directly to other human(s).

Activities for Tacit Knowledge

Assuming that tacit knowledge is inexplicable whatsoever, the tacit realm is tightly delimited, allowing just two options.

• *Transfer of knowledge holder:* making tacit knowledge available by repositioning its source (human or an artifact that embodies the knowledge).
• *Nurturing:* assisted recreation of tacit knowledge.

Motivating Activities

Strictly spoken, motivating is not a knowledge activity, but an enabler. However, we have included it in the KI Watermill model because it cannot be ignored, since motivation is a precondition for all the other activities: *Motivating:* prompting people to buy in and to apply knowledge activities intrinsically for their own good.

The meaning and impact of these eight activities will be made clear throughout this book, starting with the next section.

2.5 KI Problems and Solutions

A major challenge for companies is to recognize and solve problems they encounter during their work. The development of new products is not without problems. A considerable proportion of new products are not being developed in time, within costs, or meeting the original targets of quality and technical performance [5]. Although there are many potential causes for these problems, part of them is undoubtedly caused by KI deficiencies, for example, by a failure to trace back knowledge that has been in the company.

To illustrate the type of KI problems that can be encountered during NPD, Table 2.4 (see next page) gives descriptions and examples of problems with each of the eight activities described in Sect. 2.4.

For solving these problems, numerous amounts of solutions exist. There are techniques, such as brainstorming and story telling, but also IT-based tools, such as search engines, databases and expert systems. A solution, as in "we did such and such to solve this KI problem", is just as valuable (or even more so) for SMEs as is "we used that particular technique to solve this KI-problem". Since tacit and latent knowledge seem to be more relevant for SMEs than explicit knowledge is (see Sect. 2.2), these more 'soft' solutions are most likely to be even more significant for them.

Solutions for KI problems are not only solutions when their vendors or original inventors have labelled them as such. On the contrary, every solution that can solve a KI problem can be labelled as a KI solution. For example, a project planning software tool is not designed to support KI. However, if such a tool appears to be of great value to an SME in, for example, their process of acquiring knowledge from another company, it is in fact a KI solution. Rather than summarizing a number of solutions in this chapter, we have dedicated Chap. 4 of this book to describing and classifying types of solutions that exist for the problems mentioned in Table 2.4. Moreover, Chaps. 5-10 provide detailed examples of practical solutions for each of the eight problem types.

No matter how simple or sophisticated some solutions are, the road from KI problems to KI solutions is a difficult one. Although by no means can we provide a clear-cut step-by-step guide for KI problem solving, there are three separate steps:

1. Companies must identify and define a KI problem. After all, in order to look for solutions, they have to know what problem to solve.
2. They have to search for an effective solution that is expected to solve their problem. This can be solutions that need to be customized or even completely developed for the company, but also commercial off-the-shelf solutions.
3. This solution needs to be implemented and used in the company, after which it can be evaluated as to whether and to what extent it has solved the problem.

Table 2.4. Definitions and examples of problems with knowledge activities

Activity	Problems
Elicitation	Although it could be done, knowledge is not expressed to such a degree that it is understandable for others.
Examples	- Knowledge is not made explicit.
	- There is knowledge available somewhere, but it is 'under the surface'.
	- There is a vague idea of what is going on, but it is not known exactly.
Codifica-tion	Knowledge is not codified: there is explicit knowledge available, but it resides within people and thus cannot be transferred independently of them.
Examples	- Although it could be written down, people do not do it.
	- It is hard to capture best practices into new procedures.
	- Knowledge cannot be shared without personal contact.
Detection	Knowledge that is needed in a certain situation or its source is not found.
Examples	- Not being able to find knowledge because it is scattered or hidden.
	- There is so much knowledge available that it is hard to stay informed.
	- Not knowing what sources are the best for certain knowledge.
Assessment	Being unable to assess the value, significance, or meaning of knowledge. Although available, it is not known what its use is or why it is needed.
Examples	- Having a lack of knowledge about the real advantages of new knowledge.
	- There are no criteria to evaluate the knowledge.
	- It is unclear whether knowledge/sources are reliable or complete.
Transfer of knowledge	Although it is known where relevant explicit knowledge can be found, for some reason it cannot be transferred from the source to the company.
Examples	- Being unaware of the fact that tacit knowledge is not transferable.
	- Substituting technological contact (e.g. the Internet) for human interface.
	- Lacking a shared platform by which knowledge can be transferred.
Transfer of knowledge holder	Not being able to transfer, hire, employ, or keep people with valuable knowledge within the company.
Examples	- Being unable to get personnel with the right skills or knowledge.
	- People with unique knowledge leaving the company.
	- Finding someone relevant, but being unable to get them to the company.
Nurturing	Not being able to provide knowledge that is highly based on experience.
Examples	- Knowledge of senior staff is hard to transfer to junior staff.
	- People are unable to express all the subtleties of their work.
	- Some people are indispensable: once they leave, their knowledge has gone.
Motivation	Although certain activities can be done, they are not done, because people are not motivated or willing to do them or not rewarded for doing them.
Examples	- Knowledge is not shared because it is considered too valuable to share.
	- People do not take the time to properly archive their knowledge.
	- Not-invented-here syndrome: unwillingness to use knowledge from others.

The fact that the solution is to be implemented in the company means that it should not only fit the problem, but also the company and its strategy mode. Fitting the company means that a solution has to be suitable for a high-tech SME, e.g. in terms of costs, ease of use, organisational fit, and maturity. There are three basic strategy modes for dealing with problems [12]: problem preventing, solving, and setting. When a *problem preventing* strategy is applied, a firm acts under the basic assumption that what was right for yesterday will be right for tomorrow as well. *Problem solving* is an evolutionary approach in which problems that appear are solved as long as solutions are in line with the current situation in the company. *Problem setting* is more revolutionary and involves finding solutions to problems before they actually occur. The strategies and the criteria for SME suitability are further explained in Chap. 4. Chap. 11 provides an example of how this problem-solution matching process can be supported by an Internet portal.

2.6 Summary and Conclusions

Chap. 1 has shown the importance of KM for SMEs and has explained why KM in SMEs is distinct from KM in large companies. That chapter has argued that one of the most striking differences is SMEs' need to acquire and use external knowledge. Consequently, in this chapter we have further specified the concept of 'knowledge integration' (KI) and have provided a concise overview of KI theory that is relevant for SMEs. Of course, this overview is not complete. However, it defines and exemplifies the most important concepts, which are:

- Types of knowledge: there are three general types of knowledge (explicit, tacit, and latent) and three NPD-specific categories of knowledge (customer/market, technological, and organizational).
- Sources of knowledge: these can be characterized by dichotomies (internal-external, personal-impersonal, formal-informal, nearby-remote), and consist of a wide range of sources (including customers, suppliers, and fairs).
- KI process: this consists of eight activities (elicitation, codification, detection, assessment, transfer of knowledge and knowledge holder, nurturing, motivating) that are used in three stages (identification, acquisition, utilization).
- KI problems and solutions: there are KI problems and KI solutions associated with the eight knowledge activities and with the three KI strategy modes.

With these theoretical elaborations on KI, a central question arises: How do SMEs execute KI in NPD practice? In order to answer that question, the next chapter discusses the results of an international survey on KI amongst high-tech SMEs. Subsequent chapters provide practical examples of specific parts of the models that were outlined in this chapter. At the end of the book (Chap. 13) we come back to this chapter and discuss how these concepts have been used in practical KI.

References

1. Boer H, During WE (2001) Innovation, What Innovation? A Comparison Between Product, Process and Organizational Innovation. International Journal of Technology Management 22:83-107
2. Clark KB, Wheelwright SC (1993) Managing New Product and Process Development: Text and Cases. The Free Press, New York
3. Cooper RG (2001) Winning at New Products: Accelerating the Process from Idea to Launch, 3rd edn. Perseus Books, Massachusetts
4. Faulkner W, Senker J (1995) Knowledge Frontiers: Public Sector Research and Industrial Innovation in Biotechnology, Engineering Ceramics, and Parallel Computing. Clarendon Press, Oxford

5. Gomes JF (2001) Knowledge Infrastructures in New Product Development. In: 5th International Conference on Technology Policy and Innovation, Delft, Netherlands
6. Hoffman K, Parejo M, Bessant J, Perren L (1998) Small Firms, R&D, Technology and Innovation in the UK: A Literature Review. Technovation 18:39-55
7. Jassawalla AR, Sashittal H, C. (1998) An Examination of Collaboration High-Technology New Product Development Processes. Journal of Production and Innovation Management 15:237-254
8. Johnson JL, Kuehn R (1987) The Small Business Owner/Manager's Search for External Information. Journal of Small Business Management 25:53-60
9. Julien P-A (1995) New Technologies and Technological Information in Small Businesses. Journal of Business Venturing 10:459-475
10. Kolb DA (1984) Experiental Learning: Experience as the Source of Learning and Development. Prentice-Hall, Englewood Cliffs, NJ
11. McGee JE, Sawyerr OO (2003) Uncertainty and Information Search Activities: A Study of Owner-Managers of Small High-Technology Manufacturing Firms. Journal of Small Business Management 41:385-401
12. Mintzberg H (1973) Strategy Making in Three Modes. California Management Review 16:44-53
13. Mohan-Neill SI (1995) The Influence of Firm's Age and Size on Its Environmental Scanning Activities. Journal of Small Business Management 33:10-21
14. Nooteboom B (1989) Diffusion, Uncertainty and Firm Size. International Journal of Research in Marketing 6:109-128
15. O'Dell C, Grayson CJ (1998) If Only We Knew What We Know: Identification and Transfer of Internal Best Practices. California Management Review 40:154-174
16. OECD (2001) Science, Technology and Industry Scoreboard 2001: Towards a Knowledge-Based Economy (e-Book)
17. Olson EM, Walker Jr. OC, Ruekert RW, Bonner JM (2001) Patterns of Cooperation During New Product Development Among Marketing, Operations and R&D: Implications for Project Performance. Journal of Product Innovation Management 18:258-271
18. Pahl G, Beitz W (1996) Engineering Design: A Systematic Approach. Springer-Verlag, London
19. Ramesh B, Tiwana A (1999) Supporting Collaborative Process Knowledge Management in New Product Development Teams. Decision Support Systems 27:213-235
20. Robertson A (1974) Behaviour Patterns of Scientists and Engineers in Information Seeking for Problem Solving. ASLIB Proceedings 26:384-390
21. Rogers EM (1995) Diffusion of Innovations, 4th edn. The Free Press, New York
22. Rothwell R (1994) Industrial Innovation: Success, Strategy, Trends. In: Rothwell R, Dodgson M (eds) The Handbook of Industrial Innovation, Paperback 1996 edn. Edward Elgar Publishing Limited, Cheltenham, UK, Brookfield, US, pp 33-53
23. Rothwell R, Dodgson M (1994) Innovation and Size of Firm. In: Dodgson M, Rothwell R (eds) The Handbook of Industrial Innovation, Paperback 1996 edn. Edward Elgar Publishing Limited, Cheltenham, UK, Brookfield, US, pp 310-324
24. Simon HA (1997) Administrative Behavior: A Study of Decision-Making Processes in Administrative Organizations, 4th edn. The Free Press, New York
25. Swan J, Newell S, Scarbrough H, Hislop D (1999) Knowledge Management and Innovation: Networks and Networking. Journal of Knowledge Management 3:262-275
26. Tyre MJ, Von Hippel E (1997) The Situated Nature of Adaptive Learning in Organizations. Organization Science 8:71-83
27. Weick KE (1979) The Social Psychology of Organizing, Second edn. Addison-Wesley Publishing Company, Reading, Massachusetts

3 Knowledge Integration by SMEs - Practice

Jeroen Kraaijenbrink, Aard Groen, Fons Wijnhoven

University of Twente, Enschede, The Netherlands, j.kraaijenbrink@utwente.nl;
a.j.groen@utwente.nl; a.b.j.m.wijnhoven@utwente.nl

3.1 Introduction

Chaps. 1 and 2 outlined the relevance and difference of KM for SMEs and discussed the concept of knowledge integration (KI). These chapters were based on
theory in diverse settings. The crucial question that was dropped there was how
high-tech SMEs conduct KI in their NPD practice.

Existing studies are of limited use for answering this question for several reasons. Firstly, while concentrating on knowledge identification and acquisition,
they disregard the way knowledge is used within the company. Secondly, they pay
little attention to the different types of knowledge that are needed during NPD.
Thirdly, they do not accord the Internet the prominent position it deserves.

This chapter addresses these deficiencies of existing research by reporting the
findings of a systematic empirical investigation of KI for NPD in high-tech SMEs.
The chapter is organized as follows. Sect. 3.2 discusses the research framework,
followed by an explanation of method in Sect. 3.3. Sects. 3.4 and 3.5 present the
results of our study, and in Sect. 3.6 we conclude and discuss its implications.

3.2 Analysing KI in SMEs: Research Framework

The framework used for this research is similar to the framework that was presented in Fig. 2.1 in Chap. 2. We have included a slightly adjusted version of this
framework below in Fig. 3.1. The numbers refer to the sections in which the results on that particular part of the framework are presented.

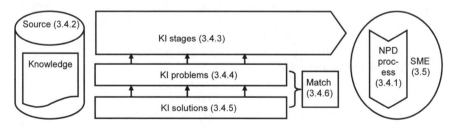

Fig. 3.1. Research framework for the empirical study

Since most of Fig. 3.1 was already introduced in Chap. 2, we will not repeat this below. However, we have made changes to the following topics:

- *Knowledge:* Rather than asking respondents which types of knowledge they use, we asked them questions on source, KI process, KI problems, and KI solutions for customer/market knowledge and for technological knowledge.
- *Match:* In addition to asking respondents about KI in practice, we asked them for their opinion about a Web portal that would match KI problems with KI solutions. Such a portal is described in Chap. 11.
- *KI stages:* Chap. 2 mentioned three KI stages and eight knowledge activities. While most of this book concerns these activities, this chapter provides 'subprocesses' of the three stages. In contrast to the activities, these subprocesses are directly related to one of the three stages. They are explained below.

The identification stage consists of subprocesses concerned with locating relevant knowledge outside the organization. Central to this stage is the level of intrusiveness (pro-activeness) of the knowledge seeker and the knowledge source [1, 5, 3]. When the levels of intrusiveness of source and seeker are seen as dichotomies, four identification subprocesses are distinguished. The first subprocess (high intrusive seeker, low intrusive source) is *intentional search*. Here, a seeker seeks actively for knowledge outside the company, for example on the Internet. The second subprocess (low-high) is *unsolicited presentation* of knowledge by the source. An example is the disseminating of knowledge on new technologies to potential partners. The third subprocess (low-low) is *accidental discovery* and occurs, for example, when a seeker browses the Internet without a particular knowledge need. The fourth subprocess (high-high) is irrelevant within this study because, dependent on who is most intrusive, it will be similar to intentional search or unsolicited presentation. For example, when the seeker is most intrusive (i.e., he finds the source), he cannot assess whether the source has been intrusive or not.

In the acquisition stage, knowledge is transferred from a source to a company. Based on possible carriers of knowledge, we distinguish six types of acquisition subprocesses. Firstly, knowledge that is codifiable can be represented and transferred in *written form*. Secondly, *physical objects* with embedded knowledge can be transferred. An NPD example is reverse engineering of competitors' products [2]. Thirdly, the *people* that carry knowledge can be transferred by hiring or employing them [7]. Fourthly, people can transfer their knowledge in the form of oral and visual communication, for example in *courses* [6]. Fifthly, when knowledge is embedded in work processes, transfer of knowledge is possible by *cooperation* between source and recipient. Finally, when knowledge is embedded in the source organization's structure or culture [cf. 14], it can be acquired by *outsourcing* a problem to the source and staying in contact.

The utilization stage consists of the subprocesses in which obtained knowledge is processed internally in the organization. The first subprocess is *application* of knowledge, in which knowledge is used for the situation it was acquired for. When knowledge is used for other purposes than it was acquired for, we call this knowledge reuse [11] or *exploitation* [9]. The third subprocess in this stage, *storage,* makes sure that knowledge resides within the organization by storing it, for example in archives. The fourth subprocess is that of *diffusion*, which is done by disseminating documents throughout an organization. The last process is the *internalization* of the knowledge. This is done by codifying tacit knowledge into explicit rules and instructions and by developing a fixed response to defined stimuli to simplify choice [10, 8]. These subprocesses are depicted in Figure 3.2.

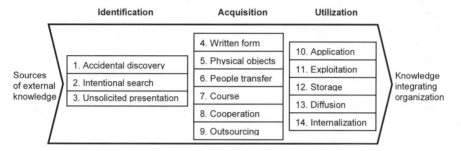

Fig. 3.2. Subprocesses of knowledge integration

3.3 Research Method

We followed a two-stage approach consisting of interviews and self-administered questionnaires, both conducted in Germany, Israel, the Netherlands, and Spain.

An interview scheme was developed in an expert panel of academics and practitioners. In the four countries, 33 interviews were done with NPD managers. They lasted between one hour and 2.5 hours. Sampling was based on convenience, but respondents covered companies of different countries, industries, and sizes.

Survey: sample

The selection of high-quality databases in each of the four countries that allowed selection on similar criteria was a challenge. Eventually, we selected Hoppenstedt (Germany), D&A HiTech Information Ltd. (Israel), Chamber of Commerce (the Netherlands), and AXESOR (Spain). We used the typology of SMEs that was given in Table 2.1 (Chap. 2) for the selection of a randomized sample of 1306 SMEs that was stratified over country, size, and industry from these databases. SMEs were contacted by phone, were asked for a key informant, received a questionnaire, and were reminded twice if they did not respond.

A total of 317 NPD managers responded, leading to a response rate of 24.3%, which is remarkably high for SME research [12]. Respondents' profiles are given in Table 3.1. A comparison of respondents with non-respondents on industry, size, and company age showed no significant differences on industry. However, younger companies and companies with 10-49 employees were underrepresented, while companies with more than 100 employees were overrepresented. A comparison of early and late respondents on all variables showed no significant differences ($p < 0.05$). Thus, substantial response bias seems unlikely.

Table 3.1. Individual and company profile of respondents

Industry	%	Founded	%	# Employees	%
Chemicals & chemical products	10.7	Before 1965	13.1	2-9	14.3
Machinery & equipment	28.4	1966-1980	13.1	10-49	28.7
Office machinery & computers	11.7	1981-1990	18.0	50-99	16.5
Electrical machinery & apparatus	4.1	1991-1995	14.6	>=100	35.1
Radio, TV, communic. equipm.	19.9	1996-1998	15.5	Missing	5.5
Medical, precision, optical equipm.	12.6	1999-2001	16.2		
Motor vehicles, trailers	5.0	Missing	9.5		
Other transport equipment	3.2				
Missing	4.4				

Position	%	Field of expertise	%	Gender	%
Director/ manager	29.9	Customers and Markets	14.9	Male	85.4
Manager/head R&D	37.8	Technology	33.5	Female	9.8
Manager/head marketing	14.3	Both	45.7	Missing	4.9
Other	12.8	Missing	5.8		
Missing	5.2				

Survey: questionnaire

For operationalization, it is important to regard validity, reliability, and practicality, of which the last concerns factors of economy, convenience, and interpretability [4]. In particular for SMEs, practicality is important, because of their general lack of time and resources [13]. To illustrate: during the interviews, one NPD manager remarked that he, at times, receives up to ten questionnaires a week. We preferred using existing scales because of their tested validity and reliability. However, a search in over 500 relevant articles did not yield any practical scales. Alternatively, we developed a new questionnaire together with targeted respondents. Based on the interviews, a draft questionnaire was developed and discussed in the expert panel, before it was tested, improved, and translated double-blindly in the four national languages. Four pre-test rounds (draft, second draft, translated, and online version) were conducted before the final versions were ready in paper-and-pencil and online format. The final questionnaire is included in the Appendix.

3.4 Results

This section answers the question of how SMEs conduct KI in their NPD practice by presenting the results on each of the variables of the framework of Figure 3.1. Where appropriate, we refer to the interviews for additional explanations.

3.4.1 NPD Process

Respondents were asked to what extent they are dependent on external knowledge during NPD. Fig.3.3 indicates that the dependency is almost the same for all three NPD stages of idea generation, selection, and realization. Considering that all three means are lower than 3 (2.76, 2.66, and 2.73 respectively), perceived dependency on external knowledge tends to be low rather than high.

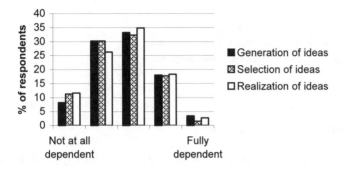

Fig. 3.3. Dependency of external knowledge during three NPD stages

In the interviews, we observed that the dependency on external knowledge was different for two NPD strategies: 1) push-strategy: SMEs pro-actively develop a product that is not tailored for a specific customer. 2) pull-strategy: SMEs develop their products based on a particular customer demand and in cooperation with that customer. For the push strategy, SMEs search actively for market and technological knowledge, whereas for the pull strategy (which is more common) they are less active and depend more on their customers. Also, the dependence on external knowledge was reported to be lower for the pull strategy.

3.4.2 Sources

Three questions were asked on the type of sources that high-tech SMEs use when they search for knowledge for their NPD process. The most important sources for knowledge about customers and markets and about technology are depicted in Fig. 3.4. It shows that customers (and to a lesser degree conferences) are the most important source for customer/market knowledge. For technological knowledge, respondents rely on a broader range of sources, including suppliers, conferences, customers, magazines, and online sources. Fig. 3.4 also shows the crucial importance of personal sources, and, in particular, of the customer as a source of knowledge (which is consistent with the pull strategy frequently pursued for NPD, see Sect. 3.4.1). It also shows that branch organizations – which are specifically founded to provide companies with relevant knowledge – are seen as the least important source for both technological and customer/market knowledge.

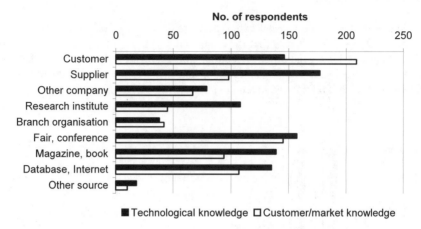

Fig. 3.4. Most important sources of information

In the interviews, we made an additional observation that is consistent with these results. It appeared that SMEs apply an inside-out strategy when selecting sources: they start searching for knowledge within their firm; next, they contact their close network of suppliers, and customers; and, as a last step, they look at sources outside their close network, such as companies, research institutes, and magazines.

The observation that companies seem to rely on a broader range of sources for technological knowledge is consistent with the results shown in Table 3.2. This table indicates that respondents use more different sources for technological knowledge than they do for customer/market knowledge.

Table 3.2. Same or different sources of knowledge

	Technology	Customers/markets
Mean (std dev)	3.05 (1.00)	2.90 (.92)
Exactly the same	2.7 %	4.3 %
(Fairly the same)[a]	23.8 %	18.0 %
(Undecided)	31.7 %	35.1 %
(Fairly different)	17.4 %	11.9 %
Completely different	7.9 %	3.7 %

[a]Only the extreme values were given in the questionnaire

Respondents were also asked about the location of their most important source of knowledge. Fig. 3.5 displays that, for both types of knowledge, the most important source is located in another country. We find this remarkable, because much research shows the advantage of nearby sources as compared to remote sources.

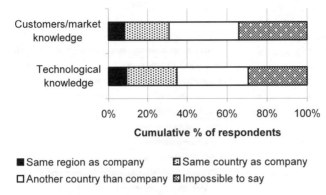

Cumulative % of respondents

■ Same region as company   ⊞ Same country as company
☐ Another country than company ⊠ Impossible to say

Fig. 3.5. Location of most important source

3.4.3 KI Process

The results of either ends of Fig. 3.1 having been presented in the previous section, this section addresses the KI process itself. Respondents were asked how often they conduct the various KI subprocesses in their company. Fig. 3.6 shows that, for virtually all subprocesses, the scores for technological knowledge are higher than for customer/market knowledge. This seems to imply that respondents pay more attention to technological knowledge than to customer/market knowledge. This is also indicated by the difference between the overall means for both knowledge categories (3.01 for technological knowledge and 2.87 for customer/market knowledge). For the identification stage, Fig. 3.6 demonstrates that most knowledge is found after a deliberate search. For customer/market knowledge, accidental discovery seems to be somewhat more important than for technological knowledge. Additionally, we observed that analysing products is the most frequently applied way of acquiring knowledge for both knowledge categories, and receiving documents and files the second frequently applied way. On the other hand, outsourcing and employing external personnel appear to be less frequently applied ways of acquisition. For the utilization stage, we observed that respondents apply the knowledge they have received and store and disseminate it for potential reuse, but do not use it again frequently for other goals.

The results from the interviews strongly support the results of Fig. 3.6, including the relative importance of active search and the low use of outsourcing problems. One additional observation was made as well: KI is not perceived as being a process in itself. It is perceived as being indistinguishable from and interwoven with the NPD process. As a result, KI-related activities are performed ad hoc.

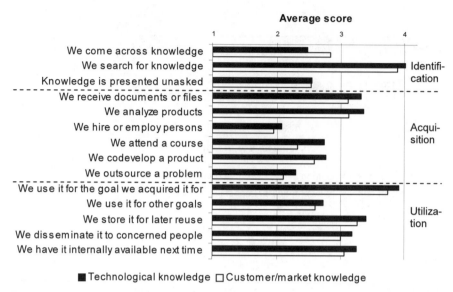

Fig. 3.6. Frequency of executing KI subprocesses

3.4.4 Problems

In addition to questions on what sources they use and how they execute their KI activities, respondents were asked how easy it was for them to perform certain activities. Fig 3.7 shows the results for these questions.

Fig. 3.7. Ease of executing KI subprocesses

In Fig 3.7, we see that, for almost all the subprocesses, it is slightly easier for respondents to perform them for technological knowledge rather than for customer/market knowledge. We would expect a bigger difference since most high-tech SMEs' core competence lies in their technological expertise. It also can be seen that none of the three stages is considered to be substantially more difficult than the others. However, when we compare the overall means for each of the stages, we observe a slight increase from identification (3.06), to acquisition (3.14), and utilization (3.30), which is a weak indicator that the early KI stage is more difficult than later stages. This observation is consistent with observations during the interviews, where identifying knowledge was mentioned as a main challenge.

In the interviews, it also appeared that the SMEs are quite satisfied with their KI and that customer/market knowledge is more problematic for them than technological knowledge is. However, virtually each of the 33 respondents also mentioned problems, some of which were clear-cut and urgent and others more general. A general problem that appeared was a lack of structure in their KI processes.

3.4.5 Solutions

A large number of solutions for KI problems exist. For some of these, we asked companies to indicate whether they used them and whether they were satisfied with them. The results indicate that companies above all use general methods, such as brainstorming, documenting and regular meetings (Fig. 3.8) and general software, such as search engines, e-mail, and catalogues (Fig. 3.9). The figures illustrate that methods are used more frequently (1855 in total) than software (1451). Another difference is the larger spread of methods compared to the frequent use of only a small set of software programs. The figures also show that most users of methods and software (M&S) are satisfied with them. When we look at the ratio of satisfied and unsatisfied users (right-hand columns of Figs. 3.8 and 3.9), it appears that particularly e-mail is highly appreciated and that the few users of extranets and mind mapping software are also very satisfied with these.

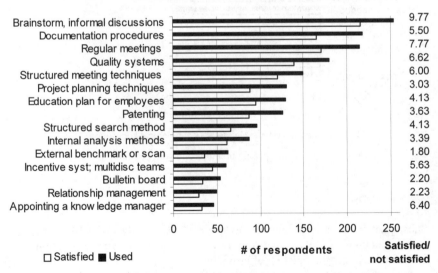

Fig. 3.8. Number of respondents that use certain methods and that are satisfied with them

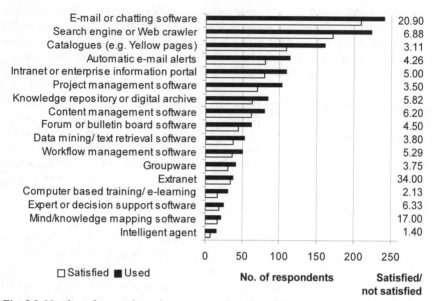

Fig. 3.9. Number of respondents that use a certain software and that are satisfied with it.

We also asked companies why they did not use more specific methods and software in each KI stage. The aggregated results are shown in Fig. 3.10, which clearly indicates that not being aware of specific M&S is the most important reason for not using them, in particular for technological knowledge.

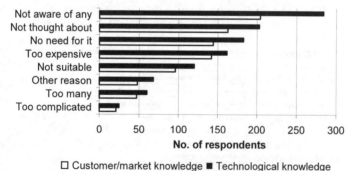

Fig. 3.10. Reasons for not using specific methods and software more often

3.4.6 Match

Subsequently, we asked companies to spend a virtual budget of € 1000 on six potential functions of a portal that would match KI problems with KI solutions. Fig. 3.11 indicates that the function of providing access to a collection of methods and techniques is regarded as most important (25 %) compared to the others.

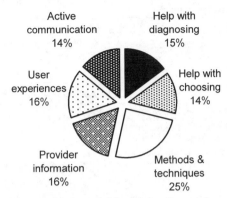

Fig. 3.11. % of budget spent on potential functions of a portal

Finally, we asked respondents' opinions about a few specific portal features by confronting them with four statements on which they could opinionate on a five-point scale from 1 (strongly disagree) to 5 (strongly agree). The results are:

- The portal's administrator should check the information that is offered: 3.87
- The portal should mention who provided the information that is offered: 4.36
- The portal should be targeted at specific types of companies: 3.09
- The portal should be in the user's native language rather than in English: 2.43

3.5 Differences between SMEs

In Chap. 2, it was argued that high-tech SMEs are a diverse group of companies. In Sect. 3.4, we have presented the aggregated results for all companies. In this section, we look for differences between companies that vary in size and country.

Regarding size, we compared four size classes (2-9, 10-49, 50-99, 100-499 employees). In general, most differences are not significant (Kruskal Wallis test, p=.05). However, there are a few significant differences. Larger companies

- use more different sources,
- use more methods and software, particularly for acquisition and utilization ,
- analyze products as a way of acquisition more often than smaller firms,
- use the acquired knowledge more often for other goals than it was acquired for,
- attach less importance to an administrator checking the KINX portal, and
- had a higher response rate than smaller companies.

Additionally, we compared the four countries in the same way as we compared the different size classes. Here, we found a lot of significant differences. This is illustrated in Table 3.3, which ranks the four countries on the variables for which the differences are significant.

Table 3.3. Differences between countries

Question/variable	Customers/markets (Low → High)	Technology (Low → High)
Dependency on external knowledge ...		
... to generate ideas	N I G E	///// (not significant)
... to select ideas	N G E I	///// (not significant)
... to realize ideas	///// (not significant)	///// (not significant)
Use of different external sources of knowledge	///// (not significant)	I E N G
Coming across knowledge without looking for it	E G I N	///// (not significant)
Intentional search for knowledge	G N E I	N G E I
Other organization presents knowledge unasked	G N I E	G I N E
Receiving documents	///// (not significant)	G N E I
Analyzing products	///// (not significant)	///// (not significant)
Hiring persons	G N I E	G N I E
Attending a course	///// (not significant)	///// (not significant)
Developing a product together	E G I N	
Outsourcing a problem to a source	///// (not significant)	///// (not significant)
Using knowledge for the goal it was acquired for	G E N I	G E N I
Using knowledge for other goals	E G N I	E G N I
Storing knowledge for potential reuse	///// (not significant)	///// (not significant)
Disseminating knowledge to everybody concerned	G N I E	G N I E
Making sure knowledge is internally available	///// (not significant)	///// (not significant)
Easily find out what knowledge is needed	///// (not significant)	///// (not significant)
Easily find the needed knowledge	///// (not significant)	E G N I
Easily obtain knowledge when it is identified	E G I N	E N I G
Easily gain ownership over knowledge	///// (not significant)	///// (not significant)
Easily disseminate knowledge obtained	///// (not significant)	///// (not significant)
Easily apply knowledge obtained	///// (not significant)	E N G I
Easily integrate market & technological knowledge	E G N I	E G N I
Access to methods and software	E I G N	
Access to information from suppliers	///// (not significant)	
Access to experiences of other companies	///// (not significant)	
Interactive communication with other companies	///// (not significant)	
Help with diagnosing problems	I N G E	
Help with choosing suitable methods and software	///// (not significant)	
Administrator should check information on portal	///// (not significant)	
Want to know who provided information on portal	N I G E	
Portal only useful if specific for companies like us	///// (not significant)	
Portal should be in own language	I N E G	

N = the Netherlands, I = Israel, G = Germany, E = Spain

///// = Not significant.
= Not split into 2 knowledge fields.

Although there is no unambiguous order in the scores of the countries, there are a number of remarkable differences. We discuss them by characterizing the different countries in comparison with the other countries:

- **German companies**
  - are moderately dependent upon external knowledge;
  - use different external sources most extensively;
  - identify, acquire, and utilize external knowledge least;

- find knowledge integration moderately easy;
- need the functions "access to methods and software" and "help with diagnosing problems" greatly; and
- strongly prefer a portal in their national language.
- **Israeli companies**
  - are most dependent on external knowledge during idea selection of NPD;
  - use the same external sources most;
  - identify, acquire and, in particular, utilize external knowledge most;
  - find knowledge integration easiest;
  - need the functions "access to methods and software" and "help with diagnosing problems" least; and
  - do not need a portal in their national language.
- **Dutch companies**
  - have the lowest dependency on external knowledge;
  - make use of rather different sources of knowledge;
  - identify, acquire and utilize external knowledge moderately;
  - find knowledge integration moderately easy;
  - need the function 'access to methods and software' most; and
  - have a low need for a portal in their national language.
- **Spanish companies**
  - are highly dependent on external sources;
  - make most extensive use of the same external sources of knowledge;
  - identify knowledge by unasked presentation most;
  - acquire knowledge by hiring persons most;
  - use least of the acquired knowledge;
  - find knowledge integration most difficult; and
  - need the function "access to methods and software" least and "help with diagnosing problems" most.
  - have a high need for a portal in their national language.

Although the differences are significant, it is impossible to draw strong conclusions about them, because the data come from four different samples. We did as much as possible to create similar samples in each of the four countries by using the same sampling procedure in each country, but we cannot exclude the possibility that differences are caused by different samples rather than different countries. However, since each of the samples was drawn randomly from a high-quality database, we suspect that, despite different samples, the discussed differences reflect significant differences between countries as well.

3.6 Conclusions and Implications

Since the number of results presented in this chapter is large, summarizing them involves a loss of detail. We therefore suggest having a look at the individual tables and figures in order to find results that are most interesting. Nevertheless, we can conclude in very general terms that high-tech manufacturing SMEs

- are, to a low to moderate extent, dependent of external knowledge all over the NPD process (Sect. 3.4.1).
- use a limited number of external knowledge sources of which the most important ones lie mainly outside of their country and of which the most used are customers and suppliers (Sect. 3.4.2).
- intentionally search for knowledge, acquire it by documents, files, and products, and apply it only for the goal they acquired it for, despite attempts to make it available for reuse. They execute most subprocesses more often for technological knowledge than they do for customer/market knowledge (Sect. 3.4.3).
- find knowledge integration relatively easy, in particular for technological knowledge. However, they all have KI problems too, which they seem to accept as inevitable. Two of the most apparent problems are obtaining property rights and a lack of structure in their KI processes (Sect. 3.4.4).
- use a number of general methods and software, like e-mail, search engines, and brainstorming and are also satisfied with them. They do not use more specific M&S because they are not aware of them or do not perceive a need for them (Sect. 3.4.5).
- prefer a portal that simply gives them access to a collection of KI methods and software rather than providing all kinds of interactive features (Sect. 3.4.6).
- differ between countries, but virtually not between size classes (Sect. 3.5).

The results and conclusions of this chapter answer our question as to how SMEs conduct KI in their NPD practice. When we compare the results on the various parts of Fig. 3.1, we observe a consistent picture of KI in high-tech manufacturing SMEs. We find that it is very difficult for them to think in terms of KI. KI is not in their daily language and it is not a specific and separate process but part of the NPD process. They are also not very well aware of the KI problems that they do have and solutions that might exist for those problems. All respondents, however, recognize the importance of external knowledge, report problems that we have identified as KI problems, and find some general solutions for those problems. Thus, we conclude that the central issue seems to be SMEs' lack of awareness about the middle part of Fig 3.1: KI stages, KI problems, KI solutions, and ways to match problems and solutions.

Consequently, the main challenge for KI is improving SMEs' awareness of these aspects of KI. Because this chapter has shown that SMEs do not think in terms of KI stages, the remaining chapters of this book will also disregard KI stages and instead focus on KI activities that are not related to a specific stage. These activities were already mentioned in Chap. 2 (the 'KI watermill') and are further explained in the next chapter. Chaps. 5-10 provide detailed examples of implementations of solutions for problems with each of the KI activities. These examples help to better understand KI in practice and, as such, improve awareness. Moreover, the KINX portal that is described in Chap. 11 is explicitly designed to address the awareness problem.

References

1. Aguilar FJ (1967) Scanning the Business Environment. The MacMillan Company, New York, London
2. Becker MC, Zirpoli F (2003) Organizing New Product Development: Knowledge Hollowing-out and Knowledge Integration - The FIAT Auto Case. International Journal of Operations & Production Management 23:1033-1061
3. Choo CW (2002) Information Management for the Intelligent Organization: The Art of Scanning the Environment. Information Today, Inc., Medford, New Jersey
4. Cooper DR, Schindler PS (1998) Business Research Methods, 6th edn. Irwin/McGraw-Hill, Singapore
5. Daft RL, Weick KE (1984) Toward a Model of Organizations as Interpretation Systems. Academy of Management Review 9:284-295
6. Devon R, Bush L (1996) Teaching Technology Decision Making for Product Design and Development: A University Course on Technology Assessment and Technology Transfer. Journal of Technology Transfer 21:16-21
7. Dyer JH, Nobeoka K (2000) Creating and Managing a High-Performance Knowledge-Sharing Network: The Toyota Case. Strategic Management Journal 21:345-367
8. Grant RM (1996) Prospering in Dynamically-Competitive Environments: Organizational Capability as Knowledge Integration. Organization Science 7:375-387
9. March JG (1991) Exploration and Exploitation in Organizational Learning. Organization Science 2:71-87
10. March JG, Simon HA (1958) Organizations. John Wiley, New York etc.
11. Markus ML (2001) Toward a Theory of Knowledge Reuse: Types of Knowledge Reuse Situations and Factors in Reuse Success. Journal of Management Information Systems 18:57-93
12. Raymond L, Julien P-A, Ramangalahy C (2001) Technological Scanning by Small Canadian Manufacturers. Journal of Small Business Management 39:123-138
13. Scarborough NM, Zimmerer TW (2000) Effective Small Business Management, 6th edn. Prentice Hall, New Jersey
14. Walsh JP, Ungson GR (1991) Organizational Memory. Academy of Management Review 16:57-91

Appendix: Questionnaire

Questions 2-5a were differentiated in two types of knowledge: 'customers/ markets' and 'technology'. For questions 1, 2c, 3, 4, and 5a, 5-point scales were used, ranging from not at all/never/strongly disagree to fully/always/strongly agree.

1. **NPD process:** To what degree are you dependent on external knowledge in product development?
   a. For generating product ideas.
   b. For selecting one out of several product ideas.
   c. For realizing a selected product idea.

2. Sources:
   a. Knowledge can come from several external sources. Check the sources that are most important to you in your field(s) (multiple answers)
      a.   Customer.
      b.   Supplier.
      c.   Other company than customer or supplier.
      d.   Research institute, university.
      e.   Branch organization, innovation centre.
      f.   Fair, conference.
      g.   Magazine, book.
      h.   Database, Internet.
      i.   Other (please specify).
   b. Where is the most important external source of knowledge in your field(s) located?
      a.   Same region as your company.
      b.   Same country as your company.
      c.   A different country from your company.
      d.   Impossible to say.
   c. Do you use the same, or different external sources of knowledge for each product development process?

3. KI process:
   a. There are several ways to find external knowledge. How often do the following ways occur in your company?
      a.   We come across knowledge without really looking for it.
      b.   We intentionally search for knowledge.
      c.   Another organization presents knowledge unasked.
   b. There are many ways to obtain knowledge if its source its known. How often do the following ways occur in your company?
      a.   We receive documents or files from a source.
      b.   We analyse products from a source.
      c.   We hire or employ persons from a source.
      d.   We attend a course given by a source.
      e.   We develop a product together with a source.
      f.   We outsource a problem to a source.
   c. Obtained knowledge can be used in several ways. How often do the following ways occur in your company?
      a.   We use it for the goal we acquired it for.
      b.   We use it for other goals than we acquired it for.
      c.   We store it for potential later use.
      d.   We disseminate it to everybody concerned.
      e.   We make sure that we have similar knowledge internally available next time.

4. Problems: Your company might find it easy or difficult to acquire external knowledge. To what extent do you agree or disagree with the following statements about this?

a. We easily find out what knowledge we need.

b. We easily find knowledge we need.

c. We easily obtain knowledge when we know where it is.

d. We easily gain ownership over knowledge.

e. We easily disseminate obtained knowledge in our company.

f. We easily apply obtained knowledge in our company.

g. We easily integrate knowledge about markets with knowledge about technology.

5. Solutions:

a. Below, you will find a large number of methods and software programs. Please tick those that your company uses or has used regarding external knowledge. For those you use(d), please indicate whether you are satisfied.

b. Which of the following reasons for not more often using specific methods of software applies to you?

    a.   Not thought about it.

    b.   There is no need for it.

    c.   I am not aware of any.

    d.   There are too many to choose from.

    e.   They are too expensive.

    f.   There are no suitable ones.

    g.   Too complicated to learn to use them.

6. Match: Below you find potential functions of a portal that matches KI problems with KI solutions. Suppose you have a budget of € 1.000. How would you spend your money?

a. Access to methods and software that help you with acquiring external knowledge.

b. Access to information about such methods and software, directly from their suppliers.

c. Access to experiences that other companies have with such methods and software.

d. Interactive communication with other companies about acquiring external knowledge.

e. Help with diagnosing problems related to acquiring external knowledge.

f. Help with choosing a suitable method or software for acquiring external knowledge.

4 Organizing the Toolbox - Typology and Alignment of KI Solutions

Doron Faran[1], Aharon Hauptman[2], Yoel Raban[2]

[1]Net Knowledge Ltd., Karmiel, Israel (dfaran@yahoo.com)
[2] Interdisciplinary Center for Technology Analysis and Forecasting (ICTAF) at Tel-Aviv University, Israel (haupt@post.tau.ac.il, raban@post.tau.ac.il)

4.1 Introduction

This is a true story about a fashion company; let us call it simply Fashion Inc. Among other events, Fashion Inc. faced a remarkable decrease in revenues which, in retrospect, was attributed to a tremendous shift in customers' tastes, that the company hadn't noticed. Undoubtedly, concluded the management, we have messed up with knowledge processing and should prevent its reoccurrence; the reaction was to hire more talented salespersons and deploy them all over the market[1]. Alas, such brilliant people soon attracted watchful headhunters, so desertion shortly became the next problem. The management did not stay passive; as a counteract they ordered the still-loyal salespersons to document their knowledge. But unenthusiastic enough, the stellar fellows did it offhandedly; it did not take long – just until the next crisis – before the "knowledge base" was considered useless and abandoned.

The story goes on and on, but most probably we have made our point: unless well matched with the problem, any solution – as good as it may be – would at best do nothing (if not harm). The lesson? Carefully classify your problem before you select the proper means. In this chapter, we develop a comprehensive categorization of KI problems/solutions and show how to distinguish among them. For example: the first step taken by Fashion Inc. was "transfer of knowledge holder" – an adequate means for tacit (hereinafter explained) knowledge; unfortunately, the knowledge at point was latent. Later, they applied "abstract codification" – effective for explicit knowledge only - whereas for latent knowledge "extracting elicitation" would have been appropriate. True, a little bit complicated; but such is knowledge – each knowledge type allows a distinct set of activities and leads to different solutions, and that is what is described below.

Incidentally, the anecdote we started with is another KI technique, known as "story telling". It is a lovely way to convey complicated knowledge in an intrigu-

---

[1] Chandrasekhar, R. The Case of Knowledge Management. *Business Today*, 22.10.1999

ing and memorable manner; so if you have got the typology's complex idea, we might have succeeded in matching a solution to the problem.

This chapter is organized as follows: in Sect. 4.2, we lay the ground with definitions and principles that underpin the rest of this book. Sect. 4.3 provides the main body with thorough explanations and examples of each knowledge activity, arranged with respect to knowledge type. Then, in Sect. 4.4, we add another parameter – the KI objective – and suggest three consistent alignments of activities to address a desired strategy. Sect. 4.5 describes how SMEs may use suitability parameters in order to choose KI tools and techniques. The chapter ends with conclusions in Sect. 4.6.

4.2 Definitions and Principles of the Typology

As shown in the present chapter, numerous solutions exist for the problems encountered by SMEs in their Knowledge Integration processes. These solutions are categorized by their support of the fundamental (generic) KI activities, which were defined in Sect. 2.4 and are explained in more detail hereinafter. Broadly speaking, these solutions can be divided into two different groups: (a) specific KI software tools, which we hereinafter call simply "tools" for short (for example, software for document management), and (b) KI techniques (for example, "Community of Practice").

The term "technique" is usually understood as some systematic procedure by which a certain (complex) task is accomplished. It is closely related to the term "method". In some definitions, the two terms are quite synonymous[2]. Other definitions assert that a method is a "higher-level" entity rather than a technique. For example, according to Bemelmans (quoted by [12]) a method is "a way of thinking and acting when approaching a scientific or practical problem" while a technique is "the specification of the method and its transfer to application".

We will not go deeply into these semantic subtleties, and at the moment we prefer to take a pragmatic approach: we label every means for KI that is not (inherently) IT-dependent as "technique". Naturally, there are KI techniques that are not inherently IT-dependent but can be assisted or enhanced by IT tools. For example, a "community of practice" can exist in a company without using computers and

---

[2] The Cambridge dictionary defines Method as "a particular way of doing something" and Technique as "a way of doing an activity which needs skill". According to the Merriam Webster online dictionary, a Method is (1) a way, *technique*, or process of or for doing something (2) a body of skills or *techniques*. According to the online dictionary Yourdictionary.com, a Method is "the procedures and *techniques* characteristic of a particular discipline or field of knowledge" (one of several definitions), and one of its definitions of Technique is "A *method* used in dealing with something: approach, attack, course, line, modus operandi, plan, procedure, tack"

communications, but it can be significantly supported and enhanced by using computer networks and suitable software.

Yet we will show later (in Sect. 4.4) that appropriate selection and application of the KI solutions require a guiding frame, which we call "KI strategy" – a concerted application of means towards a certain objective. This could be viewed as the "higher level" entity, namely the *method* ("way of thinking") mentioned before, which envelops the KI techniques and tools and makes them meaningful.

Principles of the Typology

In the scholarly literature, there are several options to categorize KI means (a shortcut for Tools and Techniques), which we skip for practical reasons. However, we reviewed the typologies suggested so far and found some weaknesses in addressing the following requirements:

- *Uniform problems-solutions classification:* however significant each by itself is, unless there is a common denominator, one would find it difficult to match. Our preferred approach was to adopt a common classification for solutions and problems, so that matching one with the other would be more straightforward. This approach proved particularly useful in the design of the diagnosis module of the KINX portal (Chap. 11).
- *Comprehensiveness:* the typology must encompass the entire KI cycle over all the types of knowledge, which most researchers regard as twofold (tacit or explicit). As explained in chapter 2 and in this chapter, we distinguish between three by adding the *latent* type. Further, we found that the knowledge type determines the classification.
- *Independency of process order:* the KI three-stage division (identification, acquisition and utilization - see Chap. 2) is helpful for illustration purposes but too broad for fine classification. Unlike many who aligned the problems along the process (implying that each stage carries unique problems), we saw their relations as web-like, or many-to-many (see Fig. 2.2.). Thus, we looked for another determinant as a criterion.

Taken together, these requirements called for another approach; we concluded that *knowledge integration activities* (KIA) would satisfy. KI activities are those transactions or manipulations of knowledge (e.g., telling, publishing or acquiring), where the knowledge is the object, not the result. For instance: to find, study and institutionalize a new production process are all KI activities, but to produce accordingly is not. Instead of theorizing hypothetical classes, we collected available tools and techniques from the field and asked ourselves which problems they address. Then, inductively, we identified the factors and the dependencies between them in this order: barrier, knowledge type and knowledge activity (see Fig. 2.3. in Chap. 2 – "The Watermill Model"):

1. *Barrier:* what impedes the KI process; choices are either *attitude* – that people do not *want* to buy in, or *skills* – that people do not *know* how to.
2. *Knowledge type:* what knowledge is in point, out of three types:

2.1 Explicitknowledge that can be articulated without attenuation. Written knowledge is explicit by definition, but not vice versa (knowledge can be explicit even if not yet articulated).

2.2 *Tacit*: knowledge that cannot be articulated whatsoever, but can be experienced (what Collins [4] calls "embodied knowledge").

2.3 *Latent:* explicable (but not explicit) knowledge that is either applied in back-of-mind or exists in potential (i.e., no new knowledge is required for its materialization). In some instances (e.g., Nonaka [15]), it is regarded as a sub-type of tacit knowledge but certainly deserves a separate attribution.

3. *Knowledge activity*: what is done upon the knowledge? We shall elaborate this criterion in Section 4.3.

Fig. 4.1 below projects the "Watermill Model" in the diagnosis order. The KI activities are explained in more detail in the next section.

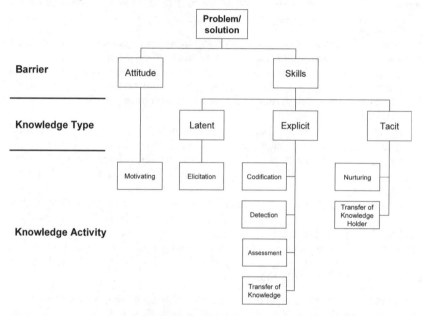

Fig. 4.1. Problems/solutions classification in the diagnosis order

4.3 Typology of KI Tools and Techniques

In Chap. 2, we distinguished eight KIA categories in a first-order division; here, we apply a finer subdivision, driven by varying distinguishers (many for some activities, few or none for others). To make things more vivid, we provide, next to each term, examples of corresponding tools and techniques and describe them in brief. Where *italic* letters, followed by an asterisk (*) are used, further explanations are available in the KINX portal (see Chap. 11).

4.3.1 Activities for Latent Knowledge

Latent knowledge should receive the most attention, since on the one hand it is highly prevalent but on the other it is susceptible to loss [13]. By definition, as long as the knowledge is latent, it can be used by its holder exclusively (others can imitate him or her, but only blindly). What can be done in this case is *Elicitation*: explication of unarticulated latent knowledge or engendering new insight(s). If successfully performed, the knowledge in question becomes explicit.

Latent knowledge has two shapes. One is the expert's knowledge, usually carried out in back-of-mind [5]; it is not uncommon to ask an expert after-the-act how (or why) he or she did what they did and to get a shrug as an answer. We tend to call it intuition or gut feeling but, actually, the expert applies a schema [10, 18] unconsciously. The other shape of latent knowledge is the question-that-has-never-been-asked: something that we could have known had we faced the necessity; as that appears, we do not need new knowledge but rather an extra thought (a famous joke tells about a child who had been considered mute until his sixth birthday, when suddenly he asked for salt at dinner. To his parents, who wondered why he had kept silent this far, he answered: "I did not need anything"). New stimuli or unfamiliar occasions are a common cause for such a need. However, each form of latent knowledge requires different activity.

To disclose expert knowledge, we use *Extraction:* unilateral elicitation by an expert; even when supported or stimulated by others, the source is sole and the flow is unidirectional. The yielded knowledge is not new – it was applied before, but in a back-of-mind manner. An example of a related technique is the *laddering interview*[3]*: asking the expert a series of consecutive Why's to unveil his reasoning structure. Consider this:

- "Why did you choose this material?" (In, say, an NPD process).
- "I thought it would be more efficient."
- "And why is it more efficient?"
- "Because it glues faster."
- "And why is faster gluing important?"

And so on and so forth. For the unprecedented question, we turn to *Cross-fertilization:* multilateral elicitation among counterparts, where none has any advantage over the others and all gain new insights through mutual stimulation. The yielded knowledge has potentially existed – it does not stem from new knowledge but from deeper inquiry of the already existing.

The most popular technique for this case is *brainstorming**, which is actually an umbrella term for a variety of nuances such as *Bohm Dialogue[4]* (a group discussion characterized by extraordinary openness, acceptance and tolerance, as

---

[3] An asterisk (*) indicates that the solution is described in detail in the KINX portal (see chap. 11). For this solution in particular, see also chap. 5.

[4] From IBM Systems Journal (2001, 40, 4): "The knowledge management puzzle: Human and social factors in knowledge management".

criticism is contained) or the *devil's advocate* (to think counter-intuitively). A nice instance of the latter is the "stance swap" game, where people are assigned to represent an idea opposed to theirs; there is nothing like that to provoke a fresh thought!

4.3.2 Activities for Explicit Knowledge

Explicit knowledge is the easiest to manipulate by the "classic" knowledge activities – "classic" as they have been associated with knowledge management since its very inception. In some sense, their over-popularity is detrimental (like in the case study we mentioned above) when – as the coin under the streetlight - applied too simplistically or for the wrong knowledge type. That is the very reason why we suggest the following subtle subdivision, taking into account a wide array of variables. Consider the case of Michael, a savvy R&D engineer in a high-tech company:

It was on a flight when I chatted with the nice lady next to me; she worked for X (a company in a totally different industry) and talked about a new material they have developed and how, and doubtlessly was very proud. It meant nothing to me but suddenly I recalled that staff meeting where Dave, from the other project, mentioned some difficulties they'd faced. "My Goodness" I thought, "doesn't the process this lady dwells on resemble Dave's?". Back at the office I e-mailed Dave the story. His team examined the details, gathered some more from magazines and successfully implemented a similar process. They also documented their lessons, so now other teams can share their experience.

What a coincidence! Or is it? Not really: this little story demonstrates four activities that, if well implemented, will render such a coincidence commonplace. These are: detection (in the form of *discovery*), transfer (twice – *continuous broadcast* and *ad hoc personal*), assessment (*value, significance or meaning*) and codification (*abstraction*) – all appropriate for explicit knowledge under different conditions. We have already mentioned that KIA are not compliant with any certain order, thus the following alignment is arbitrary.

Codification

The knowledge you are obtaining from these pages at this moment is codified; the book you are holding is the exclusive medium between us – we do not know each other and we cannot control the way you receive the knowledge or use it. On your side, you lack the opportunity to direct us towards your special interest, but it is your advantage that you can read it at your convenience. So, what is codified knowledge? *Codification* is defined here as the articulation and transit of explicit knowledge from a human source to any kind of media, either straightforward (e.g., plain text or model) or adapted (e.g., embedded in a work procedure). Once codified, the knowledge is detached from its source and independently transferable to others.

The keyword in this definition is "detached" [20], and that is the critical differ-entiator between codification and transfer. Under some circumstances, it can be very efficient, mainly when the knowledge is context-independent and repeatable; unfortunately, that is not always the case. In some exaggeration, by codifying her or his knowledge, the owner "excesses" her- or himself – which drives an under-standable discouragement (consider Fashion Inc.). The benefit of the knowledge consumer, on the other hand, is not guaranteed as well: he or she is exclusively accountable for the knowledge application. Beyond the prime question of whether to codify at all, one should select the proper codification style:

1. *Embedding:* codifying (hard-coding) knowledge into machines or software ap-plications, thus annulling any discretion of whether to apply that knowledge.

This type is appropriate when the knowledge is highly mature and no deviation is expected (or welcomed); Simon [18] called it "programmable decisions". For in-stance, in a workflow* software tool, we may conclude in advance that three days are whatsoever enough for an incumbent to approve a request, and if he or she passes up, the next step will automatically be activated. Or in an inventory man-agement system, we may predefine a threshold under which a purchase order is is-sued instantaneously. It is clear enough how such procedures may increase effi-ciency and enhance control [14] but at the same time entail rigidity.

2. *Prescribing:* codifying knowledge in a strictly guiding manner ("how-to"), like manual, procedure, rule, prescription, recipe, etc., which makes it applicable unbeknownst to the background rationale. Still (unlike embedding), the knowl-edge's application is subject to a human's compliance.

This codification is a hybrid style: a distinct rule for one but a call for discretion for the other. When is it desirable? Where the knowledge is applicable in similar situations, yet not identical; in other words, the knowledge is incomplete. A repre-sentative example of this style is *best practices**: a horizontal distribution of proven operating procedures that were established (or tested) locally. In a more re-strictive manner (i.e., a partial practice) they are named "tips".

3. *Structuring:* here, the meta-knowledge (i.e., knowledge about knowledge) is the object, rather than the knowledge itself. By framing, classifying, ordering and interrelating concepts and/or terms, a knowledge domain is constructed under a shared language.

A keywords tree in a repository (e.g., a *document management** system) is a typi-cal example. Note the difference: to construct knowledge structure is a *codifica-tion* activity, whilst to use this structure it is *detection* (explained hereinafter).

4. *Abstracting:* codifying knowledge in a form of theory, idea, reason, etc., that answers the "why" question, thus interpretation and modification are required for its usage. Examples of resulting "products" are lessons learned, research conclusions, commentary.

As with this book, such a style does not tell you what to do (or how to do it); rather, it explains the "why" or - as in Michael's story - just draws upon one's ex-perience. In that story's sense, it could be useful to apply the *learning history** [11] technique: an authentic outline of an event, accompanied by the insights of each involved party; it remains for the reader to infer the analogous.

Some combination may also apply; for instance, keywords added to free-text documents. While the knowledge within is abstracted, the meta-knowledge (i.e., the keywords) is structured – which makes detection (cf.) easier.

In Fig. 4.2, we schematize the inefficiency and ineffectiveness zones of codifying knowledge (borrowed, with adaptation, from Bohn's [1] idea "Stages of Knowledge"). Efficiency is gained when applicable knowledge is reused, avoiding the "reinvent the wheel" phenomenon. Effectiveness is contributed by reflective adjustment of the knowledge to the need. The vertical axis – "level of similarity" – represents how similar the occasions are in which the knowledge is applied.

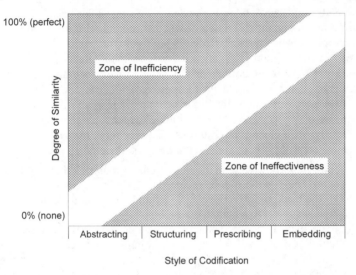

Fig. 4.2. The inefficiency and ineffectiveness zones of codification (the diagonal is symbolic, not precise). Freely adapted from Bohn [1]

Detection

When Michael encountered the new knowledge, he performed *Detection*, which is intended or accidental identification of useful explicit knowledge. In essence, there are three basic paths to do so, factored across two dimensions of the knowledge-seeker relation: (1) Is it known to be needed? (2) Is its location determined? This multiple choice yields three sub-activities, summarized in Table 4.1.

In addition, the knowledge itself (regardless of the seeker) has another attribution: it may be either codified or non-codified (but still explicit). This segmentation doubles the above threefold division, since different means support each of the six. Some examples:

For *retrieval of codified knowledge, taxonomy** would be useful; it is a method of arranging knowledge in a predefined, structured order that is shared (i.e., the order) across the organization. The documented knowledge is then stored under the proper entry.

Table 4.1. Detection subdivision by the known a priori

No	Known prior to detection		Subactivity	Description
	Need	Location		
1	Yes	Yes	Retrieval	Need-driven detection of knowledge at a predefined location (direct access).
2	Yes	No	Search	Need-driven detection of knowledge, the location of which is unknown in advance.
3	No	No	Browse/ Discovery	Opportunity-driven, by-chance detection of knowledge, the location of which is unknown in advance.

In order to *retrieve non-codified* knowledge (perhaps because it is context-sensitive or rapidly changes; see [8]), one should locate the knower; for that, internal *yellow pages** could assist. It is a directory of who-knows-what, intended to be followed by direct contact with the knowledge owner. Indeed, *yellow pages* is often panned as a naïve and empty solution that can hardly reflect one's richness of knowledge, but for the less intimate medium (or larger) companies, it may provide a clue.

Search for codified knowledge is quite synonymous with Internet (or intranet) search engines. The problem associated with them, that of low hits ratio, can be alleviated by means such as *ontology*[5]* – a sort of knowledge map to guide a finer-tuned search. Another aid is a *directory*, like in Google or Yahoo!.

In *search of non-codified* knowledge, the ultimate target is, again, the knower – only that now she or he is not identified beforehand. The well-known *community of practice** (CoP) technique can be helpful; indeed, the question "who knows…" is quite popular in such forums. Similarly effective are simple social ties – to reach a source through a mutual friend, e.g..

Means for *discovery* are rare or trivial or both; however, we must stress that they do nothing unless the discovered knowledge meets – as with Michael - a context, even if tenuous. We deliberately use the term "context" and not "need": shared context (or mutual awareness) among group members enables one to recognize knowledge as helpful even if that knowledge has never been heard of and, thus, no need was explicitly stated (we will return to this point later in Sect. 4.4).

One means for *discovery of codified* knowledge is to subscribe to *newsletters** from sites of interest; once you check a broad pertaining area, you will receive periodical updates which you might further investigate. Another tactic – trivial, as we warned, but effective – is to keep watching the leading magazines in one's field.

As for *Search for non-codified* knowledge, our advice is as simple as visiting fairs, chatting, membership in professional associations and the like. In short, apply all the activities that constitute environmental scanning.

---

[5] See also Chap. 7.

Assessment

Imagine that you encounter some revolutionary wisdom, something that totally contradicts whatever you have known about the topic in question. Would you abandon your old knowledge and embrace the new one? Not an easy question, for sure. Regardless of your answer, you must have gone through two quandaries (in that order or another): first, is this knowledge significant for me? And second, is it credible? This, in short, is the essence of the *Assessment* activity. It rests upon the paradigm that there is not a single truth and many questions are open-ended. The definition is: attaching credibility, value, significance or meaning to explicit knowledge, either actively or by omission (e.g., ignorance, unawareness).

To be specific, *credibility* concerns weighting the *sources* of knowledge. The algorithm used by Google exemplifies the point of tool-assisted credibility assessment: results are rated on popularity basis – the more links from other sites, the higher the rating. Quite similar, and common in academic research, is the count of quotations (*citation index*) – assuming that such a measure is available. Professional intelligence organizations, that diligently track their sources' reports, perform *periodical sources evaluation* in hindsight, so the next piece of information can be judged accordingly. A good credibility process pays off when one faces equivocality or lacks corroborative indications – and of course to guide the collection effort a priori.

The second aspect of assessment is *value, significance or meaning:* evaluating the *knowledge* itself. Trusting the knowledge source is just the half-way; still, even if the source is a hundred percent credible, you may ask: so what? What difference does it make for me? History is rife with misjudgments of meaning (among the most curious are: "But what... is it good for?" - Engineer at the Advanced Computing Systems Division of IBM, 1968, commenting on the microchip, or "This 'telephone' has too many shortcomings to be seriously considered as a means of communication. The device is inherently of no value to us." - Western Union's internal memo, 1876). Sure, wisdom after the fact is always easier; but – without full guarantee – some techniques may make the evaluation more than a guess.

One technique, which is described in detail in chapter 8, is the *DVT* – a systematic and systemic identification of driving forces to be focused on. Another is the *Knowledge SWOT Analysis* [19], which highlights the gaps between the currently possessed and the required knowledge in order to attain a strategic leap. The *Knowledge Tree* [1] suggests a systematic dissection of the firm's process (from input to output) into its particles, each is scored for knowledge level; consequently, the weakest links are exposed for further investigation.

Needless to say, full coverage is a Utopia; luck and intuition (the latter is actually *latent* knowledge) still have a role. But the intelligent organization should not rely on them solely.

Transfer of Knowledge

Once the knowledge exists (after elicited or detected, and assessed), the next concern is to make it available where needed. Under some circumstances, the right way to do so is by *Transfer of knowledge*: addressed transit of explicit knowledge from a human source directly to other human(s). What circumstances? Unlike codification, in transfer, the knowledge and the knower are tightly coupled; possible reasons are high context-sensitivity that requires delicate adaptation, questions of mutual trustworthiness or the source's wish to control the transmission. To be sure: when one writes down a message and selectively addresses some certain addressee(s), it is – although written – transfer, not codification; the selection as well as the tailored concoction make the difference.

Transfer of knowledge is subdivided twice, upon two dimensions: frequency and audience, and thus totals four forms. Table 4.2 summarizes the distinctions and the conditions in which each type of transfer is appropriate.

Table 4.2. Forms of knowledge transfer and their appropriateness

		Frequency	
		Continuous (On-going, routine, procedural)	**Ad hoc** (Upon request)
Audience	**Broadcast** From one to many (generally-defined audience, like entire company or sector) or from many to one (few)	Knowledge is changed in a constant rate and concerns a common interest.	Knowledge is changed continuously and concerns a common interest.
	Personal From one (few) to one (few), individually selected	A mutual accomplishment depends on constant knowledge flow among distinct individuals.	An occasional need and motive shared by distinct individuals.

Transfer of knowledge is not restricted to intra-organizational relations; rather, as Chap. 3 suggests, a great deal of knowledge is sourced from the outside. The representative tools and techniques we list below are independent of the organization's boundaries.

For *broadcast-continuous transfer,* an organization may hold *periodical gatherings and newsletters* or encourage its staff to participate in *communities of practice*. Besides the knowledge per se, such involvement has a motivating effect (cf.). Sending people to courses or professional conferences are examples of *broadcast-ad hoc transfer,* and also typify cross-organizational collaboration. Another, quite different means, is to *survey* a group's opinion (employees, customers, etc.); here, the ratio is reversed as many inform the few.

Personal-continuous transfer is more reciprocal by nature. Innovative projects, for instance, may employ *cross-functional teams*, where varied competencies are compounded to achieve "knowledge fusion". *Stand-up meetings** – related to the agile management school – ensures mutual awareness across fragmented teams and counteract the "silo" phenomenon. Do you remember Michael's so-meaningful flashback ("suddenly I recalled that staff meeting where Dave, from the other project, mentioned some difficulties they'd faced")? We bet there it was where he had heard it.

Nowhere else is the human side of knowledge work as dominant as it is in *personal-ad hoc transfer*. The *peer assist* technique, used at BP [2, 6], is a fine example: people share their expertise with others upon request, regardless of their direct benefit (a matter of culture, for sure). Or the ancient *face-to-face meeting*, irreplaceable by any modern communication, to yield a vital knowledge exchange.

4.3.3 Activities for Tacit Knowledge

Not much is doable with tacit knowledge, given its inherent properties. Actually, the list is as limited as twofold. The first activity is *Nurturing*: assisted recreation of tacit knowledge. Before the industrial revolution, craftsmen gained their skills through a long period of *apprenticeship*, where they imitated and re-experienced their master craftsman´s knowledge. Despite technological progress, some talents still require the same process (over certain innate capabilities); such as design, art, manual work, and – though different – emotional intelligence. *Apprenticeship* is laborious, long and expensive, since it requires significant co-working.

Alternatively, companies may consider the *Transfer of knowledge holder:* making *tacit* knowledge available by repositioning its source (human or an artifact that embodies the knowledge). *Outsourcing*, for example, may compensate for lack of knowledge without extra overheads. Another way of transferring a knowledge holder is hiring or enlisting an expert.

But, you may ask, aren't detection or assessment – arguably exclusive for explicit knowledge – applied for the expert's locating? Make no mistake: only explicit knowledge can be acted upon directly. As for tacit (or latent) knowledge, only their outcomes are discernible. For example: when a firm detects a skilful designer, that is the marvellous design which is explicitly detected and not her or his skill.

4.3.4 Motivating Activities

Motivation, as the Watermill model illustrates (see Chap. 2), propels the whole wheel and, hence, is a necessity. But it is not unintentionally external: while we define KI activities as acting upon the knowledge, motivating means affecting the human. For that reason, many of them are as good for general purposes as for KI. What falls under this category anyway? In short, all that is *Motivating*: prompting people to buy in and to apply knowledge activities intrinsically for their own good (which, obviously, should match this of the organization).

We divide this wide field into two subclasses, based on the criterion of directness: either the means are direct (incentives) or indirect (enablers). Incentives actively encourage involvement and are directly linked to performance. A classic example is *the Golden Banana Award** – attributed to the history of HP and standing for a symbolic reward in return for knowledge contribution (named after a Hewlett-Packard engineer who surprised his manager with an inventive solution he had found to a long-lasting challenge. The surprised manager quickly groped around his desk for some item to acknowledge the accomplishment and ended up handing the employee a banana from his lunch with the words, "Well done. Congratulations!" Soon after, the Golden Banana Award became a prestigious symbol of honor[6]). Another application is to just demonstrate recognition in public. More formal are the inclusion of knowledge contribution in performance appraisal or monetary rewards.

Enablers remove obstacles but are indifferent to their exploitation. Examples are *collective ownership* – mutual responsibility for some achievement, or *knowledge fair* – an organized opportunity to present new ideas. More in general, tolerant acceptance of innocent failure or collaborative spirit expresses knowledge-favour culture, whereas good access to external knowledge (by infrastructure, budgets, etc.) relieves the burden. By that, we covered the entire spectrum of KI activities. The question remains of how to apply them coherently, which is addressed by a broader term – methodology.

4.4 Knowledge Integration Strategies

Knowledge is a resource – some even suggest the most essential – and as any other resource (human resources, capital, etc.) its management does not stand alone but should serve the attainment of the subject organization's goals; a tight correlation must be kept between the overall and the KI strategies. Thus, stating both is the starting point of a KI initiative.

What is KI strategy? It is a concerted application of means and habits, inspired by a proper spirit, towards a common end[7]. Along this chapter, we implied several times that some knowledge activities are juxtaposed to others, thus requiring integration. For example, one may try to retrieve till one's fingers are ossified - but in vain, unless a strict knowledge structure exists. Many KM initiatives have failed due to scattered implementation of tools and techniques, all one can lay. In this section, we suggest three main modes of knowledge integration; each applies a distinct set of activities (with some overlaps) that render a coherent and synergic outcome.

It is extremely important to note that a single organization does not necessarily mean a single mode. Rather, more than one mode may coexist simultaneously in separate parts (notice, for instance, the differences between the R&D and the logistics departments in an industrial company). Thus, the mode and its derived methods should be adjusted carefully per unit.

---

[6] This popular anecdote is widely cited in myriad sources, origin unknown.(typeset too big)
[7] Elaborating about strategy in general is beyond our purpose. The interested reader can find a leading reference in [16].

As a discerning criterion between the modes, we use the concept of *problem*[8], which is a challenge, an interruption or an unanswered question that impedes the regular gear of doing; in other words, it requires a decision. On that basis, we can post three KI strategies[9]:

Static Strategy (problem preventing): the firm acts under the basic assumption that what was right for yesterday will be right for tomorrow as well; knowledge is mature and stable. Thus the optimal way is to maintain the present and avoid any variations. The main – often exclusive – measure is efficiency. This state is dominated by what Simon [18] has coined "programmable decision" – decisions for which results are completely anticipated, or semi programmable decisions – those decisions for which the considerations that have to be taken into account are likewise predefined. Indeed, such a case (especially the former) calls for intensive automation; hence, *embedding* is mostly appropriate. Semi-programmable decisions are supported by firm *prescribing* of knowledge that is accessed via *retrieval*. Further distribution is assisted by *broadcast-ad hoc* transfer (courses, workshops and the like) where guidelines are instilled. Exploitation of the long-lasting knowledge is realized through *extraction* or *nurturing* – probably the strongest form of continuation. Assessment is needless, since no new knowledge is expected. Detection is eliminated to a great extent, as knowledge is automatically pushed in. This mode emblematizes the path from "core competencies" to "core rigidities" or from experience to stickiness. It is not necessarily wrong, as long as one eye watches for disruptions (the DVT in chap. 8 suggests just that).

Evolving Strategy (problem solving) : here, the change is evolutionary and confined to clear knowledge domain(s). Variations (or innovations, if you wish) are welcome as long as they converge, so there are advances - only step-by-step and along a bright trajectory; to sustain, as labeled by Christensen [3]. Conspicuously, the need for new knowledge precedes its identification. In this mode, *cross-fertilization* is common, complemented by *personal-continuous transfer* (which together form the team organization). Since the knowledge domain is familiar, *structuring* of meta-knowledge and *search* are useful – and less, but still, *retrieval*. As for assessment, *value, significance or meaning* are cornerstones in forming preferences, whereas *credibility* is not so critical since the trustworthy sources are well known. Regarding transfer, because the need is predefined, personal mode - mostly in the form of *personal-continuous* - prevails. Still, *personal-ad hoc* is also used for solving local problems. In the case that the knowledge in point is tacit, *transfer of knowledge holder* is employed to bridge knowledge gaps.

Revolutionary Strategy (problem setting) : now we deal with revolution – absolutely new knowledge, opportunity-driven and serendipitous. Indeed, in this mode, KI is more about forgetting than retaining knowledge [7, 9]. The ideal is not regu-

---

[8] The term "problem" may confuse as, along this book, it was vastly regarded to? as? *knowledge problems*. We use it here to comply with the canonical literature, where it is akin to *deviation* or *discontinuity*.

[9] This classification integrates several points of view, although none is identical. We skip an educated, referenced discussion due to its length.

lar (incremental) innovation (more of the same), but (radical) breakthrough innovation; examples are rare, but striking: Polaroid, South West and eBay[10] come to mind. For that to happen, one relies on two bases: broad context and perpetual discovery. Thus, the most important activity is browse/discovery, backed by broadcast-continuous transfer to assure shared context (broadcast transfer is default since no specific need is recognized – and consequently no unique addressee). Also credibility is significant, since no direct references are available for assessment; here, value, significance or meaning are secondary. Abstracting is the only way of codification, which allows free interpretation from others. And in order to intercept external opportunities, one should watch around – which is what broadcast-ad hoc transfer suggests[11].

Table 4.3 summarizes the appropriate activities under each mode. Note that we skipped motivating activities: for Problem Preventing it is negligible, since knowledge is actually compelled; for the rest it is equally imperious.

Table 4.3. Modes (strategies) of knowledge integration activities per each line are ordered by significance

	Problem Setting	**Problem Solving**	**Problem Preventing**
Elicitation		Cross-fertilization	Extraction
Codification	Abstracting	Structuring	Embedding Prescribing
Detection	Browse/Discovery	Search, Retrieval	Retrieval
Assessment	Credibility is paramount; value, significance or meaning are secondary	Value, significance or meaning	
Transfer of knowledge	Broadcast-continuous, Broadcast-ad hoc	Personal-continuous, Personal-ad hoc	Broadcast-ad hoc
Nurturing			Nurturing
Transfer of knowledge holder		Transfer of knowledge holder	

---

[10] Polaroid invented the instant photo camera, South West reinvented the airline industry with cheap flights and eBay gave a new meaning to the auction concept.

[11] It may sound weird that the same activity fits so unalike strategies, as it is ascribed to Problem Preventing as well, but the orientation is totally different: there, it is a vehicle for exploitation and, here, for exploration (like conferences).

4.5 SME Suitability

The analysis in previous paragraphs is general, and may be applicable to different types of organizations. When we focus on KI in SMEs, we need to add the dimension of suitability. SME suitability refers to the suitability of KI solutions (techniques and tools) to the specific needs of NPD-performing SMEs. There are several distinct differences between SMEs and larger enterprises. SMEs have less economies of scale and fewer resources than larger enterprises. Other disadvantages of many SMEs include lack of formal skills (managerial and technical), inability to spread risks and access external capital. On the other hand, SMEs may have some advantages, such as less bureaucracy, more flexibility and rapid decision-making (for a more extensive discussion see Sect. 2.2 in Chap. 2). Suitability criteria fall into four groups: cost, ease of use, organizational fit and maturity.

Cost of purchase is applied only to tools, since using KI techniques generally does not require an outright payment to a vendor. For tools, cost of purchase is a critical criterion. For techniques, instead of cost of purchase there may be other critical criteria such as assimilation time.

Ease of use includes three criteria: assimilation time, simplicity and required effort. Assimilation time measures the time required to fully utilize the technique or the tool. Simplicity characterizes the skill level needed to use the technique or tool, and ranges from special skills (such as programming skills, in case of tools) to no skills at all. Once assimilated, a technique/tool might require different levels of efforts for routine operation. Some solutions may require a dedicated effort on an individual, departmental or company-wide level. Others may easily become part of the daily routines.

Organizational fit includes two criteria: scalability and sensibility to organizational culture. Scalability measures the capability of a solution to function in smaller and larger organizations. In some cases, KI techniques and tools are functioning well in smaller organizations, but cannot be scaled up to function in larger ones. In other cases, techniques and tools can work effectively in small as well as in larger organizations. Sensibility to organizational culture relates to the fit between the solutions and the culture of the SME. In some organizational cultures, it is a difficult task to introduce new techniques or tools. Brainstorming, for example, requires that participants can speak freely without being intimidated by their superiors. In many organizations, including SMEs, this is not always the case.

Maturity of techniques and tools is represented by industry acceptance (or experience). For tools, acceptance ranges from "limited use" to "industry standard". For techniques, the scale ranges from "new" to "common practice".

4.6 Conclusions

In this chapter, we provided an extensive framework for KI implementation; together with the previous chapters it draws a solid line from problems diagnosis to solution implementation and from theory to practice. Along this way, the complex

KI issue was disintegrated according to barriers, knowledge types and knowledge activities and then reintegrated to form coherent KI strategies. The message is clear: unless carefully matched to strategy and problems, KI efforts will all but dissipate.

At this point we can check whether we met the requirements we had set at the beginning of this chapter: uniform problems-solutions classification, comprehensiveness and independence of process order. For the first, the framework indeed enables one to precisely pinpoint the deficient piece of the KI initiative and to turn straightforwardly to a proper solution; further, the three strategic groupings that we have suggested enable one to set up a coherent combination, rather than isolated, loosely-coupled techniques. The second was achieved by covering all the three knowledge types and the entire spectrum of what is doable on them. The fulfillment of the third requirement was expressed throughout the text in several instances, as, for example, the detection-assessment interchangeable order.

The right order to proceed is strategy-first: determine the goal KI should buttress, and only afterwards pave the way of implementation. Once the strategy is settled on, the time is right to tune it with appropriate activities (although for didactic reasons, we reversed this order). But whatever your starting point is, all the factors we have passed through are of necessity.

The following chapters will be organized according to KI activities in the watermill model, as depicted in Fig.4.3.

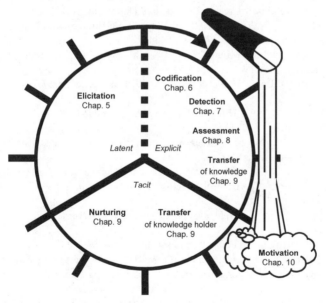

Fig. 4.3. Organisation of the next chapters according to the watermill model

All the chapters will start with a broad overview of general KI means for each activity and then discuss recent developments, which result from the KINX project and are each illustrated by case studies. They will also explain why the recent developments are suitable for SMEs. This will give valuable guidance for practitioners.

However, when practitioners encounter a specific KI problem, they need help in analyzing the KI activities affected, in understanding the KI solutions that are presently available and in selecting the right ones for their specific situation (using operationalized suitability criteria) – this is what the KINX portal will deal with, which is introduced in Chap. 11.

References

1. Bohn RE (1994) Measuring and Managing Technological Knowledge. Sloan Management Review 36 (1): 61-73
2. Browne J, Prokesch SE (1997) Unleashing the Power of Learning: An Interview with British Petroleum's John Browne. Harvard Business Review 75 (5): 146-168
3. Christensen CM (1997) The Innovator's Dilemma. Harvard Business School Press. Boston
4. Collins HM (1993) The Structure of Knowledge. Social Research 60 (1): 95-116
5. Davenport TH, Beck JC (2002) The Attention Economy: Understanding the New Currency of Business. Harvard Business School Press, Boston, MA
6. Dixon N (2000) Common Knowledge. Harvard Business School Press, Boston, MA
7. Foster R, Kaplan S (2001) Creative Destruction. Doubleday, New York, NY
8. Hansen MT, Nohria N, Tierney T (1999) What's Your Strategy for Managing Knowledge? Harvard Business Review 77 (4):106-116
9. Holan PM, Philips N, Lawrence TB (2004) Managing Organizational Forgetting. Sloan Management Review 45 (2): 45-51
10. Huff AS, Huff JO, Barr PS (2000) When Firms Change Direction. Oxford University Press, Oxford, NY
11. Kleiner A, Roth G (1997) How to Make Experience Your Company's Best Teacher. Harvard Business Review 75 (5): 172-177
12. Kraaijenbrink J, Wijnhoven F, Groen A (2002) KINX: Working Paper on Theoretical Basis of the Project. www.kinx-europe.com
13. Leonard D, Swap W (2004) Deep Smarts. Harvard Business Review 82 (9):88-97
14. Merchant KA (1982) The Control Function of Management. Sloan Management Review 23 (4): 43-55
15. Nonaka I (1991) The Knowledge-Creating Company. Harvard Business Review 69 (6): 96-104
16. Porter ME (1996) What is strategy? Harvard Business Review 74 (6): 61-78.
17. Simon H (1986) Decision Making and Problem Solving: Report of the Research Briefing Panel on Decision Making and Problem Solving. The National Academy of Sciences
18. Simon HA (1997) Administrative Behavior: A Study of Decision-Making Processes in Administrative Organizations. Free Press, New-York, NY.
19. Zack MH (1999) Developing a Knowledge Strategy. California Management Review 41 (3):125-145
20. Zack MH (1999) Managing Codified Knowledge. Sloan Management Review 40 (4): 45-58

5 Elicitation – Extracting Knowledge from Experts

Antonie Jetter

Chair for Business Administration with focus on Technology and Innovation Management, RWTH Aachen University, Germany, jetter@tim.rwth-aachen.de

5.1 Motivation and Introduction

The activity of elicitation – the explication of unarticulated latent knowledge that the knowledge owner might not even be fully aware of – is an important first step for many knowledge activities, such as codification and transfer of knowledge. Elicitation requires that people are conscious of and successfully express their knowledge and that their expressions are adequately represented and interpreted. Cognitive psychologists have long been interested in learning and have therefore developed methods to research what people know (knowledge contents), how their knowledge is organized in the human brain (knowledge structures) and how content and structure change in the course of time. Though many of the research methods they use have been adopted in other areas (e.g., marketing, managerial cognition, expert system design), they are still relatively unknown in the field of knowledge management (KM). Furthermore, some elicitation methods that have originated in psychology are applied in KM with very little consideration for their theoretical background and application domains. Consequently, the knowledge that is captured in KM practice is sometimes only an insufficient representation of expert knowledge.

This chapter will briefly discuss the psychological perspective on knowledge elicitation, and its value for knowledge management (Sect. 5.2), before it presents elicitation methods for three distinct steps in the elicitation process (identification of experts, activation and capture; interpretation and documentation) in Sect. 5.3. In Sect. 5.4 it will then present a case study of a high-tech SME that has applied the elicitation techniques of episodic interviews and free word association for building ontologies for knowledge search and retrieval.

5.2 A Psychological Perspective on Knowledge Elicitation

5.2.1 Theoretical Background

Many researchers in cognitive psychology are primarily interested in the structures of knowledge in the human brain. It is widely accepted that the brain follows the principle of cognitive economy and organizes related knowledge content in structures that can be easily accessed and processed as an entity. Elicitation results (e.g., the speed and order of a test person's statements) are used to infer these structures [9].

Models of knowledge structures vary greatly. One very influential idea of knowledge organization, e.g., grounds on the notion that de-contextualized knowledge about facts – so-called *semantic knowledge* (e.g., historical data, the members of the European Union, the differentiating characteristics of mammals) – is organized in *network structures.* These knowledge structures consist of verbal concepts and propositions about them and are usually represented through graphs, with concepts being the nodes and relations being the edges. The sentences "A tree is a plant", "Plants need sunlight", "Oaks are trees" for example, contain four concepts (tree, plant, sunlight, oaks) that are linked through the relations "is a", "need", and "are". In the case of hierarchical knowledge structures, superordinates, such as "plants", represent abstract concepts with few characteristics. Concepts of a sub-class (e.g., oaks) have detailed individual characteristics as well as all the attributes of the superordinates (e.g., "oaks need sunlight since they are specifications of plants") [2, 9].

Concept hierarchies and networks are models for the organization of semantic knowledge but cannot capture "autobiographical", so-called *episodic knowledge* about past events (e.g., a visit to an Italian restaurant). This type of knowledge is assumed to be organized in complex mental constructs, which are used to encode general knowledge (e.g., What happens in a restaurant? Who are the focal people? What is the usual order of events?) and can be applied in a specific situation. When someone reads the restaurant critique "When my bill arrived, I was pleasantly surprised that prices were very reasonable" he or she uses their mental construct (also schema, frame, script) about restaurants in general to infer that, in this particular case, the bill was brought by the waiter and that the food probably did not cost several hundred Euros [2].

The way in which the brain organizes knowledge is far from being fully understood and many competing models are discussed in the literature. It is, however, widely agreed upon that the brain uses different organizing principle for different types of knowledge. Consequently, there is no one-size-fits-all elicitation technique that can capture all aspects of knowledge [2, 7, 9]. Table 5.1 gives an overview of three common groups of elicitation techniques that are used in cognitive research [7].

None of these broadly described techniques is relevant for only one type of knowledge. Semantic knowledge and the structures in which it is organized, for example, can be researched by asking people to sort concepts (e.g., to sort pictures of plants) but also by probing and asking questions about concepts (e.g., "Is an oak a tree?"). To overcome the limitations of single approaches and to validate results, psychologists often combine different elicitation techniques. They, for example, first ask test persons to sort objects and then ask them to verbalize everything that comes to mind about and within a specific category [7].

Furthermore, elicitation techniques are usually combined with means to "activate" knowledge in order to transfer it from the long-term memory of the human brain, where it is stored, to the short-term memory, where it is processed [7].

Table 5.1. Elicitation techniques (based on [7])

Technique	Processing of results	Problems & Concerns
Thinking aloud Test persons are asked to express everything that comes to mind while solving a problem. Expressions should be spontaneous. The flow of thought is not interrupted by the researcher, who documents everything the test person says in writing, on tape or on film.	Knowledge structures are inferred from the sequence of statements. Processing takes place in two steps: Pre-processing: the content of tapes and videos is put in writing. Texts are structured to show the sequence of topics covered. Vocabulary is standardized. Text-coding: coding rules are defined and applied to attribute statements from the text to different categories. To ensure objectivity, usually different persons code the same text.	Thinking-aloud protocols of the same test person in the same situation can vary greatly and often contain thoughts that are not relevant for the problem-solving process. It seems that the technique does not capture all of the knowledge nor does it capture only the knowledge that is needed for problem-solving. Ensuring objectivity of text coding (e.g., through the use of standard vocabularies and independent coding by different researchers) is time-consuming and considered to be problematic.
Sorting Test persons are asked to group stimuli (e.g., note cards with words) in order to build categories of related objects.	Sorting results are visualized in network-like structures. Processing includes the analysis of these structures (e.g., closeness and centrality of concepts) as well as the comparison of different structures (e.g., sorting results of experts and novices).	Sorting techniques vary: sorting objects and categories can be predefined by the researcher or created by the test persons. Categories can be strict (one category per object, clear-cut boundaries) or fuzzy (objects belong to more than one category, varying degrees of membership). Categories can be hierarchically organized or all on the same level, etc. Since sorting exercises are laboratory situations, the validity of the inferred knowledge structures is often challenged.
Probing Test persons are interviewed off-line (after they have solved a problem), online (during problem-solving) or independent of a specific learning situation.	Either pre-existing models of knowledge structures are tested through interviews or knowledge structures are inferred from interview results. Processing hereby depends on the probing technique. Answers to open questions and semi-structured interviews are usually processed in a way similar to thinking-aloud protocols. Structured interviews can be assessed using quantitative techniques.	Probing can deliver rich and detailed knowledge structures. A key problem is the choice of a suitable interview technique that is understood by the test person and does not distort results. A multitude of techniques exist, such as structured interviews, advising (test person explains a topic to a novice in the field), and DOE (Demonstrate-Observe-Explain; test persons predict and explain system behaviour).

After knowledge has been made accessible through activation, knowledge contents are captured, e.g., by thinking aloud, by answering questions or by writing on note cards. Afterwards, different sorting and mapping techniques are applied to find out about the hierarchical order, links and interdependencies between elements of the knowledge content in order to elicit the knowledge structure. The three steps of knowledge elicitation – activation, elicitation of knowledge content and structuring of knowledge contents – are not always strictly separated. It is, however, assumed that this sequential approach reduces the cognitive demands on the expert and lowers the risk of mistakes [1].

5.2.2 Relevance for Knowledge Management

As can be inferred from the problems and concerns described in Table 5.1, the choice of an elicitation technique can greatly impact and possibly distort results, which is why many studies in cognitive research are restricted to very small knowledge areas (e.g. an expert's knowledge of chess constellations) that can be fully researched with carefully selected, multiple research designs. As a consequence, the 'ecological validity' of these laboratory experiments and their applicability in real-world (KM) applications is put in doubt. On first sight, KM nevertheless simply accepts the concepts and theories of psychology: e.g., semantic networks are used in knowledge maps and many user interfaces of knowledge portals to browse and navigate. They are, furthermore, core to some information retrieval methods in the form of taxonomies, topic maps and ontologies[1]. A more thorough analysis, however, reveals distinct differences between the two fields:

Cognitive psychology researches how humans interpret sensory input and use it to solve problems, how their memory works, and how knowledge is organized in the brain. To do so, psychologists analyze knowledge and knowledge processes of individuals. Usually, it is not important to them whether their research objects' knowledge is true, plausible, widely accepted and useful for other individuals. Often, the knowledge itself is unimportant (e.g. chess constellations, attributes of furniture in different rooms) and only under research, because test persons are readily available and research designs can be kept simple.

In contrast, KM always aims at capturing knowledge of importance to make it accessible and applicable to a larger group of people. This means that the knowledge domain under research is usually more complex than in many research designs in cognitive psychology. On the other hand, KM is typically not interested in the in-depth elicitation of individual knowledge structures but needs to capture and present only the most important aspects of a broad domain. Theoretical concepts from psychology, such as the idea of semantic nets, are therefore often used in a somewhat metaphoric sense: when KM practitioners use them, they usually do not assume that they are a correct representation of the memory of a knowledgeable individual, let alone the shared content of the brains of the many people who use them – they are too generic, simple and organized for this. However, they

---

[1] see Chap. 6 and Chap. 7

resemble the knowledge structure of people to some extent and it is this resemblance that makes them useful for navigation and search.

When the knowledge structures used in KM do not reflect the knowledge of people from the field – when for example, terms are used that no one understands or when topics are grouped counterintuitively – they are useless. Nevertheless, there is almost no hint in KM literature of how the knowledge for semantic nets, knowledge maps, micro articles, lessons learned, etc., should be generated to make sure that they reach beyond an ad hoc verbalisation of individual ideas and, indeed, capture the useful and valid knowledge that they are intended to codify. Even more strikingly, KM literature rarely discusses whose knowledge should be codified and how experts could be recognized. Knowledge management practice could therefore clearly benefit from the theory-driven rigor and thoroughness of psychological knowledge research, even though the detailed investigation of individual knowledge and knowledge structures are clearly not at the core of the discipline. With this in mind, the following sections will discuss practical aspects and solutions for knowledge elicitation, thus answering the question of what KM can and should learn from cognitive psychology.

5.3 Elicitation in Practice

5.3.1 Identification of Experts

The first step in knowledge elicitation is the identification of the people whose knowledge is to be captured. Usually, they are referred to as *experts*, though the term can be misleading. In the strict sense of the word, experts are people with substantially more experience than average in a relatively small field of expertise, such as fault analysis in a technical system that the expert has known for years. Because of their tremendous experience, experts only need a little information to analyze a problem and to choose the matching solution from the cases they have accumulated in their memories. Problem-solving by these experts is, therefore, almost automatic and often experts are not even fully aware of how they have solved a particular problem [6]. These "real" experts are usually well-known in an organization and are, therefore, relatively easy to identify.

In many cases, however, this type of expertise does not exist: despite experience, a lawyer does not "semi-automatically" negotiate a contract and an engineer does not intuitively choose the right component for a product he or she designs. Instead, they both apply domain specific knowledge on law and engineering that can (and usually has) been captured in books and university classes as well as context-specific knowledge of company goals, the behaviour of contract partners, the use environment of a new product, existing production facilities, etc. [5].When the knowledge in question is as broad as this, it can be difficult to identify experts, because many people have some amount of knowledge.

One solution for identifying experts is to seek the advice of people who depend on expert knowledge: they can, for example, be asked to give five names of people that they consider experts in the field and possibly also rank them. By comparing the names on different people's lists, experts often become obvious. Furthermore, people can be asked how often they consult different people on a list. People who are often consulted clearly have something to share and might qualify as experts. This approach can be systemized, using organizational network analysis [10].

When a potential expert is identified, his or her ability and motivation to share knowledge have to be carefully considered:

- Ability can be a problem when language barriers exist, when experts extensively use technical jargon and when organisational problems (distance, lack of time) occur. Lack of ability, furthermore, often occurs with "real" experts with automated problem-solving who sometimes cannot fully articulate the approach that they use [6].
- Lack of motivation is highly problematic, when experts fear that they might lose prestige and power by sharing knowledge or make themselves obsolete. Also, the expert needs to benefit from sharing knowledge, e.g., through recognition, through the satisfaction of being considered an expert or through future ease of work [6].

As a consequence, not everybody who has relevant knowledge is a suitable partner for knowledge elicitation – sometimes the expert with the greatest knowledge is not the top choice but a more accessible, better motivated or less specialized person should be asked.

5.3.2 Activation and Capture of Knowledge

As pointed out before, only knowledge in the short-term memory can be elicited. It would therefore not be wise to start a knowledge elicitation session by asking an expert to name or write down everything he or she knows. Rather, the knowledge of interest needs to be activated with the help of stimuli, such as models, photographs, role plays, etc. The choice of stimuli depends on the objective of knowledge elicitation: when knowledge about the meaning and relationship of terms is to be activated (e.g., in order to build semantic nets), note cards with words and phrases may be used as stimulus. When experts are expected to reflect about practical knowledge (e.g., about how to operate a machine) a stimulus can be created by giving the expert practical tasks that require this knowledge [7]. In so-called *episodic interviews,* experts are repeatedly asked to share stories and events – so called episodes – from their lives ("Please tell us about a situation where the process really turned critical..."; "Do you remember a situation where the customer was really satisfied?....) that trigger the memory and serve as a starting point for further investigation [3].

After activation, the expert has to express his knowledge in an interpretable and comprehensive manner. Observation-based approaches, such as thinking aloud, leave the expert more or less with the possible drawback that the expert's comments might not refer to the knowledge area in question but deal with different topics as well as with emotions. Rather than letting ideas run freely, some techniques, such as advising novices and "Demonstrate-Observe-Explain" (DOE) (see Table 5.1), are applied in order to structure the thought process.

While observation techniques leave the broadness and depth of the elicitation result almost exclusively up to the expert, interviews are a means of strongly focusing on specific aspects of his or her knowledge. Needless to say, the quality of an interview greatly depends on the interviewer and the questions that person asks. LaFrance describes probing activities with two dimensions: forms of knowledge that are investigated (e.g., scripts, metaphors, rules-of-thumb) and types of interview questions (e.g., "grand tour questions", questions about categories, cross-checking questions), which capture different aspects of knowledge. Grand tour questions, for example, cast a wide net over the knowledge domain (e.g., "Could you describe the kinds of things that key account managers do?"), while questions about categories ("When you told me about your work, you were talking about key account managers. Is this a specific type of manager? How does it differ from other managing functions?") clarify the meaning and organization of concepts. LaFrance suggests the use of a so-called "knowledge acquisition grid" – a generic table that organizes forms of knowledge and types of questions – to support interviewers in preparing questionnaires, documenting answers during the interview and identifying knowledge aspects and question types that have not yet been covered [8].

In order to ensure the validity of the knowledge capture, cross-checking questions are important. They can fulfil different tasks, ranging from simply summarizing the experts' opinions ("Did I get this right: you believe that customers should only have one person to talk to within the sales organization?...") to evoking conflicting views (e.g., "Let me play devil's advocate in response to your story about the need to involve the key account manager. What if you did not – would it really upset the customer?"). The quality and validity of the elicitation process can furthermore be improved when the expert feels well-informed about the elicitation process, feels that he or she is being taken seriously as a partner and trusts the interviewer [3, 7, 8].

5.3.3 Knowledge Interpretation and Documentation

Protocols, audio tapes and films capture data about knowledge that still have to be processed before the underlying knowledge can be documented. Researchers in cognitive psychology usually employ elaborate methods that attempt to reduce subjectivity of this translation to a minimum, such as text coding (see Table 5.1) and quantitative measures (e.g., word frequencies, answers on item scales), while knowledge engineers, who design expert systems, and strategists tend to employ more qualitative approaches and accept higher levels of subjectivity of results.

The way in which data is processed and documented obviously depends on the purpose of the elicitation process and the elicitation method that has been chosen:

- When the elicited knowledge is intended for the rule base of an expert system, it is often documented in production systems, i.e., a set of "if-then rules".

- When knowledge is used to structure a knowledge domain for navigation (e.g., to design knowledge maps – see Chap. 6), the resulting documentation consists of tree-structures and network diagrams.
- When knowledge about causality is elicited, causal maps are used to document the elicitation results.

Fig. 5.1 shows different ways of documenting elicitation results as described by Huff [4] Some of these forms of documentations are usually referred to as knowledge maps (within dotted line, also see Chap. 6) while others are less visual and provide little or no spatial information. In general, documentations that are based on simple models of cognition (e.g., concept hierarchies to capture semantic knowledge), and that are easy to use and to interpret, only have a very limited explanatory range. Visualizations of cognitive frames, schemes and linguistic codes give very broad views on individual (episodic) knowledge. They do, however, require a good deal of interpretation through the researcher and are therefore costly to produce and especially prone to misinterpretations [4].

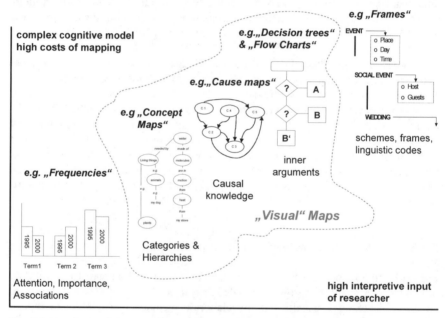

Fig. 5.1. Documentation and interpretation of elicitation results, based on [4]

5.4 Implementation Experience

The preceding paragraphs have outlined approaches to knowledge elicitation that are common in psychological research (and neighbouring disciplines) but so far have only rarely found their way into knowledge management literature and practice. To KM practitioners, especially in SMEs, this might not come as a surprise.

They could rightfully point out that their company does not employ an experienced cognitive psychologist for elicitation purposes or does not use any kind of facilitator for knowledge elicitation but simply asks experts to jot down what they know. Furthermore, many of the described methods are rather complicated, while business practice demands approaches that are simple, quick and have low resource demands.

The following section describes the application of different psychological elicitation techniques in a high-tech SME that encounters time and resource constraints that are typical for this company type. It thus challenges the view that knowledge elicitation techniques are too complicated, time-consuming, and expensive for SMEs. The SME of the case study, CEROBEAR GmbH, is a producer of high-tech bearings that are used in a variety of demanding and very different use environments, such as racing cars, NASA space shuttles, semiconductor machinery, and the food industry. The purpose of the elicitation exercise was to build an ontology about CEROBEAR's customers that could be used to identify possible new application fields and customers on the Internet. The use of the ontology for Web intelligence is described in Chap. 7, while the knowledge elicitation necessary for ontology building is covered in this chapter.

The research described was two-fold: (1) the systematic use of psychological knowledge elicitation techniques was to be tested for feasibility, applicability in an SME setting, time demands, possible improvements etc. and (2) the ontology that was derived through a systematic approach was to be compared with an ad hoc ontology that was created without any methodological support. The following paragraphs describe the systematic approach.

5.4.1 Identification of Experts at CEROBEAR

Since CEROBEAR offers mainly customized products, the company's sales force and marketing group consists of highly qualified engineers, who not only know their present and similar future customers but who are also able to assess potential new product application domains. Nine members of the group, which is subdivided into teams in accordance with the different customer groups, were therefore considered to be experts in the knowledge domains of interest (customers and new applications/markets) and were included in the elicitation exercise. To ensure their co-operation, they were informed about the objectives of the research project prior to the elicitation sessions. All individual interview sessions took place on one day, thus reducing time demands for travel, preparation and general organization to a minimum.

5.4.2 Activation and Capture: Free Association & Episodic Interviews

In order to activate expert knowledge, *free word association* [3] was employed: for a short time span of about 5-8 minutes experts were asked to name everything that came to mind when describing CEROBEAR's customers and their needs.

Response times were relatively slow at first – possibly because of a feeling of inhibition – but the speed and number of responses soon increased. The exercise resulted in a list of 6 (minimum) to 10 (maximum) items, such as "...can be divided into racing cars and future industries", "...should be grouped according to their needs", "...ask for different types of bearings".

In a second step *episodic interviews* were administered that were intended to capture experience about past events, as well as individual expectations. Typical interview questions were: "When you look back at the time when you joined the company, what happened the first time you contacted a customer? What has changed in the meantime?"; "What did your working day look like yesterday?"; "How do you think a customer would describe the product?". Also, topics addressed in the free word association exercise were elaborated on. Asking for episodes of individual experience proved to trigger many responses and great interests of the experts. Interviews lasted about 20 minutes and were recorded on tape.

5.4.3 Interpretation and Documentation: Building an Ontology

The objective of the elicitation process was the construction of an ontology to be used in a software tool. The software thus provided a template for knowledge documentation: knowledge had to be captured in a graph of concepts and relations (see Chap. 7). A multi-step process was employed to achieve this objective:

1. Interview transcripts were searched for topics that a) had been mentioned in the free word association sessions and b) were mentioned by all or most of the experts. These topics were considered to be key elements of the ontology and were marked in the interview transcripts.
2. Desk research (thesauri, internet, engineering and marketing publications) was employed to identify synonyms and related words for key elements of the ontology.
3. A preliminary ontology was designed and presented to two of the experts at CEROBEAR. They made suggestions for improvements that were used to modify the ontology. The new and improved ontology was again evaluated and modified by the experts. In the third and final feedback cycle, the ontology was presented to some of the other experts who commented that they were able to find their sales team and activities easily. A comparison between the first and the final ontology showed that the number of concepts and links had substantially decreased, but that also information had been added that was only hinted at during the interviews but not discussed in detail: it became obvious that different groups of customers (e.g., space industry, racing cars) generally ask for different types of products (e.g., hybrid bearings, ceramic bearings). The ontology was extended to answer the question "which customer has bought which product type?"

The final ontology was employed in the software tool (see Chap. 7) and provided substantially better results than the ad hoc ontology that was developed without the use of psychological methods.

5.5 Discussion and Conclusions

The case study at CEROBEAR has followed the three elicitation steps well-known in cognitive research – identification of experts, activation and capture and interpretation/documentation – and has applied elicitation methods, that are not commonly applied in KM, to build a company specific ontology about customers and markets. Results were promising: a knowledge search that was based on the developed ontology delivered better results than standard search engines did and by far exceeded the results that were achieved with an unsystematically elicited, ad hoc ontology. Also, acceptance for both the methods and the results was high: CEROBEAR uses the newly developed ontology to restructure its website in order to make it more easily accessible for potential customers.

The total efforts necessary for the elicitation process, however, are still unclear. While interview times could be limited to less than 30 minutes per expert, considerable time was needed for feedback loops and improvements. Now that the multi-step approach for ontology-building has been designed and tested, feedback cycles in new ontology projects can probably be substantially shorter, but future research is needed for reliable data.

Another possible problem is the fact that the elicitation process requires a facilitator, such as the researcher in the case study. SMEs will need some guidance in identifying suitable facilitators within their company, such as employees with good communication and analytical skills or relevant education (e.g., in qualitative (market) research or in (job) interviewing techniques). This does, however, not pose unsolvable problems.

References

1. Dann, H-D (1992) Variation von Lege-Strukturen zur Wissensrepräsentation. In: Scheele, B. (Ed.). Struktur-Lege-Verfahren als Dialog-Konsens-Methodik: Ein Zwischenfazit zur Forschungsentwicklung bei der rekonstruktiven Erhebung Subjektiver Theorien. Aschendorff, Münster pp. 2-9
2. Eysenck, MW, Keane MT (1990). Cognitive Psychology. Lawrence Earlbaum Associates, Hove, London, Hillsdale
3. Flick U (1995) Qualitative Forschung: Theorie, Methoden, Anwendung in Psychologie und Sozialwissenschaften. Rowohlt, Reinbeek bei Hamburg.
4. Huff, AS. (1990). Mapping Strategic Thought. In: Huff, A.S. (Ed.) Mapping Strategic Thought. John Wiley & Sons pp. 11-49
5. Iansiti, M (1998) Technology Integration: Making critical choices in a dynamic world. Harvard Business School Press, Boston.
6. Ignizio, JP (1991) An introduction to expert systems: the development and implementation of rule-based expert systems. McGraw-Hill, New York
7. Kluwe, RH. (1988) Methoden der Psychologie zur Gewinnung von Daten über menschliches Wissen. In: Mandl, H., Spada, H. (Eds.).Wissenspsychologie. Psychologie Verlags Union , München, Weinheim pp. 359-385

8.   LaFrance M(1988) Knowledge Acquisition Grid: a method for training knowledge engineers. In: Gaines, BR, Boose, JH (Eds.) Knowledge Acquisition for Knowledge-Based Systems. Academic Press, London pp. 81-91.
9.   Wessels, MG (1982) Cognitive Psychology. Harper& Row, New York
10. Westermayr (2002) Organizational Network Analysis (ONA) – Basis für die erfolgreiche Einführung von Wissensmanagement; conference presentation Knowtech 2002, Munich; available at: http://www.knowtech2002.de/Westermeyr_SerCon.pdf

6 Codification – Knowledge Maps

Antonie Jetter

Chair for Business Administration with focus on Technology and Innovation
Management, RWTH Aachen University, Germany, jetter@tim.rwth-aachen.de

6.1 Introduction

Knowledge codification takes place when knowledge is written down in books
and manuals, stored on films (e.g., instructional videos) or embedded in everyday
work procedures or software (e.g., diagnosis software, expert systems). These media are widely used and serve the purpose of articulating, transferring and storing
explicit human knowledge. Knowledge maps, in contrast, do not attempt to codify
the knowledge itself, but rather to codify "knowledge about the knowledge". Like
geographical maps, they guide the way and help to find knowledge, either in the
form of knowledgeable people and experts or in the form of knowledge media.
Furthermore, knowledge maps are used to structure a knowledge domain in order
to provide a shared understanding and common vocabulary and to preserve meta-
knowledge about a topic.

The following chapter will briefly discuss means and objectives of knowledge
codification in general and then focus on knowledge maps in particular. Knowledge maps can be differentiated according to their purpose: while some maps codify knowledge to provide means for knowledge detection, others are used to support knowledge assessment. These aspects will be discussed in Sect. 6.2.
Knowledge maps, furthermore, differ in the knowledge contents they codify (e.g.,
causal knowledge, knowledge about knowledge sources), which will be explained
in Sect. 6.3. Sect. 6.4 introduces the case of a high-tech SME that has successfully
used a newly developed knowledge mapping approach to analyse its knowledge
flows in new product development and has subsequently used an intranet knowledge application map to codify its processes for easy navigation. The chapter
closes with a discussion of the results in Sect. 6.5.

6.2 Knowledge Codification and Knowledge Maps

As discussed in Chap. 4, knowledge codification is the process by which explicit
knowledge is detached from its source and put in a state in which it can easily be
transferred via different media, such as software or books. Different types of codification can be differentiated: knowledge can be embedded in machines or software (e.g., robots, workflow software) or codified in detailed process descriptions

and manuals, that prescribe how knowledge should be used. Though in varying degrees, both approaches efficiently ensure that the same knowledge is applied in all similar occasions (e.g., in reoccurring production steps or to answer standard questions in a call centre). Embedding and prescribing, however, can be problematic when new situations occur. In these cases, the type of knowledge codification employed needs to leave room for reflection and adjustment of the codified knowledge to new needs. Knowledge structures, which represent the elements and interrelations of a particular knowledge domain, rather than its detailed content, and learning histories, which explain why a particular event has occurred, are examples of such abstract, relatively context-independent types of codification. They leave it up to the knowledge user to see analogies between situations that are not completely similar and to adjust the knowledge accordingly.[1]

Knowledge maps are visual representations of "knowledge about knowledge", rather than of the knowledge itself [5, 6, 20]. They, for example, point towards experts that have knowledge, rather than codifying the expert knowledge. Often, geographical maps are therefore used as a metaphor for knowledge maps: they provide abstract models of a domain that simplify a complex reality (e.g., a mountainside), downsize it to the important aspects, add relevant information (e.g., about the months in which mountain passes are open) and thus help to find locations and the paths that lead to them. Knowledge maps basically serve the same purpose: they help to detect the sources of knowledge and information (e.g., people, databases) and structure the knowledge landscape by representing the elements and structural links of knowledge domains. As is the case with geographic maps, this requires that someone – the cartographer – knows and understands the knowledge territory that is codified in the map. The map is useful if the cartographer understands the knowledge domain and successfully translates it into the map and if the territory - the context in which the map is used - is relatively stable and does not change during map use.

In many cases, however, knowledge domains are instable: because of shifting business environments (e.g., new markets, technological progress), formerly important knowledge can lose its relevance, while new knowledge becomes important. Knowledge maps can be employed to analyse shifting knowledge territories by codifying the different individual views or "mental models" people have about reality. These models can be transferred to other people, assessed, updated, and improved, subsequently leading to increasingly adequate shared mental models of reality [19]. This view of knowledge maps as means to codify mental models and support knowledge assessment is shared by researchers in the field of managerial cognition, who investigate the mental maps (or, cognitive maps) of decision-

---

[1] The different types of knowledge codification have been characterized in Chap. 4 as embedding (hard-wiring knowledge e.g., in software), prescribing (giving "how-to" instructions, e.g., in manuals), structuring (framing, classifying and ordering knowledge elements, e.g., in keyword trees), and abstracting (developing hypotheses and theories about events, e.g., in learning histories). They all depend on the existence of explicit knowledge that can be obtained through elicitation (see Chap. 5)

makers [1, 8]. Mental maps hereby contain the subjective knowledge that managers have and use, such as their knowledge of the general business environment, the future evolution of technologies or the probable moves of a competitor [8].

The two different objectives of employing knowledge maps have some implications for the way in which knowledge is codified in them:

- When maps are intended for knowledge detection, they focus on efficient (re-) use of knowledge in a knowledge domain that is considered to be well understood. The resulting maps therefore tend to be context dependent and to leave relatively little room for re-interpretation of reality and adaptation to new situations. When, for example, a knowledge application map instructs an employee on what knowledge to use or yellow pages point towards expert knowledge, these maps imply that it is the knowledge on the map that is relevant for the company. The importance of knowledge that is not codified in the maps might be missed. Knowledge maps for detection should, therefore, ideally only be codified after the knowledge territory has been thoroughly analysed, possibly with the help of knowledge maps for assessment. Furthermore, they should be designed in a way that leaves maximum room for questioning the map without losing its efficiency in knowledge (re-)use.

- Knowledge maps that codify different world views show "snapshots" of the perception of a knowledge domain, including its key elements, boundaries, influencing factors, and structural and dynamical properties, at a given time. The resulting maps, for example, visualize cause-and-effect relations, driving forces, and strategy roadmaps (also see Chap. 8). Since these maps tend to be abstract, they demand a good deal of interpretation, analogy-building and transfer from the map user before they can be applied – the knowledge codified in them might, therefore, be applied quite differently by different persons. They could, for example, derive different strategies for dealing with changes in a business environment that is codified in the map. The maps are thus able to provide a starting point for (re-)defining the knowledge territory, but do not give answers to how knowledge should be used.

Mapmakers need to clearly focus on one of the two objectives of codifying knowledge in knowledge maps to make sure they serve their intended purpose.

6.3 Types of Knowledge Maps

The last section has emphasized that all knowledge maps codify "knowledge about knowledge" but with different intentions. The underlying purpose of a knowledge map, however, is not easily recognizable by the map user, since many types of knowledge maps can be and are applied for both purposes: a visual description of knowledge flows in a given situation can, for example, be descriptive, with the purpose of assessing the knowledge domain or prescriptive with the intention of instructing map users on how to apply knowledge. The following sections will, therefore, briefly present examples of four commonly known types of knowledge maps and will discuss what type of knowledge they codify and how this relates to assessment and/or detection. Some of these maps resemble the visualizations of knowledge elicitation results that are described in Chap. 5. Indeed, many knowledge maps have originated as models of the human memory in cognitive psychology. Today, however, they are only loosely linked to their origins and are not considered to represent the way in which knowledge is organized in people's brains but understood as practical tools of knowledge management.

6.3.1 Hierarchical or Radial Knowledge Structure Maps: Concept Maps and Mind Maps

Hierarchical knowledge structure maps are strongly related to psychological models that are grounded on the notion that the human brain organizes semantic knowledge in networks or hierarchies of concepts and propositions (see Chap. 5). Often, these models are depicted as graphs, with nodes (mostly visualized as bubbles or squares) that represent the concepts and edges that stand for propositions.

Concept maps provide one model for the hierarchical organization of knowledge: top-level concepts are abstract with few characteristics. Concepts on the levels below have detailed individual traits, as well as all the characteristic of the superordinate concept. The propositions between concepts are described verbally and can represent any type of relation ("is part of", "influences", "can determine", "maybe disturbs", etc.) [14]. Concept maps have been extensively used in education to provide orientation about the structure of courses, textbooks and single lectures and to check the knowledge level of students by comparing the concept maps they draw (or that can be inferred from their statements) with a concept map that represents the teaching objectives. Most importantly, they are said to facilitate learning by providing students with the means to externalise, question and improve their individual mental models [14].

A similar approach, though with a slightly different theoretical background, is mind mapping. *Mind maps*, too, consist of concepts that are linked through propositions. They are, however, radially organized. The mapping process starts with a key topic in the centre of the map. More specific concepts are added to the map by drawing lines that branch from the central concept. These concepts are again expanded outward into branches and sub-branches. In the resulting mind map, the most specific aspects of the key concept are, therefore, at the edge of the map, the more general ones in its centre [3].

As is the case with concept maps, mind maps can simply be built with paper and pencil, but software packages are available. They make it possible to use concept and mind maps not only to codify, communicate and gain clarity about a knowledge domain, but also to provide access to knowledge resources (e.g., documents, software applications, contact data of experts) that cover a specific knowledge domain [5]. Ramesh and Tiwana [15], for example, use concept maps to model and store team knowledge in a software system for collaborative product development.

6.3.2 Networked Knowledge Structure Maps: Causal Maps

Causal mapping is characterized as a technique "for linking strategic thinking and acting, helping make sense of complex problems, and communicating to oneself and others what might be done about them" [3]. The outcomes of the mapping exercise, so-called "causal maps", codify knowledge about cause and effects. They are digraphs that consist of nodes ("concepts") and edges ("arrows") that represent causality.

Fig. 6.1 (below) shows the positive and negative causal links (black and dotted lines) between environmental forces (white boxes) and the desired characteristics (dark boxes) of a specific technology (laser diode pumped Nd-YAG lasers). The example is taken from a case study and reflects the mental model of a technology manager [10]. It has been generated in order to investigate the possible future availability (or non-availability) and attractiveness of a particular product technology. One of the desired attributes of the new product technology is "high pulse energy". It is, among others, causally influenced by the "total demand for YAG-Laser". When this concept increases, the concept "high pulse energies" increases as well. Furthermore, the concept "price degression through competition" is causally decreased.

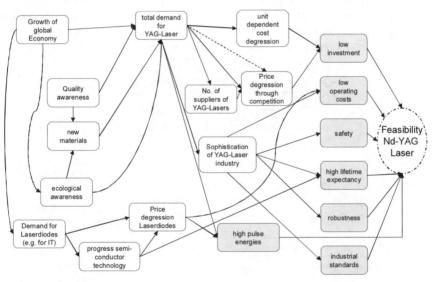

Environmental Forces   **Technology characteristics**

Fig. 6.1. Causal map of environmental forces and characteristics of a technology [10]

Causal maps are widely used to capture complex mental models of individuals, to provide a starting point for strategic business analysis [2] and to visualize systems for modelling and simulation design [17]. They are referred to by different names, such as "cognitive maps" [1], "oval maps" (for collectively generated causal maps

[2]) "influence diagrams", and "patterns of interactions" [18]. Other than concept and mind maps, causal maps encode dynamic behaviour ("something happens because and after something else has happened"). Because of map complexity, occurrence of feedback loops and the possible compensation of incoming arrows with different signs, causal behaviour is not easily inferred from maps [1]. A variety of approaches have been developed to analyse the structure and the underlying dynamics of causal maps, such as Vester's "paper computer" [18] or a Fuzzy Cognitive Map (FCM)-based action support system suggested by Jetter [9, 10, 16]. The latter translates the mental models of product development experts into FCM models and thus makes them computable to support product planning and design decisions. Cause maps are also at the core of the decision-validity tracking approach suggested by Faran in Chap. 8. As can be inferred from these applications, causal maps are mainly used to support knowledge assessment, rather than knowledge detection.

6.3.3 Knowledge Source Maps

Knowledge source maps, sometimes also referred to as knowledge carrier maps, can be interpreted as organizational charts that do not depict functions, responsibility and hierarchy, but expertise. They help to detect experts in a specific knowledge domain so that managers can find people for their teams, as well as advisors for particular problems that cannot be solved within the team [4, 5].

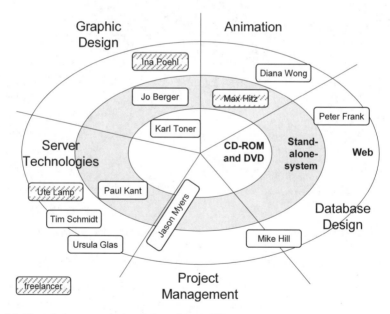

Fig. 6.2. Knowledge source maps (adapted from [5])

Fig. 6.2 shows a simple knowledge source map for a multimedia company that offers and develops three different product groups (websites, stand-alone systems, such as terminals and CD-ROMs/DVDs – see concentric circles). Relevant fields of expertise are depicted as sectors of the circles (graphic design, animation, database design, project management, server technologies). The names of the experts are placed according to their expertise: Jason Myers, for example is an expert in project management (regardless of the product), while Mike Hill has expertise in project management and database design for Web applications. Additional information can be coded in the map, such as the fact that three people (Ute Lamp, Ina Poehl and Max Hitz) are freelancers. Knowledge source maps can be extended through so-called "yellow pages" or "blue pages" that contain information on the individual internal experts (yellow pages) or external experts (blue pages), such as name, photo and contact data, position, fields and level of expertise (e.g., true expert, some experience, novice), membership in professional organizations, and personal interests [4, 6].

Knowledge source maps point towards the location of explicit, as well as tacit knowledge and are clearly intended for detection purposes. When knowledge about the expertise of employees is available, it can, however, also be used to assess capabilities in given knowledge domains. For example, in the map above, it becomes obvious that the company has no expert knowledge of database design for the domains of stand-alone multimedia terminals and CDs/DVDs. Results of this assessment can be used to optimise the structure of project teams (e.g., no redundancies, all important knowledge domains covered) as well as to support human resource management in planning training programs and career paths and systematic knowledge retention. [5].

6.3.4 Knowledge Flow Maps

Knowledge flow maps - sometimes also referred to as knowledge application maps - show the order in which knowledge resources are and should be used. They are, basically, representations of knowledge-intensive business processes that are supplemented by visualizations of the information and knowledge that is needed to handle specific steps of the process [5]. Fig. 6.3 shows a process flow chart for a routine business process.

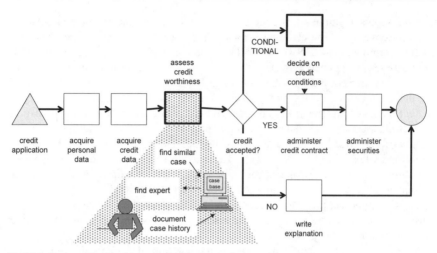

Fig. 6.3. Process flow and knowledge flow map (adapted from [7])

One process step ("assess credit worthiness") is considered to be knowledge-intensive and, therefore, is supported by a knowledge flow map. The latter shows sub-processes of the process step (e.g., find similar cases in case base; find expert; document the case history) and the knowledge resources needed for these steps (electronic case base, expert) [7]. Sub-processes, such as "find expert" can be divided even further into process steps such as "define search context", "search yellow pages", and "assess expertise" [7]. In contrast to this great level of detail, Eppler presents a knowledge application map of a market research company that covers the firm's value chain in only four process steps that are supported by a large variety of specific methods (e.g., interview techniques, statistical analysis) [5].

The "correct" level of detail is determined by the intended use of the knowledge application map. The map described by Eppler only presents procedural knowledge and leaves it fully up to the user to decide what process step he or she is currently in or which one of the offered methods should be used. In contrast to this "pull" approach, Kang et al. [11] and Hinkelmann et al. [7] suggest the use of knowledge flow maps in workflow management systems that control the execution of business processes, "push" knowledge resources towards users in accordance with their process needs and also guide the storage of results (for a discussion of "pull" and "push" strategies, see Chap. 3). Needless to say, for this type of application, knowledge flow maps have to give very fine-grained descriptions of activities and knowledge resources.

Knowledge flow maps can be used to codify and support knowledge assessment, as well as to detect relevant knowledge, as will be demonstrated by the following case study of a high-tech SME that has successfully employed a mapping technique to analyze its knowledge flows and has codified and communicated its improved process in an intranet knowledge application map.

6.4 Case Study: Knowledge Maps to Improve NPD

AIXTRON[2] is a relatively large SME with approx. 400 employees worldwide. The company develops manufacturing equipment for the production of semi-conductors. It serves specialty needs in this extremely dynamic and volatile market through highly innovative products. Product development is a core process in which the re-use of formerly acquired experience and the creation of new knowledge have to be carefully balanced.

At the start of the case study, new product development at AIXTRON had, for some time, been organized around a so-called "development and qualification order"(DQO) – a procedure, supported by paper documents, that guides the development process from kick-off to final documentation of development results. Though the process was generally accepted because it provides structure and transparency, some problems existed: the DQO could only capture some aspects of the necessary knowledge, such as the final test results for an accepted new development, but not the test results for those developments that did not meet the requirements. It was, therefore, possible that the same unsuccessful development efforts were repeated again in different projects. Also, a lot of knowledge was documented in media (e.g., database for quality management, project management software) that were not part of the DQO documentation or "hidden" in e-mail communication, memos and minutes of meetings. Electronic file storage did not always follow a transparent and consistent system, making it difficult to find documents. The forms of the DQO furthermore contained some information that was only necessary for some people (e.g., quality management) - nevertheless the complete set of forms including attachments was passed around, making the process difficult to handle and time-consuming.

Using the DQO as a starting point, AIXTRON therefore decided to analyse its knowledge flows in new product development (NPD) in order to come up with an improved process.

6.4.1 Process Assessment

The purpose of the process assessment step was twofold: it should be investigated (1) whether all relevant knowledge (and only relevant knowledge!) was codified, stored and made accessible in AIXTRON's NPD process and (2) which methods and media were used and could possibly be improved.

In a first step, 11 people were interviewed, who were involved in NPD in different functional areas and on different hierarchical levels. The exploratory interviews lasted between 1.5 and 2.5 hours and surfaced a multitude of information on problem fields, concerns and ideas for improvement, as well as contrasting views about processes and the suitability of the media in use. In many cases, interviewees also addressed topics outside the scope of the DQO. To structure the multi-

---

[2] www.aixtron.com

tude of information, an abstract, but nevertheless easy-to-comprehend map visualization of knowledge flows, was created, which served as the basis for discussions [12, 13].

The smallest element of all knowledge flows is the transfer of knowledge between a sender and a receiver. Senders and receivers can, for example, be single persons, teams, organizational units, databases, and files. Once a receiver has obtained knowledge (e.g., a sales person has learnt about a specific product requirement from a customer), he or she can serve as a sender by transferring this knowledge to other receivers (e.g., a product developer).

Thus, chains of knowledge transfers can be built that capture the knowledge flows within and between organizational units in processes, such as AIXTRON's NPD process (see Fig. 6.4): The process starts with knowledge transfer activity 100 ("project initiation") which can trigger different types of development (activity 21x) from the creation of a new machine concept (activity 211) to a simple change order (activity 214). All knowledge transfers are described in detail through the template presented in Fig. 6.4 for the case of knowledge transfer activity 221. Results of the design process are transferred to manufacturing and service with transfer activity 250.

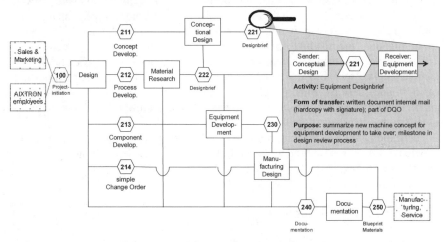

Fig. 6.4. Top-level knowledge transfer map for AIXTRON's NPD

The sender-receiver model of knowledge transfer can be applied on different levels of analysis: in Fig. 6.4 it is used to describe knowledge transfers between functional areas but it can also be used to represent detailed knowledge transfers within one design team or an individual's knowledge transfers. Since the map looks the same for all levels of aggregation, it is relatively easy to employ and can serve as a basis for discussion. Furthermore, it supports process improvement by facilitating the use of heuristics. Among others, the map can be used to identify

- knowledge dumps (e.g., receivers, such as databases, that receive knowledge but are rarely sending it anywhere),

- inadequate communication methods (e.g., the attempt to transfer tacit knowledge, such as experience, with written documents),
- people and divisions who do not communicate (lack of paths),
- parallel stream knowledge transfers (different paths between the same senders and receivers) that can lead to costly redundancies and problems with different versions of the same knowledge, and
- single paths of knowledge transfers that would break if the senders/receivers involved were to disappear (in the case of people: e.g., retirement).

In the case of AIXTRON, the knowledge mapping exercise yielded a variety of suggestions for small process improvement (e.g., the use of a database, that was already being used in one department, in another department), as well as to a few key findings:

- The knowledge transfer between functional areas was not as transparent to some employees as originally assumed – they were sometimes not fully aware of what other departments did with the knowledge they provided.
- File storage was a key problem, because the storage in project folders made it difficult to search for files using other criteria (e.g., same technological solution regardless of the project). The often criticized apparent "lack of discipline" in storing electronic files only once in the most up-to-date version in project folders could partially be attributed to a lack of know-how about where to store documents.
- Though sometimes questioned because of its complexity, the DQO proved to be a powerful approach to ensure transparency and communicate responsibilities within the NPD process. However, access should be more customized to make sure that people do not have to handle documents that they do not need for their everyday work.
- Every project creates knowledge about the duration of specific development tasks that can be valuable for future time and cost estimates. However, this knowledge was not codified with a sufficient level of detail.

To solve the problems identified through the mapping exercise, AIXTRON designed an intranet-based knowledge application map.

6.4.2 Improved Processes: AIXTRON's Knowledge Application Map

The knowledge application or process map designed by AIXTRON is based on the former hardcopy versions of the DQO. The forms are published on the intranet and supplemented by a large number of additional functions:

- The entire DQO flow is visualized and explained on intranet pages and in supplementary documents, which can be downloaded. Documents, databases, software applications etc., are accessible on the DQO intranet page that covers the development step that they are used for. Documents created within the DQO-system are automatically stored without the user having to make decisions how and where to store them.

- All DQOs are registered and can be viewed using different search and sorting criteria, such as keywords, project number, development stage or release status, and responsible persons and departments.
- Depending on their roles and responsibilities, users are given access to different documents, thus only dealing with documents they really need.
- Comments, as well as acknowledgment and approval of development steps and changes, take place electronically. An e-mail system informs the individuals involved in the process.

The process map is implemented in a trial version currently under test. Acceptance among the users is high. Based on preliminary results, AIXTRON expects a substantial reduction of the time it needs to process a DQO, as well as an improved intra- and inter-project knowledge transfer. For the final version, additional functionalities are planned, such as integration of a project control system that gathers information on the time spent on different development activities.

6.5 Discussion and Conclusion

This chapter has discussed knowledge maps as means to codify "knowledge about knowledge" and has pointed out two distinct objectives of any mapping exercise – (1) codification of knowledge with the intention to assess reality in order to identify relevant knowledge and to improve processes and (2) codification of "navigational" knowledge to improve the map-based detection of knowledge. Navigational knowledge maps are only useful when they point towards knowledge sources, such as people and databases that contain relevant knowledge, when they represent knowledge domains correctly and when they capture and prescribe knowledge processes that "make sense". Consequently, knowledge assessment should always take place prior to the creation of knowledge maps for detection.

This two-step approach – first codification with the purpose of assessment, then codification in a "navigational" knowledge application map – is at the core of the case study presented in this article. The case thus demonstrates that the knowledge integration activity "codification" is not isolated, but relies on successful elicitation of knowledge through interviews (also see Chap. 5) and also touches upon the knowledge activities of assessment and detection.

The newly developed knowledge mapping approach applied in the assessment stage of the case study proved to be a powerful means for the codification of different views on the NPD process under investigation. Its relative simplicity and the scalable level of detail made the map manageable for people with different backgrounds. Throughout the study, people actively employed the "language" – the different symbols – of the map to make suggestions, such as additional process steps. An alternative interview approach, in which interviewees draw the map themselves and explain it to the interviewer, is thus feasible. This could reduce the strain on the facilitator of the mapping exercise, which will most likely be a bottleneck in SMEs, where no researcher is present to adopt this role. Suggestions for process improvements were often expressed in the interviews already, but the map-based heuristics used to analyze knowledge processes, such as the search for redundancies or knowledge dumps, nevertheless were helpful: They offered alternative views on established processes and hinted at additional improvements.

In the case of AIXTRON, the assessment indicated the need for an intranet knowledge application map. Process analyses in other situations will most certainly yield different results and could, for example, demonstrate the need for another type of knowledge maps (e.g., knowledge source maps and yellow pages), other means of codification and communication or changes in knowledge cultures. The knowledge application map should, therefore, not be considered an inevitable result of the mapping exercise. Furthermore, it is presently still in a trial phase.

Though preliminary results are promising for AIXTRON, it is quite obvious that the solution will not suit the needs of all SMEs, especially since AIXTRON has developed the technical platform of the DQO –process map in-house and has thus come up with a solution that, at best, is applicable for larger SMEs with strong IT departments. Among the many reasons for not choosing existing commercial solutions, one was dominant: existing software packages – workflow systems, product data management systems, content management systems and other – were inadequate because they failed to provide both   process orientation and enough flexibility to deal with a non-routine process, such as NPD. Future research, but especially development efforts in the commercial domain, are necessary to solve these problems.

References

1. Axelrod R (1976) (ed) Structure of Decision. The Cognitive Maps of Political Elites. Pinceton University Press, Princeton
2. Bryson JM, Ackermann F, Eden C, Finn CB (2004) Visible Thinking. John Wiley & Sons, Chichester
3. Buzan T, Buzan, B (1996) The Mind Map Book. Plume
4. Davenport TH, Prusak L (1997) Working Knowledge. Harvard Business School Press
5. Eppler MJ (2001) Making Knowledge Visible through Intranet Knowledge Maps. Concepts, Elements, Cases. (Proceedings of the 34th Hawaii International Conference on System Sciences 2001)
6. Haun M (2002) Handbuch Wissensmanagement: Grundlagen und Umsetzung, Systeme und Praxisbeispiele. Springer, Berlin
7. Hinkelmann K, Karagiannis D, Telesko R (2002) PROMOTE – Methodologie und Werkzeug für geschäftsprozessorientiertes Wissensmanagement. In: Abecker et al (eds) Geschäftsprozessorientiertes Wissensmanagement. Springer, Berlin pp 293-322
8. Huff AS (1990) Mapping Strategic Thought. In: Huff, A. S. (ed) Mapping Strategic Thought. John Wiley & Sons, Chichester, pp 11-49
9. Jetter A (2003) Educating the Guess: Strategies, Concepts and Tools for the Fuzzy Front End of Product Development. In: Kocaoglu DF, Anderson TR (eds) Technology Management for Reshaping the World. OR, Portland, pp 261-273

10. Jetter A (2005) Handlungsunterstützung für die frühen Phasen der Produktentwicklung. DUV in press, Wiesbaden
11. Kang I, Park Y, Kim Y (2003) A framework for designing a workflow-based knowledge map. Business Process Management 9: 281-294
12. Müller-Baum P (2003) Optimierung des Wissenstransfers in Entwicklungsprojekten. Industrie Management 19: 54-57
13. Müller- Baum P (2003) Wegweiser zum Projekterfolg. In: Lange D. (ed) 20. Internationales Deutsches Projektmanagement Forum 2003. Dokumentationsband, Stuttgart, pp 301 – 311
14. Novak JD, Gowin DB (1984) Learning how to learn. Cambridge University Press, Cambridge et al
15. Ramesh B, Tiwana A (1999) Supporting Collaborative Process Knowledge Management in New Product Development Teams. Decision Support Systems 27: 213-235
16. Schröder HH, Jetter A (2003) Integrating market and technological knowledge in the fuzzy front-end: an FCM-based action support system. International Journal of Technology Management 26: 517-539
17. Sterman JD (2000) Business Dynamics. Systems Thinking and Modelling for a Complex World. Irwin McGraw-Hill, Boston et al
18. Vester: F, von Hessler A (1980) Sensitivitätsmodell: Ökologie und Planung in Verdichtungsgebieten. Forschungsbericht 80-101 040 34. Frankfurt am Main
19. Weick KE (1990) Cartographic Myths in Organizations. In: Huff AS (ed) Mapping Strategic Thought. John Wiley & Sons, Chichester, pp 1-10
20. Wexler MN (2001) The who, what and why of knowledge mapping. Journal of Knowledge Management 5:249-263

7 Detection – Electronic Knowledge Retrieval

Dina Franzen

Chair for Business Administration with focus on Technology and Innovation Management, RWTH Aachen University, Germany, franzen@tim.rwth-aachen.de

7.1 Introduction

The need for external knowledge is growing continuously: in particular, companies which are acting in knowledge intensive fields have to be informed about their environment. The World Wide Web (WWW) can be a valuable source for the detection of external knowledge since it offers a large variety of information. The huge amount of information that is available on the Web can hardly be measured[1] [3, 10, 13, 17]. The central characteristics of the WWW with respect to knowledge detection are that the access to information is not dependent on time or place and that the information offered is supposed to be always up-to-date [13].

In spite of these advantages, knowledge detection on the WWW suffers from problems. Information from the WWW is ill-structured and cannot be accessed directly, so that a satisfaction of the individual demand for knowledge by using common keyword-based search engines (e.g. Google)[2] is often inefficient and ineffective [8]. The users often "drown" in a mass of so-called hits and the information cannot be turned into knowledge, because the output cannot get processed further. The information meeting the user's need has to be filtered out of the huge amount of data returned to be turned into knowledge [17]. An additional screening of the hits is time consuming and does not guarantee that the user's information demand is satisfied [12]. This chapter is structured as follows: Sect. 7.2 provides an overview of currently used information retrieval (IR) systems for knowledge detection. In Sect. 7.3, one of these, ontology, is applied in a real life case. The chapter closes with a conclusion and discussion (Sect. 7.4).

7.2 IR Systems for Knowledge Detection

Knowledge detection can be subdivided into need-driven and opportunity-driven, by-chance detection of knowledge (see Chap. 2). Need-driven knowledge detec-

---

[1] Baeza-Yates, Ribeiro-Neto (1999), p. 367: in 1999, the amount of textual data available on the Web was estimated to be in the order of one terabyte.

[2] www.google.com

tion includes "retrieval", referring to knowledge detection at a predefined location, as well as "search", the detection of knowledge whose location is unknown in advance. "Browse/discovery" is an activitity for opportunity-driven, by-chance detection of knowledge whose location is unknown in advance.[3] Information Retrieval (IR) was originally employed for locating or relocating scientific literature in large document inventories [8]. Driven by the development of modern information and communication technologies and, in particular, by the WWW, the area of activity of IR systems, however, has expanded. Whereas originally, the term IR systems referred to systems which were confined to need-driven detection of knowledge at a predefined location, thereby providing direct access to knowledge, modern IR systems, in addition to classical retrieval, also include search and browsing /discovery. Thus, need-, as well as opportunity-driven knowledge detection may be implemented by modern IR systems [17]. In addition to performing the knowledge detection activities of retrieving, searching and browsing, modern IR systems represent, organize and store information and make it accessible [1]. They are not restricted to textual documents, but also cover visual and auditory items [15].[4]

Filing of documents is done by classification and indexing, by which the knowledge items are transformed to a searchable data structure. Either the full text of the knowledge item can be indexed, which is called total document or full text indexing, or the item can be represented by keywords, so-called "index terms". Indexing can be done manually, automatically or semi-automatically. Due to the development of computers with increasing processing power and memory, nowadays indexing is usually carried out automatically. Access to knowledge is realized by queries that are formulated by the user. Matching of queries and knowledge items can be carried out using several methods that will be discussed in the following section [19].

7.2.1 Traditional IR Search Methods

The Boolean retrieval, the vector space model and the probabilistic retrieval are the classical matching methods in IR. Whereas Boolean retrieval is based on set theory, probabilistic retrieval is based on formal probability theory; the vector space model employs statistical methods. When the classical methods of IR are used, documents are represented by index terms.

A Boolean search checks whether a defined condition is met or not without admitting any deflection from the condition specified. Concerning the search for documents, Boolean retrieval checks if an index term is contained in the document or not; it rests on the assumption that the documents browsed are either relevant or not [1, 8]. A query is formulated with Boolean expressions which follow an exactly defined semantic. Several search arguments can be connected with the Boo-

---

[3] please refer to Chap. 4 of this book

[4] in the literature, the term "document" is used for all kinds of information items

lean operators such as AND (intersection), OR (set union) and NOT (exclusion union) [20].

In contrast to Boolean retrieval, the vector –space model acts on the assumption that a partial matching is admissible. This is achieved by assigning non-binary weights to index terms in documents as well as in user queries so that their importance concerning the description of a document can be expressed. The documents, as well as the user queries, are represented by vectors [8, 15]. As a result of the description of documents and queries through vectors with real-valued entries, the documents which are most similar to the query can be determined in the collection of documents.[5] Through the calculation of the degree of similarity, not only exact matchings – as in the Boolean retrieval – but also partial matchings are considered [1, 17].

The probabilistic model of IR is based on the idea of estimating the probability that a document is relevant for a user's query [17]. For the calculation of this probability, formal probability theory is applied [15]. The documents are ranked in order of decreasing probability of relevance to the user [7].

7.2.2 Information Retrieval and the WWW

The WWW contains a tremendous amount of online knowledge items which do not follow a consistent definition and structure. Knowledge items may differ with respect to their format, length, distribution, quality and up-to-dateness [1, 8]. Concerning the satisfaction of an individual user's knowledge demands on the WWW, two methods in particular are well known: (Web) directories and search engines [1, 8, 17].

(Web) directories are hierarchical classification systems for the arrangement of information. They support the opportunity-driven, by-chance detection of knowledge because the user can browse through the categories, which are often subdivided into (sub)classes, and make use of the links offered there to get to the knowledge which satisfies his or her needs, as well as need-driven search by offering a search function. The topical placement of the knowledge offered in categories is usually done manually by editors who also check knowledge, provided by a variety of sources, for its quality [1, 8].

In contrast to the manual indexing employed for the creation of Web directories, search engines perform indexing automatically without additional human checks. The knowledge items to be indexed are detected by specific programmes – so-called "robots", "crawlers" or "spiders" – on the WWW and indexed [6]. The Web content is regularly scanned so that the index stays up-to-date. All indexed knowledge items, which can range from single words up to complete documents, are filed in a database. Users formulate a query by entering a single or a series of buzzword(s) which may be linked, e.g., by Boolean operators [1, 6]. The results usually are presented to the user via the user interface in form of a ranking list.

---

[5] for details please refer to Baeza-Yates/ Ribeiro-Neto, 1999, pp. 27 - 30.

Ranking methods which are used by search engines often make use of the number of hyperlinks which refer to a certain website as a measure of relevance [1, 8].

Search engines also may be meta-search engines. These systems offer the possibility to the user to have his or her query processed by several search engines in parallel. The search results are presented to the user altogether [6, 8].

7.2.3 New Impulses in IR Systems

The amount of knowledge stored and made available electronically has grown tremendously due to the availability of the WWW on the one hand, and the price decrease and concurrent performance increase of computers since the mid-nineties on the other hand [1, 13]. In order to cope with the new challenges, IR systems have extended their capabilities.

Since documents and queries are normally expressed in natural language, the development of natural –language processing systems for the analysis of documents has been an important step towards meeting the human need for knowledge acquisition through IR systems [17, 19]. Knowledge detection based on keywords is often of rather low quality because either the user's query context is poorly represented or the keywords generated to represent a document fail to summarize its semantic content [1].

Whereas syntactic approaches for language processing which employed statistical approaches were the focus of research during the eighties, today the challenge of such systems is language processing on the semantic level.

The goal here is to improve the results of knowledge detection, especially their quality, and at the same time to reduce the number of irrelevant hits in the set of results by taking into account the semantic context within the matching process, thus including the *meaning* of words [9, 14]. Human language processing that models a part of the human thinking process, makes great demands on the knowledge base which lays the ground for the system [17]. In order to model natural language, methods and techniques are required that are able to represent human knowledge, so that the process of matching queries and knowledge items provides results that meet the knowledge demand of the IR system user.

To represent knowledge, Computer-based Artificial Intelligence (AI) uses the model of human language processing by Collins and Quillian [4], which is based on the assumption that human knowledge and memory consist of an associative network of terms, known as *Semantic Network.* A semantic network is a formal model which consists of concepts and relations and is represented through a generalized graph which consists of nodes and edges. The nodes describe concepts (e.g. objects, events, actions) which are linked through edges representing relations [11]. The definition of relations and the way of crosslinking items is not standardized. Semantic networks serve to represent natural language knowledge and are derived from associative networks taken from cognitive psychology [11]. A commonly known semantic network is WordNet, which organizes words by concepts (e.g., word meanings) and uses homonymity, synonymity, hyponymity[6] and the like, as a semantical relationship between words [17]. Fig. 7.1 shows a semantic network for the representation of a bicycle:

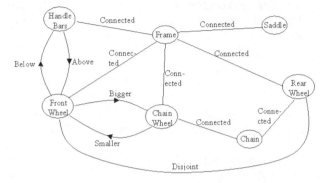

Fig. 7.1. Semantic network for a bicycle [17]

Thesauri

One of the variants of semantic networks is the *thesaurus*. A thesaurus covers words, terms and expressions of a certain domain and describes the connections among them. It is an arranged "treasury of words". A controlled vocabulary forms the basis of a thesaurus within IR. The vocabulary, which is at the bottom of the knowledge domain, is defined with the objective of avoiding ambiguity and different spellings, which can occur when uncontrolled vocabulary or the whole band width of natural language is used [8, 17, 19]. A given knowledge domain (e.g., bicycle) is characterized and represented as precisely as possible through unambiguous definition of items which are called descriptors. The definition of links between items supports the indexing of documents and improves the specification of the query specified by the user of an IR system. A thesaurus is particularly used for the disambiguation of a knowledge domain, not for its structuring and systematisation [2, 8, 17, 19]. The ISO standards 2788:1986 (guidelines for the establishment and development for monolingual thesauri) and 5964:1985 (guidelines for the estabishment and development of multilingual thesauri) may be used for the construction of a thesaurus [17].[7]

Topic Maps

A more sophisticated model for the representation of a semantic network is that of *topic maps*. They enable the development of knowledge structures and aim to im-

---

[6] A word that is conceptually included within the definition of another word (e.g., rose is a hyponym of flower)
[7] www.iso.org

prove search and navigation processes concerning a knowledge domain, e.g., via the WWW. Topic maps consist of so-called "topics" as the smallest entity of the model (e.g., persons, locations), "associations" (relations between topics) and "occurrences" (instances of or documents about topics). Topic maps are standardized by the ISO standard 13250 (specification of syntaxes that describe the possible expressions in a topic map). In contrast to thesauri, they aim at structuring and systemating a knowledge domain [21].

Ontologies

Another, more formalized alternative for the realization of semantic networks is that of *ontologies*. The term "ontology" originates from philosophy, where it is the discipline that deals with the nature and organization of being. In computer science, "..an ontology refers to an engineering artefact, constituted by a specific vocabulary used to describe a certain reality, plus a set of explicit assumptions regarding the intended meaning of the vocabulary" [16]. Ontologies promise to support a shared and common understanding of a specific knowledge domain that can be communicated between people and computer-based systems [5, 18]. An ontology aims at capturing a specific knowledge domain. Furthermore, ontologies provide a commonly agreed vocabulary by defining the basic terms and relations of a domain's vocabulary and by providing the rules for using the terms and relations. [16].

7.3 Implementation at a High-tech SME

7.3.1 The High-tech SME: CEROBEAR

CEROBEAR is an SME producing ceramic bearings. Operating in a highly dynamic environment, the company is confronted with fast changes. The company sees new potentials on the WWW for the detection of external knowledge because of its worldwide accessibility. The company's problem is how to detect knowledge about potential customers on the one hand, and about potential suppliers on the other hand. CEROBEAR's main goal in this context is to find new customers who may need its specific products. Furthermore, the company is interested in finding certified suppliers for some of its business units. When using common search engines to meet the company's knowledge requirements, CEROBEAR has come across several problems: the search engines do not deliver results in line with CEROBEAR's knowledge requirements and the further screening process of the results obtained via search engines is very time-consuming.

The main problem for the company arises from the common search engines' search strategy: they only search single buzzwords and do not consider a company's whole vocabulary of concepts. CEROBEAR is aware of the knowledge the WWW may provide, but has no suitable method for accessing the knowledge the company needs.

7.3.2 Focus: Development of a Customer-Specific Ontology

The objective at CEROBEAR was to improve WWW-based detection of knowledge about customers and suppliers through the use of ontologies. Ontologies represent the company-specific vocabulary ("concepts") of a knowledge domain and the relations between the concepts. They are said to have the potential to improve the quality of WWW-based knowledge detection, because the search process is not based on single words or a sequence of words, but on the company's associative network of knowledge. Ontologies "enrich" the queries with additional knowledge about the relevant knowledge domain and thus enable the search engine to consider meanings of words in specific contexts, as well as related words.

The use of ontologies involves technical, as well as human aspects: technologies for ontology-based search are currently under development and are being, at a progressive rate, integrated into knowledge management systems and intranet solutions, but are still far from having reached a "stable phase". At the beginning of the project, some systems, however, were already commercially available. The human aspects were only poorly researched: little was known about how to efficiently build ontologies (especially in the context of SMEs) and how useful these ontologies might be in supporting knowledge acquisition from the WWW.

The KINX approach was to use commercially available software for ontology building and ontology-based search as a platform, on the basis of which it was possible to evaluate

- how latent domain knowledge that experts and experienced employees have gained in their daily work should best be elicited,
- how this knowledge can best be translated into an ontology,
- whether ontology-based knowledge detection is more effective than traditional search methods.

Work in this project involved two areas: first of all, an ontology-based software had to be selected from the different commercially available products as well as from programs under development in universities and research groups. It was decided to choose L4 from Moresophy, a four-layered tool consisting of an analysis process and three modules: a document indexing function, a support tool for graphical concept modelling and a navigation function for internal and external/WWW-based knowledge detection. It thus supplies the platform necessary to model and use ontologies.

Furthermore, means to elicit and capture latent knowledge about specific knowledge domains had to be identified, evaluated and applied. These activities were genuinely human-oriented and used, among others, concepts and techniques from cognitive psychology.[8]

After the selection of software and a thorough assessment and pre-test of psychological and other elicitation techniques, a customer-specific ontology was cre-

---

[8] Please refer to Chap. 5 of this book

ated and the result was presented to CEROBEAR. This gave rise to further refinements before the ontology could be finalized:

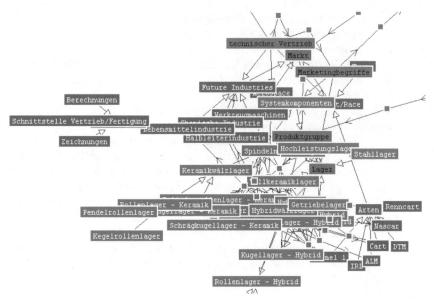

Fig. 7.2. Extraction of the semantic network developed at CEROBEAR

7.3.3 Results and Evaluation

During the search process, which is initiated by entering a query, the software considers the underlying ontology. The hits are presented, as usual, in the form of a ranking list. In order to evaluate the results of the ontology-based search, the L4 based search was compared with Google, because this is the most widely used search engine. Queries formulated by CEROBEAR employees were entered in L4 as well as in Google. L4 and Google searched through a collection of documents that were evaluated prior to the search by CEROBEAR employees with respect to their relevance for answering the queries. Since the relevance of the documents was known, precision and recall, the basic measures used for the evaluation of search strategies, could be calculated for both search strategies. *Recall* is the ratio of the number of relevant documents retrieved to the total number of relevant documents in the database, whereas *precision* is the ratio of the number of relevant documents retrieved to the total number of documents retrieved. They are usually expressed as a percentage [1, 15, 19].

The values of precision and recall for six queries with Google and L4 (given in Table 7.1) show that, in five of the six cases, L4 provided better recall results than Google; one recall is identical with Google's. In three cases, the precision of L4 is better than that of Google, two results for precision are identical and in only one case did Google provide results with higher precision than L4. The results demonstrate that an ontology-based knowledge detection approach provides better search results than a common search engine (Google) and thus better meets the user's knowledge needs.

Table 7.1. Recall and precision of L4 and Google

	L4		Google	
	Recall	*Precision*	*Recall*	*Precision*
Case 1	0	0	0	0
Case 2	0,22222	1	0,0020	1
Case 3	0,13333	0,66666	0	0
Case 4	0,4	0,33333	0,4	1
Case 5	0,03	1	0	0
Case 6	0,04545	1	0	0

7.4 Discussion and Conclusion

Ontology-based search has great potential for improving WWW knowledge detection: In contrast to common search engines (Google), an ontology enables an associative search process that does not only search for single buzzwords, but considers a company's specific vocabulary of concepts. It thus improves the quality of search results.

A survey of the state-of-the-art of ontology-based software shows that the technology is still rapidly evolving. The technology is increasingly able to meet SMEs' requirements in terms of price, infrastructure requirements and ease of use, though some development is still needed. In the following years, the bottleneck of ontology-based search in SMEs, therefore, will not be software, but the ability to efficiently create and update valuable ontologies without the help of costly consultants.

The research shows that ontologies should not be built ad hoc, e.g., solely by the knowledge engineer, but should be generated in a systematic process.[9] Such a multi-step process has been successfully developed in the KINX project. The process was tested and applied in an SME that encounters ressource problems typical for small and medium companies (availability of key persons, only very few experts - and these always very busy -, scarce time and concern for topics that lay outside everyday work, little prior knowledge about ontologies, etc.). Therefore, the approach presented may be suitable for many other SMEs, as well.

> "The ontology-based approach provided better search results than a common search engine! It really supported the structuring and defining of specific knowledge domains a t our company." **CEROBEAR Representative**

---

[9] Within the project it could be shown that a model based on knowledge that was elicited by using psychological methods provides better search results than a model based knowledge that was elicited without using psychological methods.

References

1. Baeza-Yates R , Ribeiro-Neto B (1999) Modern Information Retrieval. ACM Press, New York, Addison-Wesley, Harlow et al
2. Buchberger E (1994) Form and Substance: Knowledge Representation by Thesauri. In: Best, H. et al. (eds) Informations- und Wissensverarbeitung in den Sozialwissenschaften. Westdeutscher Verlag Opladen, pp 91 - 100
3. Cockburn C, Wilson TD (1996) Business Use of the World-Wide Web. International journal of information management 16: 83 – 102
4. Collins A M, Quillian R (1969) Retrieval time from semantic memory. Journal of Verbal Learning and Verbal Behavior 8: 240-247
5. Davies J, Fensel D, van Harmelen F (2002) Towards The Semantic Web – Ontology-Driven Knowledge Management. Wiley, Chichester et al
6. Dong X (1997) Search Engines On The World Wide Web And Information Retrieval From The Internet: A Review And Evaluation. Online & CDRom Review 21: 67-82
7. Ellis D (1996) Progress and Problems in Information Retrieval. 2nd edn. Library Association Publishing, London
8. Ferber R (2003) Information Retrieval – Suchmodelle und Data-Mining-Verfahren für Textsammlungen und das Web. Dpunkt.Verlag, Heidelberg
9. Gaus W (2003) Dokumentations- und Ordnungslehre – Theorie und Praxis des Information Retrieval. 3rd edn. Springer-Verlag, Berlin, Heidelberg
10. Griesbaum J (2003) Unbeschränkter Zugang zu Wissen? Leistungsfähigkeit und Grenzen von Suchdiensten im Web – zwischen informationeller Absicherung und manipulierter Information. (Article in the course of the Online-conference Competence in Content 3rd- 5th June in Frankfurt a. M.)
11. Helbig H (1996) Künstliche Intelligenz und automatische Wissensverarbeitung. 2nd edn. Verlag Technik, Berlin
12. Jaros-Sturhahn A, Löffler P (1995) Das Internet als Werkzeug zur Deckung des betrieblichen Informationsbedarfs. Information Management 1: 6-13
13. Jaros-Sturhahn A, Schachtner P (1998) Betriebswirtschaftliches Anwendungspotential des World Wide Web. WiSt-Inforum 2: 85-90
14. Korfhage R R (1997) Information Storage and Retrieval.Wiley, New York
15. Kowalski G J, Maybury M T (2000) Information Storage and Retrieval Systems – Theory and Implementation. 2nd edn. Kluwer Academic Publishers, Boston, Dordrecht, London.
16. Maedche A (2002) Ontology Learning for the Semantic Web. Kluwer Academic Publishers, Boston, Dordrecht, London.
17. Mußler G (2002) Retrieving Business Information from the WWW. Ph.D. thesis, Konstanz University. http://www.ub.uni-konstanz.de/kops/volltexte/2002/844/, 23.1.2005
18. Oppermann et al. (2001): Die Bedeutung von Ontologien für das Wissensmanagement. http://www.ontoprise.de/documents/Bedeutung_von_Ontologien_fuer_WM.pdf, 23.1.2005
19. Salton G, McGill M J (1987) Information Retrieval – Grundlegendes für Informationswissenschaftler. McGraw-Hill, Hamburg et al.
20. Stock W G (2000) Informationswirtschaft – Management externen Wissens. Oldenbourg Verlag, München, Wien
21. Widhalm R, Mück T (2002) Topic Maps. Springer-Verlag, Berlin, Heidelberg

8 Assessment – Making Sense of It All

Doron Faran

Net Knowledge LTD and Ort Braude Academic College, Karmiel, Israel
(doronf@ort.org.il)

8.1 Introduction

The knowledge integration (KI) process, depicted in Chap. 2, consists of three stages: identification, acquisition and utilization – definitely in this order, as each stage presupposes its former. Clearly, then, right identification determines the effectiveness of the entire process since – as in any value chain – the pendulum's principle works: a small deviation at the outset causes a huge shift down the road.

Identification is mainly actualized through two knowledge activities: *assessment* and *detection*, in that order or the other. In this chapter, we deal with assessment, which – despite its centrality – is hardly regarded in the KM literature; worse, even when it is, implicitness reigns supreme or the issue is left ambiguous[1]. Indeed, few make the effort to decipher – even to themselves – how assessment has been done; most often it is regarded as a "black box" behind the KM stage. In order to close this gap, we draw upon cognitive and information[2] science for theoretical ground and mainly upon the business strategy literature for more practical aspects. The chapter is proceeding from a broad theoretical perspective to specific devices and is structured as follows: Sect. 8.2 defines the term and introduces its conceptual elements; Sect. 8.3 lays out a theoretical framework by cross-referencing three information paradigms, which we then use to classify available assessment techniques and to explore deficiencies; in Sect. 8.4, we address the gap by presenting the KINX-outcome method – the DVT, and Sect. 8.5 evaluates the experimental implementation of this method throughout the project, backed by the user's firsthand evidence. In Sect. 8.6, we conclude and tie the assessment framework to KM strategies.

---

[1] A typical example: Davenport [3:49-52] posits the "what-to-focus-on" question as first and foremost among information (see footnote 2) strategy's considerations, but notwithstanding, avoids any detailed discussion on "how-to" work it out.

[2] Since *assessment* of knowledge and of information are identical from any practical aspect, we refer to both interchangeably along this chapter.

8.2 What Is Knowledge Assessment?

Assessment, in our view, attributes the merits of relevancy and worthiness to a piece of knowledge, which are derived from the meaning and significance of that knowledge and result in attention. This general definition may be clarified by the typical problems associated with improper assessment (as listed in Chap. 2), like: "lack of knowledge about the real advantages of new knowledge", "there are no criteria to evaluate the knowledge" or "unclear whether knowledge/sources are reliable, complete, or trustworthy". To be sure, we eliminate the notion of economic valuation (akin to intellectual capital) from the scope of this discussion[3]. More to the point, assessment addresses two distinct questions: (a) What knowledge does one need? And (b) Once noticed, what significance does this knowledge have?

These questions are consistent with the distinction (made in Chap. 2, Sect. 2.4) between *need-driven* and *opportunity-driven* identification, respectively. They also dictate the activities' order along the identification stage: assessment precedes detection in the former while vice versa in the latter.

An example might be a good starting point. This one [13], demonstrating opportunity-driven knowledge assessment, is about IBM (not exactly an SME, but the lesson is nevertheless valid). In 1994, shortly before the Internet boom, IBM was the official technology sponsor of the Winter Olympics in Norway, responsible for collecting and displaying all the results. David Grossman, a midlevel IBM programmer, watched the games on his TV and was proud to see his employer's logo on the screen. Less satisfied was he to discover, after turning to his computer and surfing the Web, that those results had been copied and distributed all over the net under the banner of... Sun Microsystems. At that time, the Internet was unheard of at IBM, which was still mainly corporation-orientated. Grossman was smart enough to assess its relevance, and fortunately succeeded to convince a higher-ranked executive that jumping on the fledgling Internet wagon was an imperative for IBM. To make a long story short, this minded freak caused the giant to turn around and to make the Internet its flagship, all because of this momentary enlightenment.

This fascinating story encapsulates all the elements of assessment – meaning, significance, relevancy, worthiness and attention. The million-euro question is: should it remain occasional, depending on healthy gut feeling, or can it be institutionalized? Obviously we shall try to prove the latter.

---

[3] What is exactly eliminated is the conversion of the knowledge value to financial measures, derived from its assessment.

8.3 Critical Analysis of Assessment Practices

8.3.1 Theoretical Background and Practical Framework

In the Watermill Model (Chap. 4), we subdivided the assessment activity into two classes: (a) credibility and (b) value, meaning and significance (hereinafter *meaning*, for short). This practical classification can be projected on a theoretical distinction between two prominent paradigms: information-centric vs. user-centric, or – the other side of the same token – objectivism against subjectivism, respectively [6]. Both regard assessment as an interaction between information and a user, but from opposing points of view: the former centers on the information whilst the latter on the user. Very briefly, the objectivist paradigm considers information "to be something objective in the external reality" [1]. Regarding information as a "thing", humans and information are viewed as two separate entities; information, therefore, exists by itself and trueness is one of its inherent attributes. On the other hand, the subjectivist paradigm identifies meaning exclusively with the user [4:68–69, 6, 16]; and instead of assuming information to be already "there", it focuses on the cognitive process of evoking information *needs*. This process is depicted, for example, by the sense-making model [5] as a triangle of situation-gap-use, where each information's use instance is a time-space unique (situational), determined upon the specifics of a particular gap. A gap in this context is wherever the user loses the thread of sense-making due to a disruption. So – back to our practical subdivision – since credibility refers to the knowledge itself (regardless of its usefulness) and meaning is user-specific, the analogy to objectivism and subjectivism (respectively) is obvious.

But this is not the whole picture: against the shared fundamental of both these paradigms – that knowledge and the knower are two separate constituents – a third paradigm calls for a totally different viewpoint: the *hermeneutic*[4] paradigm argues that instead of viewing people via information's lens or vice versa, they are both interwoven in the same world; thus information is neither an object, transferred from source to receiver, nor a subjective representation, but an existential dimension of being or "the articulation of a prior pragmatic understanding of a common shared world", which is called *pre-understanding* [2]. The idea of pre-understanding relies on several disciplines and is a cornerstone of the paradigm. In brief, it is the model of reality that has been carved in the mind through life-time experience and demarcates its horizon. Pre-understanding comprises, according to one observation [18], cognitive, social and emotional elements; by another [19], albeit differently entitled, it is more about rooted habits and mental routines. The antidote for pre-understanding captivity is openness which, according to the paradigm, is achievable through a spiral series of self-questioning in order to unlock the mental confinement and to discover "new horizons" (where horizon means the restricted view enabled by the pre-understanding lens) [2]. Based on these para-

---

[4] The term "hermeneutics" originally relates to the interpretation of the Scriptures, but has been used later for interpretative and explanatory research in general.

digms, we suggest an extended, threefold framework to categorize assessment practices, which is summarized in Table 8.1. The right-hand column, titled "Counter pre-understanding", is aimed at discovering these "new horizons".

8.3.2 Alignment of Available Practices

As this framework demonstrates, no practices are available under the counter pre-understanding category – a void we intend to address. But before that, some critical explanations are given about each of the presented groups to clarify what is actually missing.

Table 8.1. Framework for assessment practices

	Information-centric	User-centric	Counter pre-understanding
Grounding paradigm	Objectivist	Subjectivist	Hermeneutic
Useful for	Credibility	Meaning	Openness
Driven by [a]	Opportunity	Situational need	Self-enforced need
Groups of available practices	Experts survey Relation-based (networked) techniques	Gap analysis Issue management	--Empty--

[a] Equivalent to the criteria what-question-is-answered and order-in-identification-stage – see Sect. 8.1.

Information-centric Assessment

As implied by its name, techniques in this category address the knowledge already existent and are widely used in macro-level instances or for basic research [14]. The experts' survey group, where experts are asked to assess knowledge (e.g., "peers review"), is older and more commonly used, chiefly in basic research. It has some vulnerabilities, such as scarcity of domain experts or biases [10], but is nevertheless popular – most likely because of the lack of better alternatives [14]. The less developed relation-based techniques (also called retrospective or network approaches – ibid) assess knowledge by analyzing relations among pieces of knowledge, for example, cite indexing or mutual terms analysis [14].

Above all, the information-centric type of techniques is criticized for low usability, from two aspects. One is the distance of scholars from real-world interest; the second is the ambiguous link between the knowledge and its implications, which is too often unbridgeable from decision-makers' points of view. Goshal & Westney [12] found it a main obstacle for business managers' effective information use.

User-centric Assessment

In this category, the focus turns to *needs*, thus – contrary to the former – assessment precedes the knowledge; also, its purposefulness makes it much more business-oriented, however, in two very different contexts. The *gap analysis* perspective presupposes distinct goals with a strict plan to attain them; the goals – held constant – provide the yardstick for the user to distinguish what is known from what is *needed* and target the remainder [20]. This assessment style, much likening control, is a natural companion to planning-mode strategy[5] [17, 20]. In contrast, *issue management* is a wide umbrella-term that complements the adaptive mode (see footnote 5) and goes hand-in-hand with foresight. The idea is to identify issues as early as possible; issues are emerging changes that "the organization must respond to... and may reasonably expect to exert some influence" [9:252], which may become either opportunity or threat. Once identified, knowledge concerning their emergence is focused [9:252–268].

The user-centric techniques for knowledge assessment have been criticized twofold: once for issues' misunderstanding and then for languid information requests. The former, much more difficult to overcome, is a sheer consequence of the aforementioned pre-understanding phenomenon by which the "issues" are filtered [21]. The latter is empirically evidenced: managers at all levels are ineffective askers [12, 15]. As we noted earlier, the counter pre-understanding category remained unchallenged by current assessment practices. This hole we wish to address by a new method, depicted below.

8.4 The Decision-Validity-Tracking (DVT) Method

A brief reminder: the hermeneutic paradigm assaults the other information paradigms for being confined to pre-understanding, which restricts the perceivable problems and consequently the information search. The reflection of this limitation on strategy in general, and that of business in particular, is management's inability to anticipate, sense and identify potentially problematic discontinuities, specifically where they emerge gradually [7:21–38].

Whereas the user-centric techniques aim at serving the decision-making process (and their contribution is measured alike), the DVT method takes place after the (strategic) decision has been made. It counteracts the common threat of inertia that

---

[5] Mintzberg [17] observes three strategic modes: (a) *planning* – "systematic attainment of goals stated in precise, quantitative terms"; (b) *adaptive* – flexible goals that are incrementally adjusted to address an uncertain environment, and (c) *entrepreneurial* – "active search for new opportunities" and "dramatic leaps forward in the face of uncertainty". The user-centric category encompasses modes (a) and (b) as for both the need is predefined, whilst (c) calls for the missing techniques that apply the hermeneutic paradigm. Mintzberg's classification underlies the three KM strategies we suggested in chapter 4, to which we will return in the concluding section.

is so prevalent in organizations, assuming that even if the decision was justifiable upon taking, it is not necessarily so along its life span. As the name of the method implies, it tracks the decision's validity (see Fig. 8.1), acting on the assumptions: (a) that people can anticipate only what they already know [11:22–37], and (b) that they pay the utmost attention to information that directly answers their explicit questions [8]. It is apparently paradoxical: how can one ask about the yet unknown[6]? The answer is a bit counterintuitive: by looking after the foreseeable but intentionally trying to refute it; as long as the refutation fails, the knowledge is revalidated.

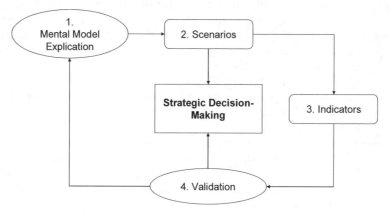

Fig. 8.1. The DVT four-step process in the strategic thinking context

Considering all these impediments, the method follows the four steps shown in Fig. 8.1, all of which – except for step 4 – involve the organization's management through a series of brainstorming. While the method consists of several well-known techniques, its novelty is in the way they are bundled. It is supported by dedicated software along the entire process. Below we elaborate the steps, each illustrated by the proper screenshot of that software (for confidentiality reasons the labels are fictitious, but reasonable):

1. **Mental model explication**: the most difficult and elusive in the process, this step qualifies the entire implementation. Its goal is to elicit (cf.) the participants' hidden assumptions (or mental model) regarding the environment in which the organization operates and to reach a shared representation of it. Since mental models are by and large about causality, it is a *causality map* that represents the model (see Chap. 6). An example is given in Fig. 8.2.

The model is a set of driving forces – external, interrelated variables that destine the organization and its mission at large. An effort is made to break out of the

---

[6] Note the difference between "uncertain" and "unknown": the former refers to a range of identified (future) possibilities that which of them will materialize is uncertain; the latter means that the possibility itself is inconceivable.

firm-centric familiar, pre-determined envelope of first-order constituents and to identify farther industry-level influencers; also, only dynamic forces are taken into account (for instance: *pace* of deregulation). Interrelations are notated by arrows from cause to effect, as either positive or negative relation (where positive (negative) relation means that if one force increases the affected force increases (decreases), too). In addition, truisms (postulates) that are not cause-and-effect expressions (like "hardware is always a step ahead of software") may explain some relations. Finally, within the model's frame, a distinction may be established between primary forces – those that affect but are not affected – and other forces.

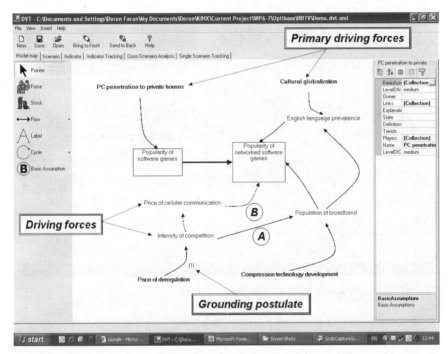

Fig. 8.2. Mental model map. The arrow marked A represents a positive relation, whereas B represents a negative relation (explained above).

2. **Scenario construction (hypothesizing)**: now there is a subset of primary forces that, by assumption, determine the potential future directions – as long as the model is valid. Apparently each primary force has endless nuances to develop, so in order to simplify only two forces – the most uncertain and influential – are singled out and the spectrum is reduced to increase/decrease extremes (compared to the present); the remaining primary forces are held constant in the most reasonable direction (increase/as-is/decrease). The four resulting scenarios (two primary forces by two directions), thus, are different realizations of the same model (which is the refined representation of the pre-understanding), each subject to other planning assumptions (see Fig. 8.3 for an example).

What, then, is the hypothesis? That if the model is (and remains) valid, and if the planning assumptions materialize, than one and only one scenario may be realized[7]. From now on, the goal is to reject the hypothesis – and if that happens – to retest the entire model altogether; that way, the aspired requirements of openness, horizon-widening questions and from-known-to-unknown-reflection [2] are met.

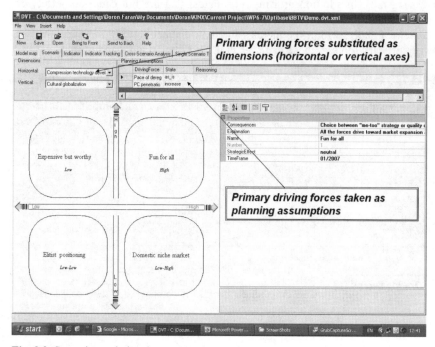

Fig. 8.3. Scenarios and planning assumptions

3. **Determination of indicators**: in this step, each scenario is dissected into discernible facts – and only facts, to prevent misinterpretation – that, if observed, indicate (or negate) the emergence of this specific scenario; for instance: "higher than 5% increase in sales of product X (total industry), year over year". Actually, this step embodies the purest form of assessment in the process since it generates the information needs. The indicators become a target for surveillance by any legitimate means (see Fig. 8.4).

---

[7] The notion of properly-done scenarios is that all of them are feasible in foresight but each excludes the others upon materializing.

An important imperative is to select only indicators with discriminatory power, meaning to include only those indicators that can distinctively tell one scenario from the others. It is also recommended to assign weights for each indicator-scenario coupling[8], which helps to evaluate the scenarios' likelihood.

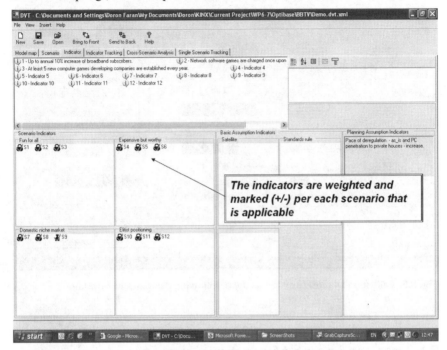

Fig. 8.4. Scenario-related indicators

4. **Validation**: unlike the previous steps, that are passed once (per process) and are consecutive, the fourth is repetitive. Periodically (once or twice a year, depends on the stability of the industry), the indicators' status is checked and scored[9]. The result is the scenario's likelihood: which, if any, scenario is in line with the evolving reality. As mentioned before, each scenario assumes a different state of the driving forces, thus, in any case, other than *one* likely scenario the hypothesis (i.e., the model) is rejected. Fig. 8.5 exemplifies a "benign" case, as only one scenario (the upper one) is likely.

---

[8] We use three ranks: high, medium or low. For arithmetic computation, they are scored as 3, 2, or 1 (respectively), positive if the indicator verifies the scenario and negative if it negates.

[9] We use a six-rank scale: highly regressing, regressing, constant, advancing, highly advancing and completed, which – for arithmetic computation – are scored from (-2) to 3, respectively.

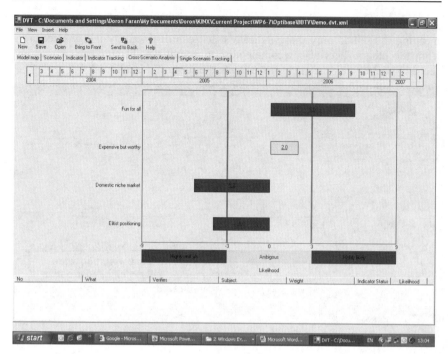

Fig. 8.5. Validation by cross-scenario analysis, following the indicators' tracking

8.5 Lessons Learned from the Implementation at Optibase

We conducted an experimental implementation with our project's partner, Optibase[10], a high-tech manufacturing SME in the video-streaming industry. The implementation process consisted of two phases: one of prior information collection and another of active intervention (by applying the DVT method). Comparing the state before the DVT implementation (phase 1) and the situation afterwards provided valuable insights into the method's effects.

Phase I

The first phase included in-depth interviews with four key employees, in which we studied how knowledge needs have been assessed in the past. The main findings from these interviews are as follows:

---

[10]   Optibase, based in Herzlia, Israel, is a high-tech manufacturing SME in the video-streaming industry. For more details, see www.optibase.com.

- Rather than to information needs, interviewees referred to information sources or to what decision the information was needed for.
- Knowledge needs, if expressed at all, almost exclusively alluded to planning assumptions (for instance, "market X will increase"); assumptions underlying mental models were not challenged.
- Interviewees were overwhelmed by information overload, arising from the mass of fragmented stimuli and resulting in an overvaluation of quantitative and repetitive items.

In summary, knowledge assessment was clearly restricted by a predefined horizon. The dominant issue-management assessment approach fitted well the adaptive strategic mode (see footnote 5) employed. There was a permanent worry about "black holes" – that is, unquestioned areas – yet it was perceived as an immanent constraint. These observations are consistent with previous theoretical and empirical findings [5, 7].

Phase II

In this phase, we implemented the DVT method in two separate strategic business units (SBU). Each implementation involved about five 3-hour brainstorming sessions with 4–5 executives each. Approximately three sessions were devoted to model explication, one for the scenario construction and one for indicators determination. The findings at both units were quite similar, and are summarized below:

- The models consisted of 9–12 driving forces and 2–3 postulates each, less than half of which had been identified in phase 1 (thus not scrutinized). In contrast, most of those forces that had been stated before were now eliminated.
- The four scenarios that emanated from the model clearly demonstrated the pre-understanding limitation: as one participant witnessed, they matched exactly the previous market life-cycle – implying that the strategic mental model was an authentic duplication of the past.
- The number of indicators – the "cornerstones" of information needs – decreased from an order of magnitude of "tens" to about 10 in each SBU.

> **Optibase Strategic Thinking**
>
> Optibase´s business in the Video-over-IP innovative world is characterized by continuous changes due to fluctuating customer needs, new technologies and many other forces that a medium-sized, high-tech company is affected by; strategic adaptation therefore is vital. The way Optibase looked at its environment was very subjective. Therefore, it had to be validated continuously to make sure that the model was still correct.
>
> Optibase´s top management got many new ideas from implementing the DVT method, such as revealing some hidden assumptions or how to define Optibase's business environment in a less straightforward manner. The final outcome will be used in the years ahead for strategy validation.
>
> The DVT method has benefited Optibase for the short term by generating common concepts and common understanding of top management's thoughts and assumptions. Tracking the DVT indicators may shield Optibase against unexpected surprises.

In summary, the exercise evidenced how powerful pre-understanding was, both through framing the present perception and through inhibiting doubts – a hurdle that scenarios by themselves did not overcome. The method clearly hones attention to information needs through diminishing quantity and enhancing quality, as well as by knowledge explication and sharing. The encouragement of openness with its positive side-effects upon strategic planning which may arise from model validation in the long run still has to be demonstrated. Table 8.2 summarizes the DVT contribution.

Table 8.2. The DVT contribution

	Before	After
Driving forces	"Tens"	9-12
Mental model	Unconscious	Explicit, visual
Common understanding	Implicit, assumed	Shared, assured
Knowledge preservation	Gone with leaving employees	Stored, inheritable
Espoused scenarios	One	16 (reduced to 4)
Strategic information needs	Innumerable	About 10 clear topics
Surveillance	Scattered, occasional	Focused, systematic
Sources	Others' (e.g. market-research companies) judgment	Facts

8.6 Conclusions

Assessment is about ascribing relevancy and sense to knowledge, either before having it (to guide detection) or while at hand (for use). Three different paradigms attempt to explain how it happens – one focuses on the knowledge, another on the user and his or her subjectivism, and the third sees both the user and the knowledge interwoven so that they define each other. The latter – the hermeneutic paradigm – argues that a dedicated effort is required to break out of one's knowledge shield (named pre-understanding) in order to discover new horizons. The method we have developed is a trial to take this advice.

The effect of the DVT (Table 8.2) was remarkable in two aspects: improved strategic thinking and focused information needs. Regarding strategic thinking, the process formalized the dynamic approach that formerly had been latent, but undoubtedly in use. Needless to say, it is much more adequate for such a turbulent market. Concerning information needs, the impact was clear, measurable and immediate in both elucidation and mutual explication. Furthermore – and in line with our main goal – the method placed the hidden layer of basic assumptions on the surface and made it accessible to analyses. Strikingly illuminative in this sense was the boundedness manifested by the scenario exercise which, traditionally, is regarded as a mind-opener but failed to break out of the box.

The practice also reaffirmed the theory, with all three paradigms reflected in one phase or another. Before our intervention, we can identify both the information-centric and the user-centric approaches. The former, associated with the formal planning mode, was demonstrated by the almost desperate wish to find the single true answer; the latter, prevalent in the actual adaptive mode, echoed the sense-making model by emphasizing help (sources) rather than needs, as mentioned in phase 1's findings. The spiral questioning process we experienced with the DVT and its consequences represent the hermeneutic paradigm and shed light on the burden of pre-understanding.

Now we can close the loop and couple KI activities with tools and techniques that fit different strategies. A reminder: we practically divided knowledge assessment into two sub-activities – one of judging credibility and another of ascribing value, meaning and significance. In chapter 4, we suggested a threefold framework for KM strategy – static, evolutionary and revolutionary; and here (in Sect. 8.3.2) we reviewed available groups of practices. How do they all match each other?

Credibility refers to knowledge per se, user- (and strategy-) independent; for that both experts' survey and relation-based (networked) techniques, entitled information-centric, are commensurate. In contrast, value, meaning and significance are user-specific; hence the user-centric approach is most adequate. Here, strategy is definitely a factor: the control-oriented gap-analysis techniques match the static, whilst the problem-solving-oriented issue-management practices go hand-in-hand with the evolutionary strategy. For the revolutionary strategy, which we have found unaddressed from a knowledge assessment perspective, we proposed the hermeneutic-inspired DVT.

Our real-life experiment with Optibase highlighted the difficulties faced by executives in a dynamic and information-swamped environment, and how systematic assessment can alleviate this stress. We still have to watch whether the DVT method contributes to openness in the long term.

References

1. Capurro R (1992) What is information science for? A philosophical reflection. In: Vakkari P, Cronin, B (eds) Conceptions of Library and Information Science: Historical, empirical and theoretical perspectives, Taylor Graham, London, pp 82–98
2. Capurro R (2000) Hermeneutics and the Phenomenon of Information. Metaphysics, Epistemology, and Technology. Research in Philosophy and Technology 19: 79–85
3. Davenport TH (1997) Information Ecology. Oxford University Press, New York
4. Davenport TH, Beck JC (2002) The Attention Economy: Understanding the New Currency of Business. Harvard Business School Press, Boston
5. Dervin B (2003) From the mind's eye of the user: The Sense-Making qualitative-quantitative methodology. In: Dervin B, Foreman-Wernet L (with Lauterbach E) (eds)

Sense-Making Methodology reader: Selected writings of Brenda Dervin. Hampton Press, Cresskill, NJ, pp 269-292
6. Dervin B, Nilan M (1986) Information Needs and Uses. Annual Review of Information Science and Technology (ARIST) 21: 3–33
7. Drucker PF (1995) Managing in a Time of Great Change. Truman Talley, New York, NY
8. Faran D (2002) What Impedes Your Intelligence Effort? Competitive Intelligence Magazine 5 (2): 18–20
9. Fleisher CS, Bensoussan BE (2003) Strategic and competitive analysis. Prentice Hall, Upper Saddle River, NJ
10. Frederiksen F, Hansson F, Wenneberg S (2001) Knowledge Assessment in the Agora. (Working Paper No. 14/2001 of the Department of Management, Politics and Philosophy, Copenhagen Business School, presented at the 5th ESA-conference, Helsinki)
11. Geus A (1997) The living Company. Nicholas Brealey, London
12. Goshal S, Westney DE (1991) Organizing competitor analysis systems. Strategic Management Journal 12: 17–31
13. Hamel G (2000) Waking Up IBM: How a Gang of Unlikely Rebels Transformed Big Blue. Harvard Business Review 78 (4): 137–146
14. Kostoff RN (1995) Research requirements for research impact assessment. Research Policy 24: 869–882
15. McGee K (2004) Give Me That Real-Time Information. Harvard Business Review 82 (4): 26
16. Miller FJ (2002) I=0 (Information has no intrinsic meaning). Information Research 8 (1)
17. Mintzberg H (1973) Strategy-making in three modes. California Management Review 16 (2): 44–53
18. Nystrom M, Dahlberg K (2001) Pre-understanding and openness – a relationship without hope? Scandinavian Journal of Caring Sciences 15: 339–346
19. Prahalad CK, Bettis RA (1986) The Dominant Logic: a New Linkage Between Diversity and Performance. Strategic Management Journal 7 (6): 485–501
20. Rockart JF (1979) Chief executives define their own data needs. Harvard Business Review 57 (2): 81–92
21. Schwenk CR (1984) Cognitive Simplification Processes in Strategic Decision-Making. Strategic Management Journal 5 (2): 111–128

9 Transfer - Knowledge Transfer in Networks

Aard Groen

University of Twente, NIKOS, Enschede, The Netherlands, a.j.groen@utwente.nl

9.1 Introduction

This chapter presents material on knowledge transfer activities aiming at knowledge integration. As discussed in Chap. 2, the latter involves a process of identifying, acquiring and using external knowledge. New product-developing small firms often need external knowledge due to the staff deficiencies and specialisation of these firms (see Chap. 1). In earlier chapters, it was shown that knowledge integration may be achieved by transferring explicit knowledge, and/or knowledge holders and that nurturing this process is important. This chapter shows that differences in knowledge and experience between a firm in need of external knowledge and the supplier of this knowledge are both a main source of advantage of knowledge transfer, as well as a barrier to successful transfer. It will be shown that, even if one knows which knowledge is needed, and where this knowledge is, an intensive process is needed to successfully implement external knowledge in an NPD process.

The structure of the chapter follows this logic. The theoretical part (Sect. 9.2) shows that, considering the nature of knowledge and structures of networks especially in NPD processes, knowledge transfer involves methods of network management. The role of interaction in networks and the concept of absorptive capacity are described and ways to overcome these difficulties are outlined in the last part of the theory. The second part of the chapter (Sect. 9.3) describes the WAP case in which mechanisms of network-based knowledge transfer are illustrated. Conclusions for practice and research implications conclude this chapter

9.2 Theory on Knowledge Transfer in NPD Processes

In this part, a theoretical approach to the role of knowledge characteristics in relation to interactions in networks is discussed. Some backgrounds are described from innovation adoption theory, knowledge management and network theory (Sect. 9.2.1). This provides the basis for a discussion of the role of cognitive distance and network characteristics in effective knowledge transfer. In Sect. 9.2.2, some consequences of the theory are described.

9.2.1 The Character of Knowledge and Networks in Transfer Processes

The goals of knowledge integration in NPD processes is to find and use external knowledge in order to improve the knowledge base, which is an important resource for NPD. The typical character of external knowledge for such purposes is that this knowledge does not automatically fit into the existing knowledge base. Therefore, it could be seen as an adoption of innovation in itself. In the domain of innovation adoption research, Gatignon & Robertson [2] pointed out that actors with a high propensity for innovation decide and learn in a different way than "non-innovators" do. This implies that knowledge integration processes involving firms with a different innovation culture, which will often be the case, involve different types of learning processes. Furthermore, knowledge in learning processes is often not easily made explicit for the actor. Michael Polanyi's [12] concept of 'tacit knowledge', implying that individuals know more than they can explain (for details see Chaps. 1 and 4), offers insights into why firms with the same kind of information about an innovation neither necessarily behave in the same way [8, 9] nor communicate easily. The interpretation of information in communication concerning knowledge integration depends upon cognitive skills built up in earlier interactions with other actors and other contexts of the actors involved. This is referred to as know-how: "accumulated practical skill or expertise that allows one to do something smoothly and efficiently". Know-how is a part of a firm's value-system, defining more or less acceptable/possible (changes in) behaviour. It is often assumed that 'blue-print' information about an innovation would be applicable in most cases, but it might not fit into the firm´s know-how. In that case, the cognitive distance between the firm´s know-how and the cognitive skills necessary to adopt this new knowledge is too large and the innovation is rejected. In Rogers' [13] words, compatibility in relation to current practice in the adopting unit is relatively low. The important aspect here is that one has to assess the knowledge available in the firm to explain or predict whether an innovation is compatible with this situation. Or in other words: Is the firm able to realize the adaptations necessary to adopt an innovation? Cohen & Levinthal [1] developed the concept of 'absorptive capacity' to indicate the ability of a firm to adapt to new knowledge. It can be measured by employees´ levels of education and vocational training and experience with (new) technology [5]. Higher levels of education in a firm increase formal, documented explicit knowledge, while experience with modern technology and vocational training tends to include a large amount of tacit knowledge. Taken together they indicate the absorptive capacity of a firm.

Nooteboom [9, 10] discussed the importance of specialization for knowledge creation and noticed that specialization leads to higher value creation in the specialized area. As many NPD processes involve more then one specialized area, normally several specializations are combined. Furthermore, if knowledge is for a large part developed in a situation-specific and path-dependent way, then in order not to miss other relevant knowledge development paths, one needs complementary cognitive competence from outside partners. For several reasons, small firms are more situation-specific than large ones, so that this requirement applies especially to small firms.

Now consider the notion of "cognitive distance" as a generalized notion of distance, with cognitive "proximity" as its inverse. Cognitive proximity enables understanding. But there must also be novelty, and hence sufficient cognitive distance, since otherwise the knowledge is redundant: nothing new is learned. If we specify effectiveness of communication as the (mathematical) product of communicability and novelty, learning is most effective at a distance which is neither too large nor too small, as illustrated in Fig. 9.1.

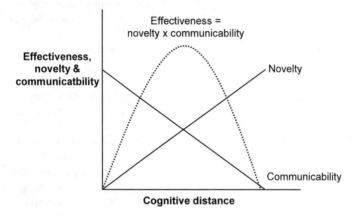

Fig. 9.1. Effectiveness of knowledge transfer

9.2.3 Some Consequences of Cognitive Distance for Networking of Small Firms

As shown above, specialisation of collaboration partners affects the effectiveness of collaboration in NPD processes. Moderate cognitive distance is presumably most productive for knowledge transfer. Whenever firms, however, need relatively new forms of knowledge in their NPD processes, implying that the cognitive distance is large, transfer of knowledge is difficult. Typical examples are found in university-industry interaction when firms integrate scientific knowledge into their NPD processes. Due to the high specialisation necessary for contributing to the advancement of science, scientific knowledge tends to be ill-suited for practical, often multi-disciplinary questions of firms - a problem usually referred to as non-fit of fundamental research to product-market related problems. Indeed, the cognitive distance between fundamental research and market application is mostly very large, but still it can be necessary to use such knowledge in a firm's R&D processes to generate more radical new products.

An attractive means to solve problems created by a large cognitive distance is interactive networking. The work of Granovetter [3, 4] in network theory shows how important "weak and strong ties" are in these circumstances. A weak tie exists when the frequency of contact and intensity of (knowledge) exchange is low. Often, the function of a weak tie is to link developments in two groups, bringing something new, a novelty, into the discussion of each group. In order to bridge large cognitive distances, weak ties, however, have to be enhanced to strong ties. This may be achieved by employing the process of *maieutics*, or intellectual midwifery, going back to Socrates who was a master in this: He discussed extensively with his students on complex issues until they came to a shared insight. In the knowledge integration process, the collaborating partners discuss in the same way extensively to make their own implicit knowledge explicit for each other (called "externalization" by Nonaka & Takeuchi [9]). When large cognitive distances exist, adoption of novel technology by small firms often requires *maieutics*. For firms with low levels of knowledge, this requires information sources that are able to communicate on an appropriate level of abstraction and with which one can interact intensively.

Collaboration between organisations with different ways of specialisation also supports the idea that more heterogeneous networks, in which different types of organisations, like academic institutes, large firms, small firms, knowledge-intensive firms and very market-oriented firms collaborate, form more viable clusters of new product development. This network perspective is underpinned by the principle of specialisation outlined above.

The importance of networks for small firms is further enhanced by the fact that they cannot afford specialist staff support in legal, technical, environmental, and personnel affairs: the problem of "staff deficiency". This is due to economies of scale: Specialist staff would not be sufficiently employed to yield viable utilization of the fixed capacity that the staff represents. Thus, for smaller firms, there is a need to acquire such intelligence from the outside. Such reliance on external intelligence requires both competence and intentional trust [7]. Competence trust stands for the belief that the outside source of advice is competent not only in a narrow, technical sense, but also able to judge the viability of technology in the context of the small firm's priorities and in view of the specifics of the firm's history. Intentional trust means that the advisor has no axe to grind, and will fairly and objectively take the firm's interest to heart and give disinterested advice. In Klein Woolthuis' study it was shown that trust is created by interacting. This way, actors learn to understand each other's position in the knowledge chain and ways of behaving in collaborative processes. For example, if a partner is very much focussed on contracts for distributing future risks, costs or profits, most collaborative relations break up before the problems are solved. On the other hand, when in the beginning of the process much attention is paid to making a plan contract, in which goals and an outline of scheduled activities of the future collaboration are described, this facilitates the process in a positive way (see [7]).

The analysis can be used to predict what kinds of sources by what types of firms will be used for what kinds of knowledge. Family and friends are cognitively close and merit intentional trust, but often their knowledge is more or less redundant, and their competence is often limited. But when the latter restrictions do not apply, they will be a preferred source. Colleagues are cognitively close while possibly making available important non-redundant knowledge, but to the extent that colleagues are also competitors, intentional trust is limited. They will be a preferred source when the subject of exchange is less sensitive to competition. Local accountants and local branches of banks tend to be both cognitively and geo-graphically close and are perceived as competent and trustworthy. Therefore, they are expected to be frequently used sources. Trade or craft associations may also be competent and trustworthy, but their cognitive distance is generally larger (of course, some trade organisations have consultants who are cognitively close). Suppliers of technology should clearly be important sources of information in adoption, provided that they achieve sufficient cognitive proximity. Governmental institutions may be perceived to be trustworthy, but are often not very competent and not very advanced, thus generally cognitively very distant, and therefore also hard to communicate with (see Fig. 9.1.). In cases where knowledge exchange is necessary, for example in implementing new policies, this is a difficult hurdle to take.

9.3 The WAP Project, an Example of Knowledge Transfer in a Network

University-industry interaction (UII) can take many forms. Recently in Twente, the university, intermediary parties and industrial actors have co-operated in a pro-ject aimed at providing (potential) entrepreneurs with information that might lead to the recognition and exploitation of new business opportunities in the field of in-formation and communication technology. This chapter focuses on one of the technologies that was promoted during this project, namely Wireless Application Protocol (WAP) technology as an example of collaboration for knowledge trans-fer, where cognitive distances between partners are large. The case shows that, in a situation where something really new is present, and actors do not know each other very well (so initial trust levels are low), the application of the principle of maieutics facilitates knowledge transfer to a certain extent in NPD processes.

9.3.1 Context of the Project

The WAP project is part of a larger project called Transuniverseel. Transuniver-seel is one of the university-industry-interaction programmes (UII) of the Univer-sity of Twente. The Liaison Group of the University of Twente (LG) and a large telecom firm initiated this programme. The project provides the opportunity to ex-periment with new forms of UII in a high-technology context, specifically in the ICT sector. The partners jointly formulated the main goal of the programme as follows: *To stimulate knowledge-intensive entrepreneurial activities in the field of ICT, in the region of Twente by means of technology transfer between the Univer-sity of Twente, intermediary parties and companies and (potential) entrepreneurs.*

WAP stands for Wireless Application Protocol; it is an open, global standard that empowers model users with wireless devices to easily access information or business services instantly (WAP-forum, 2000). The basic technology for WAP has been developed by commercial organisations. At the start of the project

(March 2000), the number of applications that had been developed on the basis of this technology was limited. However, even then it was obvious that it could offer opportunities for both firms active in the telecom sector (including providers and developers of handheld devices) and WAP-page designers, as well as for any other business that wants to interact with both internal and external partners in new ways. Those already involved in WAP-related activities indicated that WAP could be seen as the first step towards Mobile Commerce.

At the start of the WAP project, the general public (consumers and entrepreneurs) in the Netherlands was not yet very familiar with WAP technology and existing applications. Even fewer people were aware of business opportunities (for instance, in the form of new types of applications) it would offer for them or their company. What is important to note, is the fact that WAP is not a business opportunity in itself. The technology should be seen rather as a source of ideas from which business opportunities can be developed. This means that (potential) entrepreneurs had to be provided with more information about the technology than would be necessary with a ready-to-use type of innovation. Consequently, the technology transfer process had to start with the first element of the innovation adoption process (dissemination of knowledge) and had to complete as many steps as possible. As the timeframe of the project was limited, it was not expected that entrepreneurs would attain the implementation stage at the end of the WAP project.

Nine different actors were involved in the WAP project as a *project team* that can be classified as belonging to one of three basic groups:

1. actors originating from the University of Twente: the Liaison Group, department of marketing, strategy and entrepreneurship (MSE), Center for Telematics and Information Technology (CTIT, a large research institute) and the University Student Enterprise (USE)
2. intermediary actors: the regional development agency (OOM), ICTwente, and Technology circle Twente (TKT), which is an association of high tech firms in the region
3. commercial actors (firms): a large telecom firm (which will be called Commercial actor 1) and a large technical consultancy firm (which will be called Commercial actor 2)

Apart from the project team, the WAP project also included a large number of knowledge receivers who will be called the target group of the project. The target group included three groups of actors:

1. existing SMEs considering new product development in this area
2. student entrepreneurs (already in business)
3. potential entrepreneurs (both student and professional entrepreneurs)

Seen from the theoretical perspective described above, it is clear that this was a rather heterogeneous network of collaborative partners. Furthermore, most actors had, at best, weak ties which each other. Some of the individuals knew each other, but on the institutional level, this network process was the first effort at collaboration. So one would expect that much intensive interaction is necessary for bridging these cognitive distances for a productive collaboration.

9.3.3 Knowledge Transfer Mechanisms

In the WAP project, we distinguish between three broad categories of activities

1. information transfer from project team to the target group
2. providing testing facilities for interested entrepreneurs
3. setting up networks or forming clusters.

Each of these categories of activities will be discussed in the next three sections.

Ad 1. Information Transfer

In the WAP project, several of the methods of information transfer described in Chap. 4 of this book were used. In particular, two types of activities were undertaken to transfer knowledge from the project team to the target group: information meetings and publications.

The WAP project started with a large information meeting. This event was jointly organised by the Liaison Group, OOM, ICTwente and USE. During this meeting, about 200 participants (including members of the project team) were introduced to the technology by several presentations. The presenters were well acquainted with the technology through their field of business (technology trend watching and telecommunication). These presentations aimed at raising awareness and explaining the basics of the technology. After the presentation, a panel discussion took place during which members of the target group could ask questions. Both activities could not transcend tacit knowledge borders or bridge large cognitive distances. This reflects the primary function of "weak ties", as proposed by Granovetter. Interested people only get a short glance at what might be possible with the new WAP technology. It does not require intensive interaction, but it might arouse awareness and interest.

The second step was to involve interested persons in more intensive interaction. Thus, after the large-scale meeting, two smaller-scale workshops were organised during which more information regarding technological aspects was provided. About 15 individuals (both professional and student entrepreneurs) participated in these workshops. Here, the typical *maieutics* approach was followed. In-depth discussions where people interact with each other in a profound way were initiated, leading to more in-depth understanding including externalisation of tacit knowledge.

Another means used was information dissemination through the Internet. A large number of publications on the latest developments in the technology were gathered and publicised on a web site devoted entirely to WAP. These publications consisted of new paper articles in both popular and scientific journals. Regional or national WAP-related activities (organised under the Transuniverseel programme or by others) were also announced on this web site. This mechanism, too, serves to create awareness; only specialists in the technology, however, are able to read the academic journals on this topical area. Although the novelty level is high, and potential use might be of high value, communicability is rather low. Since the potential knowledge gap jeopardizes the effectiveness of this form of knowledge transfer, additional interactive ways of communications also have to be available.

Commercial actor 1 and Commercial actor 2 furthermore installed a WAP-forum on the Internet, open to questions from the target group. During the first three months of the project, it became obvious that this forum did not have sufficient added value because most public information about WAP can be found at other official WAP sites from companies and governmental bodies. Entrepreneurs, who have very specific technical information requests or want to discuss potential opportunities, would use direct (face-to-face) communication with the specialists of the companies, rather than through the more impersonal and less interactive IUnternet. Again *maieutics* serve as a process to bridge cognitive distance.

Ad 2. Testing Facilities

One step further in the knowledge transfer chain is offering the possibility to learn by doing: In order to offer entrepreneurs, that were already interested in either using or developing WAP based applications, a possibility to test their ideas and preliminary services, several facilities were offered. These testing facilities consisted of a server and a gateway, provided by Commercial actor 2 and a WAP telephone. The facilities were located at the USE premises. In practice, these facilities were only used for demonstrations during the information meetings; furthermore, students used the infrastructure informally. The use of these facilities by regional NPD performing SMEs, however, was one step too far in this stage of knowledge development. Also, not being able to use the facilities at their own premises contributed to the low utilization rate. This might be related to low trust levels: Using testing facilities outside ones own "house" might result in leakages of ideas to competitors. It is also possible that the staff deficit problem caused their low utilisation: Testing involves time-intensive processes and requires a high degree of know-how on design of testing procedures. Anecdotal evidence showed that both problems of limited trust and staff deficits did occur for some of the potential users.

Ad 3. Networking Activities

Besides offering a possibility for informal networking during the information meetings, more formal attempts to develop a network or cluster were initiated as well. First, TKT contacted a number of participants from the target group that had indicated (on the questionnaire) that they were interested in such a cluster. However, at that time, most participants considered it too early to set up the cluster. The reason for this hesitance seemed to be that the participants did not see directly a business idea in the new technological possibilities, or they did not yet know what they could do with the relative unknown participants in the project. The first problem is probably a consequence of too little knowledge of the technology, whereas the second issue is most likely related to trust issues.

At the same time, one of the students working for USE in the project became interested in WAP technology himself. With the help of investor organisations, he set up a more informal network of people interested in the technology. His efforts were more successful since they resulted in a cluster consisting of about twenty entrepreneurs. This cluster met several times to discuss their commercial activities that were related to WAP and Wireless in general. The entrepreneurs were willing to co-operate if this could lead to commercial profits. After some time, however, the meetings became less frequent. Yet, after a while, they tried to breathe new life into the cluster with some success. Again, close interaction in a diverse group rendered results.

The student entrepreneurs proved to be more willing to share ideas and to co-operate with others than the professional firms were. A good example can be found in the workshops. No professional entrepreneur or firm was interested in participating in workshops aimed at idea generation, because they "did not want to give away good information or ideas to potential competitors". This is rather surprising in view of the fact that, at project start, the market for WAP technology was still in the pre-competitive stage. The student entrepreneurs, on the other hand, believed that, because of the innovative character of the technology, enough business opportunities could exist for everyone.

At a later stage however, it became clear that a group of entrepreneurs was eventually interested in co-operation. Trust had apparently developed to such a level that co-operation in NPD became a feasible process.

The WAP project has resulted in the creation of two new ventures: WAP5 and Yucat. Both firms have been founded by student entrepreneurs. As Schumpeter already observed, newcomers are often more open to radical new possibilities, so maybe the students are the typical Schumpeterian entrepreneurs.

Interestingly, the founders of WAP5 have been closely involved in the WAP project. They were working for USE as student assistants and were responsible for several practical issues in the WAP project. Before the project, these students were not very familiar with WAP technology and had no plans to start a business venture. Therefore, it can safely be concluded that the establishment of this new firm is a direct result of intensive interactions which these students had during the course of the project. The firm started in June 2000 and is presently involved in the contract-development of WAP-based services. Yucat was founded several weeks after WAP5. The founders were not involved in the project team. They participated, however, in several meetings and frequently interacted with members from USE (especially with the founders of WAP5). They indicated that the fact that another firm had already started gave them confidence that a market would exist for WAP-based firms. In network research, this imitation process is attributed to direct interactions between a leading actor and a fast follower.

9.4 Conclusions

The theory section of this chapter showed that knowledge transfer can rarely be done by a sort of "box shifting" process. Especially for NPD processes in SME knowledge transfer, considerable cognitive distance has to be overcome. If there is not much difference in the cognitive positions of the actors in the transfer process, the learning effect tends to be small, normally resulting in a knowledge transfer process of low effectiveness. However, when cognitive distance is very large, the potential of learning something new is big, but difficult to realize. In this situation, as well as in the situation where cognitive distance is moderate, knowledge transfer processes often have to involve "maieutics": Intensive interaction is needed to enhance the product creation process with knowledge from external actors. In network theory terms, relatively strong ties (frequent and intense interactions) have to be developed to be able to construct the NPD process using the dissimilar knowledge sources.

In the case described, several of the knowledge transfer mechanisms were used. The experience from this case illustrates that knowledge transfer in a relative new technological area is not a matter of simply shifting a box of knowledge. It rather involves a complex process of initiating interest using mechanisms of creating "weak ties" between potential innovators in a network, as done here with large-scale meetings. This was followed by small-scale events in which interested persons were educated about possibilities in their own context. In addition, for bridging the cognitive gap the principle of *maieutics* was used by creating a cluster of product development and providing an infrastructure for testing. This infrastructure, however, was used most intensely by "stand alone" student companies set up by students who were intensively involved in the project - again an example of *maieutics*: a knowledge transfer effect based on intensive interaction.

IT means to enhance this are important in several ways. As shown in the case described, Internet sources may be used for making information on the new WAP protocol accessible. From this analysis it seems, however, very important to also allow for interactivity and possibility for face-to-face discussions. Furthermore, alignment of knowledge transfer with strategic positions of the actors involved seems to be an important factor for success of transfer activities.

For closing the gap between university and SMEs, intermediary actors can play a fruitful role. Not only in the literal role of transfer offices, but also by generating heterogeneous networks in which the ultimate cognitive distance is reduced by multiple actors on the scale from fundamental knowledge providers over demonstrators of principles to knowledge integrators in market-oriented product development processes. In finding such partners, a portal such as the KINX portal (see Chap. 11) could play an important role diminishing geographic distances for first contacts on a subject of knowledge management, and enabling the creation of new networks of collaborative NPD across Europe. This chapter has illustrated that, after taking this first step, more intensive social interaction is called for to transform initial knowledge transfer by the portal into concrete new knowledge co-production processes by organisations aiming at new product development. The old practice of Socrates of stimulating learning processes by "maieutics" has nothing lost of its power.

References

1. Cohen WM., Levinthal WD (1990) Absorptive capacity: A new perspective on learning and innovation. Administrative Science Quarterly 35: 128-152
2. Gatignon H, Robertson TS (1985) A Propositional Inventory for New Diffusion Research, in: Journal of Consumer Research 11(4): 859-867
3. Granovetter M (1973) "The strength of weak ties" in: American Journal of Sociology. 78:1360-1380
4. Granovetter M (1992) Problems of Explanation in Economic Sociology. Nohria & Eccles
5. Groen AJ (2005) Knowledge Intensive Entrepreneurship in Networks: A Multi-level / multi dimensional approach based on social system theory. Journal of Enterprising Culture. In Press.
6. Johnson JL , Kuehn R (1987) The Small Business Owner/Manager's Search for External Information. Journal of Small Business Management. 25: 53-60
7. Klein, Woolthuis, Rosalinde (1999) Sleeping with the Enemy, PhD thesis. University of Twente
8. Kogut B, Zander U (1992) Knowledge of the Firm, Combinative Capabilities, and the Replication of Technology. Organization Science, 3(3): 383-397
9. Nonaka I; Takeuchi H (1995) The Knowledge-Creating Company: How Japanese companies create the dynamics of innovation. Oxford University Press, New York
10. Nooteboom B (1994) Innovation and Diffusion in Small Firms: Theory and Evidence. Small Business Economics 6: 327-347
11. Nooteboom B (2000) Inter-firm alliances. Routledge
12. Polanyi M (1966) The Tacit dimension. London: Cox & Wyman Ltd.
13. Rogers EM (1983) Diffusion of Innovations, 4th edn. The Free Press, New York

10 Motivating – Incentive Systems for Knowledge Provision

Hannah Zaunmüller

Chair for Business Administration with focus on Technology and Innovation Management, RWTH Aachen University, Germany, zaunmueller@tim.rwth-aachen.de

10.1 Introduction

The management of knowledge as a central factor of production can only be successful if it considers company employees as individual knowledge carriers. This proves to be a challenge to the employees' normal perception of roles and tasks and can meet with numerous hurdles, like a lack of awareness for the relevance of knowledge, the attitude that "knowledge is power" or the opinion that "knowledge management is too time-consuming" [2]. The objective of incentive systems for knowledge management is to help to tackle hurdles like these and to support certain behaviour patterns (e.g., the sharing of knowledge).

An incentive system consists of all incentives consciously offered, or rather all consciously devised incentive tools that support behaviour patterns that promote corporate goals [16]. Incentives may be intrinsic or extrinsic. The former are, almost without exception, immaterial. They are closely linked to the work (or the task) and its definition: The work (or the task) itself or the results directly obtained from it are an incentive and offer satisfaction *per se* [10]. Assigning tasks and specification of behavioural norms are particularly relevant for intrinsic incentives [10]. Extrinsic incentives are linked to the achievement of certain work (or task) goals and relate to rewards or goals that are not directly connected to the work (or to the task) and/or to the work (or to the task) goals. They may be immaterial or material. Immaterial extrinsic incentives comprise, above all, social incentives and incentives associated with career advancement and training [9]. Material incentives may be subdivided into monetary incentives or direct financial remuneration, e.g., fixed salary, social benefits, bonuses, commission and profit participation, and non-monetary or indirect financial remuneration, such as company car and company housing.

This article deals with the design (Sect. 10.2) and implementation (Sect. 10.3) of incentive systems for knowledge management in SMEs and how they are concretised for the provision of employee knowledge. The insights are elaborated and extended by a case study at HEAD Acoustics (Sect. 10.4).

10.2 Design Areas of Incentive Systems for Knowledge Provision

When an SME has decided to design an incentive system for knowledge management, it has to define (1) knowledge management goals, (2) the areas on which the incentive system should concentrate, (3) incentive tools, and (4) the measures for the evaluation of employee performance in providing relevant knowledge (Fig. 10.1).[1]

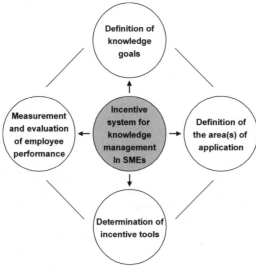

Fig. 10.1. Design areas of incentive systems

10.2.1 Definition of Knowledge Goals

Knowledge goals are fundamental to incentive systems for knowledge management in SMEs. SMEs have to formulate dedicated knowledge goals and integrate them into the goal hierarchy of the company before an incentive system for knowledge provision can be designed. Employees should participate in this process.

In order to find out what kind of employee knowledge is strategically important for the company, SMEs have to determine future and long-term knowledge requirements of the company. Strategic knowledge goals must be defined that relate, for example, to the development of certain core competences or to the access to new areas of technology.

The transformation of strategic into operative knowledge goals makes it possible to show the application-orientation of knowledge goals and their compatibility

---

[1] See here also general requirements concerning incentive systems (e.g., [16]).

with other company goals and to activate their concrete implementation [13]. Operative knowledge goals should be precisely formulated so that they can be directly pursued [12].

10.2.2 Definition of the Application Area

The definition of the application area of an incentive system for knowledge provision by employees is fundamental. The departments as well as the employees to be included have to be defined on the basis of the established goals. [1] In SMEs, in particular the service, support, sales, marketing, purchasing/procurement and development departments have contact with manifold knowledge, mostly customer knowledge. They are likely to be involved in the definition of knowledge goals and, thus, in an incentive system for knowledge provision.

An ideal incentive system for knowledge provision in SMEs is not confined to executives only, but involves all employees in the areas concerned . Hierarchical levels are irrelevant for knowledge provision. It is the knowledge of each employee that counts.

10.2.3 Definition of Incentive Tools

Information, communication/feedback and participation are fundamental to motivating knowledge provision and will be referred to in the following as "basic incentives":

- Incentive tools which provide the incentive information are, e.g., informative events, brochures, notices and information e-mails on particular knowledge topics.
- Examples of incentive tools which provide communication/feedback are regular staff meetings, staff appraisal and feedback/reflection circles. Managerial style also impacts upon motivation via the communication/feedback incentive.
- Incentive tools which offer the participation incentive for knowledge provision include all those tools which allow employee participation in decision-making relating to knowledge management, particularly participation in target agreements, employee surveys and staff meetings. Managerial styles that emphasize participation also offer the participation incentive.
- Incentive tools which offer the appreciation/awards incentive for knowledge provision are multi-faceted and range from expert presentations by employees with significant contributions to the organizational knowledge pool, and variable income parts (bonus and provision) and promotion opportunities to awards, such as "knowledge contribution of the month" or the "knowledge employee of the month".

Furthermore, appreciation/awards also have strong incentive effects [14]. They may be offered for extraordinary achievements [18].

10.2.4 Measurement and Evaluation of Employee Performance

Another important decision-making area regarding the design of incentive systems for knowledge provision is the measurement and evaluation of employee performance. For this purpose, indicators are needed. In general, employee performance can be measured and evaluated by a single indicator for performance or by several indicators that may be interlinked [1]. With regard to knowledge provision in the context of knowledge management, usually however, single indicators of performance do not suffice. The goals agreed upon for knowledge provision provide the standards for measuring employee performance in knowledge provision [16].

Design and implementation of incentive systems have to be tailored to the specific needs of each company. If the company has established, for example, that a specific part of knowledge management involves difficulties, it may focus its incentive system on that particular part.

10.3 Implementation of Incentive Systems

Experience shows that success or failure in the introduction process is due to the design of the introduction process rather than to the systematics of the system [11]. The implementation of incentive systems for knowledge management in SMEs can be split into four phases: analysis of the status-quo, development and elaboration of the concept, system introduction and system checking (Fig. 10.2).

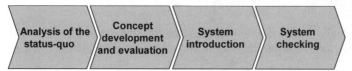

Fig. 10.2. Implementation phases of incentive systems

10.3.1 Analysis of the Status-quo

The analysis of the status-quo is a core element of the implementation of incentive systems for knowledge provision in SMEs – irrespective of the type of incentive system employed [6]. It should begin with the discussion and definition of strategic and operative goals for knowledge provision and the determination of the incentive system's area of application. The primary goal of the status-quo analysis is the identification of the conditions for knowledge provision by employees prior to system implementation. Business processes in the application area of the system have to be identified and analysed, in particular from the perspective of knowledge provision by employees. To this end, process flow charts and in-depth and detailed interviews may be employed. Employees should always participate in the process of identification of opportunities for the improvement of knowledge provision.

Operative goals for knowledge provision can be defined with the aid of a top-down approach: Strategic knowledge goals are derived from strategic corporate goals and are transformed into operative goals for knowledge provision.

The definition of *strategic* knowledge goals requires thorough analyses of the strategic corporate goals with regard to knowledge aspects. The future and long-term need for knowledge in SMEs – in order to reach the strategic enterprise goals – has to be determined. Above all, relevant customers and markets – both actual and potential – and those abilities and competences of the company, which are needed both now and in the future, have to be analyzed carefully.

The transformation of strategic into *operative* goals for knowledge provision includes mapping strategic knowledge goals to corresponding target groups and time schemes on the operative level, matching the operative goals for knowledge provision with the existing conventional operative goals and finally assigning the operative goals for knowledge provision, which were established for a certain area, to projects, work groups and individuals. [13]

The application area of the incentive system is defined by allocating target groups to knowledge goals. Since in SMEs, the service, support, sales, marketing, purchasing/procurement and development departments are usually in touch with manifold knowledge, these departments form the backbone of incentive systems for knowledge provision in SMEs.

The question of whether all employees in these departments should be included in an incentive system for knowledge provision can only be answered by evaluating the requirements for simplicity and profitability such a system has to meet [16]. The fewer areas and the less employees that are included in an incentive system, the lower the administration effort of the system will be. Furthermore, simple and easily administrable incentive systems promote the profitability of the system.

If the implementation of an incentive system starts from base zero, the analysis of the status-quo includes identification of the central business processes within the application area of the incentive system. Furthermore, these processes have to be analysed with respect to knowledge provision, Generally, the analysis of a process starts with its decomposition into single tasks and the identification of their operational sequence [15].

Many different systems which make knowledge available – such as folders, files on hard disks and databases, but also individual persons or groups – have to be analysed in this context. Forms of communication, forms of reports and ways of reporting should be analysed from the perspective of knowledge provision. Moreover, it should be checked what other tools (employee suggestion schemes, employee journals, etc.) exist in the company to motivate employees to make their knowledge public.

A general (rough) survey on business processes and potential incentive tools for knowledge provision may be provided by simple process flow charts; showing the breakdown of a process into tasks and their flows and visualizing each possible action [7]. The result of the process analysis using process flow charts is an overview of processes and, most importantly, of potential incentive tools for knowledge provision in the processes.

Existing incentives for knowledge provision can be analysed by means of the defined operative goals for knowledge provision, the process flow charts and in-depth and detailed interviews. It should be verified for each operative goal for knowledge provision whether the three basic incentives for knowledge provision are adequately provided for by potential incentive tools supporting the pursuit of that goal. Opportunities for the improvement of knowledge provision through in-centives or incentive tools arise whenever at least one of the three basic incentives (information, communication/feedback and participation) for knowledge provision are not (sufficiently) provided for by the existing incentive tools. Furthermore, opportunities for additional appreciation/awards incentives rewarding special achievements in knowledge provision have to be uncovered on a one-by-one basis.

10.3.2 Concept Development and Elaboration

Based on the analysis of the status-quo, the concept for the incentive system is de-veloped and elaborated. The process analysis of the status-quo analysis provides the direction for the development and elaboration of the concept.

The development and elaboration of incentive tools starts with those opportuni-ties which have been identified in the analysis of potential incentive tools on the basis of process flow charts and in-depth, detailed interviews. Though it begins with identifying single opportunities, however, the design of incentive tools is governed by a holistic perspective, taking into account potential interactions be-tween single tools. The design process has to be tailored to the specific needs and conditions of each company [6] and should explicitly integrate the employees us-ing employee surveys. Cost-benefit analyses are helpful for providing a formal evaluation of alternative incentive tools for a specific improvement opportunity.

Presently not available basic incentives for the operative goals of knowledge provision are the starting points for the improvement of knowledge provision in SMEs; they are complemented by improvement opportunities identified by em-ployee surveys. When selecting specific incentive tools, general requirements for incentive systems have to be observed. Above all, in addition to the potential benefits, the corresponding costs of each incentive (tool) have to be considered [16]. Potential company priorities with regard to different operative goals for knowledge provision also have to be taken into account.

Each company has to determine individually what incentive tools it wants to apply to exploit the opportunities identified for improving knowledge provision [5]. The design of incentive tools has to take into account the company´s situation – incen-tive tools have to be tailored to the needs of each company. Table 10.1. presents incentive tools which are listed frequently in the knowledge management literature and their effects on the four basic incentives as well as on the additional incentive "appreciation/awards". Depending on its improvement opportunities, a company may select incentive tools from Table 10.1 and adjust them for the pursuit of the corresponding goals for knowledge provision; alternatively, it may establish simi-lar company-specific incentive tools.

Table 10.1. Incentive tools and their incentive evaluation for knowledge provision[2]

	Information	Communica-tion/ Feed-back	Participation	Appreciation/ Awards
"Pass on what you know and let the company grow" (Allotment of Points for achievements in knowledge management to colleagues at work)	-	+++	++	+++
Suggestion schemes	-	+++	++	+++
Workshops concerning special knowledge topics	+++	+++	+	-
Regular meetings concerning important knowledge topics	+++	+++	+	-
Communities of practice in the context of knowledge management	+	+++	+++	-
Kick-off event for knowledge management	+++	++	+	-
Public recognition of contributions to knowledge management by superiors	-	+++	-	+++
Yellow pages, knowledge maps	+++	-	-	++(+)
Job rotation in the context of knowledge management	+++	+	+	-
(Advanced) Training in the context of knowledge management	+++	++	-	-
Information events for special knowledge topics	+++	+	- (+)	-
Expert presentations of employees who contributed considerably to the organisational knowledge pool	-	+	-	+++
Notice displaying the names of those persons excelling in knowledge management	-	+	-	+++
Mention of persons performing far above average in knowledge management in the company journal	-	+	-	+++
Nomination of the "knowledge contribution of the week"	-	+	-	+++
Public recognition of special achievements and knowledge awards, for example "knowledge worker of the month"	-	+	-	+++
Linkage of frequent of contributions to knowledge management to career opportunities	-	+	-	+++
Accentuation of knowledge management support by the management	+++	-	-	-
Information systems to support knowledge management	+++	-	-	-
Information on basic knowledge topics in the company journal or special brochures	+++	-	-	-
Notices or info emails (newsletters) with information about specific knowledge topics	+++	-	-	-
Attractive work contents and environments with respect to knowledge management	-	-	+++	-

[2] In Table 10.1, only tendencies of incentive impacts are indicated: „+++" = very high incentive impact, „++" = high incentive impact, „+" = incentive impact", „-" = no incentive impact. Agreement on objectives, staff meetings and employee surveys are not stated again as incentive tools in Table 10.1 because they are already taken care of in the implementation of an incentive system for knowledge provision.

When selecting individual incentive tools, it has to take into account that incentive tools may affect several improvement opportunities simultaneously. Since the measurement and evaluation of employee performance in the context of knowledge management are complex, such an evaluation in SMEs should not only consider results, but also behaviour. Therefore, the evaluation, on the one hand, should be implemented via the compilation of the individual contributions towards the achievement of the agreed objectives for knowledge provision within the framework of an ex-post result evaluation. On the other hand, the evaluation should also be implemented via the consideration of the estimated quality of the performance behaviour during the pursuit of the agreed objectives for knowledge provision within the framework of an ex-post behaviour evaluation [16].

10.3.3 System Introduction

The output of concept development is a preliminary plan for the realisation or the introduction of the incentive system. Even with flawless and context-fitting concepts, however, system introduction is no "self-runner" but has to be systematically supported [17].

Within the framework of a context-orientated approach, the implementation of an incentive system for knowledge provision should pursue the following goals regarding the employees involved: information on new or modified incentive tools, command of the skills required for the new or modified incentive tools (e.g., database application skills), preparedness to (passively) modify one's behaviour – knowledge provision has to be accepted and supported by the employees – and preparedness to (actively) take on the role of knowledge provider [6]. Information and communication, qualification and motivation tools can support these goals in the introduction phase [17].

10.3.4 System Checking

The effectiveness and efficiency of an incentive system for knowledge provision should be examined following implementation. The specific goals of an incentive system for knowledge provision and the (company-prioritised) requirements of the system can be used as starting points for the effectiveness evaluation. If incentive tools are used in different areas, an internal benchmarking may provide evidence of their effectiveness [3]. In order to monitor the effectiveness of incentive system projects, acceptance indicators, such as the results of employee surveys or feedback circles with superiors may be used [6].

The evaluation of the (economic) efficiency of an incentive system for knowledge provision involves substantial problems, because the influence of operational incentive systems on the economic success of a company is always partial and indirect and, ultimately, diffuse [8]. Therefore, incentive systems share a similar fortune with organisational structures and leadership concepts or further training programmes, the economic efficiency of which can also rarely be measured exactly, but at best be plausibly justified [8].

As a matter of principle, incentive systems for knowledge provision should not only be checked immediately after implementation, but also later on at regular intervals. Strategic knowledge goals and operative goals for knowledge provision should be regularly monitored, since they are subject to change. The application areas of an incentive system for knowledge provision can be checked against these goals. If the operative goals for knowledge provision have changed, it should be checked, with the help of up-to-date process flow charts and in-depth interviews, whether new "incentive opportunities" [4] have turned up. Also, a modification to the measurement and evaluation of employee performance may be necessary as a consequence of changes in knowledge goals.

10.4 Case Study at HEAD Acoustics

Within the KINX project, an incentive system for knowledge provision by employees was designed and implemented at HEAD Acoustics, a German high-tech SME. Following a brief description of the company and the objectives of the project, design and implementation of the incentive system at HEAD Acoustics are discussed.

10.4.1 HEAD Acoustics and the Focus of the Project

HEAD Acoustics is an internationally operating SME with more than 100 employees worldwide, developing, producing and distributing hard- and software in the acoustics industry. The relatively young SME consists of the mother company in Germany and subsidiaries in America, France and Japan. The project was carried out at the mother company in Germany, at which around 80 of the more than 100 employees work.

The success of the SME is highly dependent on its knowledge. A main knowledge source is the knowledge of its customers. Through their close customer contacts, the employees of HEAD acoustics acquire knowledge of individual customer wishes in addition to customer knowledge concerning markets, competitors or technical developments. This knowledge, however, is not automatically provided to the entire company and, therefore, cannot always be used by other employees. The provision of this knowledge is essential for the development department in particular. As it does not directly communicate with customers, it is dependent on the provision of this knowledge by other company employees.

The status-quo analysis, which was conducted in cooperation with the company, resulted in the following problem formulation: How can we improve the flow of knowledge, especially of customer knowledge, to the development department? Apparently the provision of the multifaceted knowledge of the employees had to be specifically stimulated. The motivation of employees to provide their knowledge, in particular customer knowledge, should be stimulated by incentives, or rather incentive tools. Thus, the concrete project objective was to design and implement an incentive system for the provision of knowledge, in particular customer knowledge.

10.4.2 Results

Results of the analysis of the status-quo

The overall aim of the analysis of the status-quo at HEAD Acoustics was the identification of opportunities for the improvement of knowledge provision.

In a workshop for the managers and department heads, the strategic goals of the company were discussed and knowledge aspects investigated. Participants decided to focus on external knowledge aspects because, among other things, the company operates primarily in high-tech industries and is therefore confronted with a very dynamic environment. The discussions in this meeting showed that, for the competitiveness and the long-term success of the company, it is becoming increasingly important to acquire trend information concerning technological developments, which is crucial for the early identification of trend breaks and new trends. Furthermore, it became obvious that, for the achievement of the strategic company goal "customer orientation", it is crucial to acquire customer knowledge and to disseminate it in the company, in order to influence product development and modifications. Consequently, two strategic knowledge goals were finally defined: "acquisition of trend information" and "acquisition of customer knowledge".

These strategic knowledge goals were then allocated to departments. The strategic knowledge goal "acquisition of trend information" turned out to be particularly relevant to the development and the sales departments. The strategic knowledge goal "acquisition of customer knowledge" was particularly relevant to the development, sales, service and support departments. Afterwards, in interviews and workshops with employees and the managers of the corresponding departments, the knowledge goals allocated to each department were discussed and subsequently transformed into one or more operative goals for knowledge provision in the corresponding departments. Figure 10.3 shows the knowledge goal pyramid that evolved in the SME.

Since the development, sales, support and service departments were responsible for the achievement of the knowledge goals, these departments were selected as the application areas of the incentive system for knowledge provision. Furthermore, it was decided that all employees in these departments should be involved.

Afterwards, the department heads in the application areas of the incentive system were required in interviews to reflect on their main internal department activities. These activities were then discussed with the department heads and, in this way, the main business processes in the application areas were identified. Finally, analyses of the business processes and especially of the actual - primarily multidepartmental - incentive tools for knowledge provision in the participating departments were made. The process analyses resulted in the compilation of process mappings, which were carefully checked and finally validated in workshops, and to the identification of opportunities for the improvement of knowledge provision. These were discussed in a workshop and supplemented by an employee survey.

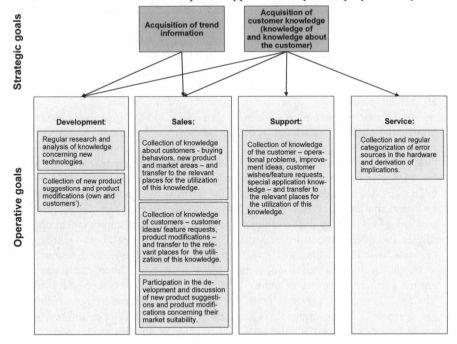

Fig. 10.3. Strategic knowledge goals and operative goals for knowledge provision in the company

At HEAD Acoustics, several opportunities for the improvement of knowledge provision were finally identified. It was decided to prioritise both of the improvement opportunities which had been identified in the development department - "regular research and analysis of knowledge concerning new technologies" and "collection of new product suggestions and product modifications (own and customers')" - and the improvement opportunity identified in the employee survey -"a multi-departmental Intranet for information on knowledge goals".

Results of the concept development and elaboration: In the concept development and elaboration phase at HEAD acoustics, first of all company-specific web sites were conceptualised – an incentive tool, which above all supports the information, communication/feedback and participation incentives aiming at the know ledge goal "regular research and analysis of knowledge of new technologies" (first improvement opportunity in the development department) and the communication/feedback and participation incentives aiming at the knowledge goal "collection of - own and customers' - new product suggestions and product modifications" (second improvement opportunity in the development department). In a meeting, in which these incentive tools were presented and discussed with the managers and the head of the development department, participants decided to give priority to the "simplicity" and "cost effectiveness" requirements of the incentive system. Furthermore, the focus was to be placed primarily on incentive tools that support the (immaterial) basic incentives.

The technical concept development and elaboration of the so-called "knowledge web sites" were realized by the Chair for Business Administration, with focus on Technology and Innovation Management at RWTH Aachen University. The contents regarding knowledge management and knowledge goals were developed by the author; following the principle "Turn the employees involved into participants", all other contents were gathered or developed by employees of HEAD Acoustics.

The knowledge web sites consist of five areas: "knowledge management and knowledge goals", "knowledge about technologies", "knowledge about the competition", "knowledge on the Internet" and "product creation process". The area "knowledge management and knowledge goals" serves to provide information on knowledge management and knowledge goals. Three further areas of the knowledge web sites were designed to support the information, communication/feedback and participation incentives relating to the knowledge goal "regular research and analysis of knowledge concerning new technologies" (first improvement opportunity in the development department). The area "knowledge about technologies" contains basic knowledge, such as information on technologies used, research projects, etc. In the area "knowledge about the competition", Internet links to cooperation partners, competitors and to different markets of the company are offered. The area "knowledge on the Internet" includes further interesting Internet links for the company, for example, links to fairs/exhibitions, developer information or hardware news. To provide the participation and communication/feedback incentives, input options for comments are incorporated in these areas which are evaluated, and feedback is given by the development department or the research department head. In addition, it was suggested to the management of the company that the communication/feedback, participation and appreciation/awards incentives should be supported by regular discussion circles and/or by a discussion forum as part of the internal knowledge web sites. The decision concerning this suggestion was postponed to a later stage of expansion of the system.

The fifth area of the knowledge web sites, "product creation process", supports the information and communication/feedback incentives relating to the knowledge goal "collection of new product suggestions and product modifications (own and customers')". In this area, the function of the "product steering committee" is described, its process flow is illustrated, example suggestions are presented and example subjects are provided. Moreover, the template for product suggestions and product modifications is provided and suggestion hand-ins are asked for. Due to security considerations, the management of the company objected to a "direct suggestion" input option on the Intranet. To support the communication/feedback incentive, the names of the persons who have recently handed in suggestions are listed and thanks are given to them. The names of the persons whose ideas are followed up are underlined.

In addition to the construction of the internal web sites, the employee performance measurement and evaluation system in the company was analyzed. The criteria-orientated performance assessment form used in the company stems from the 1990s, and was analysed in a workshop together with the department heads. All participants agreed that knowledge aspects were totally missing in this form. They decided, therefore, not only to update and improve the form, but also to enhance it with knowledge aspects and general goals, particularly knowledge goals, so that it could be used for the determination of knowledge objectives and the corresponding measurement and evaluation of employee performance.

Together with the department heads, it was decided to evaluate not only knowledge provision but also knowledge acquisition. Therefore, attributes and criteria for these two knowledge aspects were discussed and included. Voluntary information acquisition, trend awareness/market observation, ideas and suggestions, breadth of interest areas and candidness are the criteria that were finally agreed upon with regard to "knowledge acquisition". Accurate documentation, internal departmental collaboration, multi-departmental exchange of information, willingness to discuss and far-sightedness are the respective evaluation criteria for "knowledge provision".

Results of system introduction

The updated and enhanced performance evaluation form with the additional knowledge objectives was forwarded to the superior staff members responsible for its use in the forthcoming staff meetings. Concerning the implementation of the internal knowledge web sites, e-mails were sent in advance to the employees involved, providing notice of the internal knowledge web sites and their introduction. Several employees, that had participated in the construction of the internal knowledge web sites, were provided with ongoing information about the project status and the forthcoming implementation. The web master of the knowledge web sites was trained for the forthcoming new tasks.

Results of the system check

Since the developed incentive system focuses upon improvement opportunities and since opportunities for the improvement of knowledge provision by incentives occurred primarily in the development department, it was considered to conduct initial evaluations of the incentive system with regard to its effectiveness and efficiency in this department.

The knowledge and, in particular, the behaviour of the employees with respect to knowledge activities, particularly knowledge provision, were observed before and after the introduction of the incentive system, in order to find out whether the incentive system had impacted knowledge management/provision or not. For this purpose, a semi-standardised interview with a questionnaire was conducted with almost all employees of the development department before and one month after the introduction of the internal knowledge web sites. In addition, three months after the introduction of the knowledge web sites, a feedback discussion was conducted with the head of the development department. They showed an increase in the awareness of the relevance and motivation for knowledge management in general and an increased consciousness of the relevance of knowledge acquisition and provision in particular.

10.5 Summary and Conclusion

This chapter has discussed the design and implementation of incentive systems for knowledge management, in particular for knowledge provision in SMEs. It has argued that there are four central design areas for incentive systems: definition of knowledge goals, determination of application area, selection of incentive tools and measurement and evaluation of employee performance. Furthermore, it was argued that the implementation of incentive systems for knowledge management in SMEs may be divided into four main phases: status-quo analysis, concept development and elaboration, system introduction and system checking.

The design and the implementation of an incentive system for knowledge provision at HEAD Acoustics gave evidence of the importance of the design areas and the support through the definition of implementation phases. The experience at HEAD acoustics evidences that the involvement of all employees potentially affected by the incentive system in the implementation phase analysis of the status-quo is crucial for the overall acceptance of the system.

> "We see that our employees are now much more aware of the relevance of knowledge management and much more motivated with regard to knowledge management... The relevance in the whole company of knowledge acquired and provided has increased... Especially concrete knowledge goals seem to influence the behaviour of our employees!"
> **Representative HEAD Acoustics**

References

1. Boenigk M (2001) Umsetzung der Integrierten Kommunikation. Anreizsystem zur Implementierung integrierter Kommunikationsarbeit.Gabler, Wiesbaden
2. Bullinger HJ, Wörner K, Prieto J (1997) Wissensmanagement heute: Daten, Fakten, Trends. Fraunhofer-Institut für Arbeitswirtschaft und Organisation, Stuttgart
3. Dörries K (2002) Revision des Wissensmanagements. Interne Revision 37 (5):194-200
4. Evers H (1992) Zukunftsweisende Anreizsysteme für Führungskräfte. In: Kienbaum J (ed) Visionäres Personalmanagement. Schäffer-Poeschel, Stuttgart, pp 385-401
5. Fank M, Döring-Katerkamp U, Trojan J (2002) Aktivierung der Mitarbeiter beim Knowledge-Management. Institut für e-Management , Köln
6. Grewe A (2000) Implementierung neuer Anreizsysteme: Grundlagen, Konzept und Gestaltungsempfehlungen. Mering: Hampp, Hannover
7. Hunt VD (1996) Process Mapping: How to Reengineer your business Processes. Wiley, New York
8. Kossbiel H (1993) Beiträge verhaltens- und wirtschaftswissenschaftlicher Theorien zur Beurteilung der Effizienz betrieblicher Anreizsysteme: Eine Vorstudie auf der

Grundlage einiger ausgewählter Ansätze. In: Weber W (ed) Entgeltsysteme; Lohn, Mitarbeiterbeteiligung und Zusatzleistungen. Schäffer-Poeschel, Stuttgart, pp 79-103

9. Kupsch PU, Marr R (1991) Personalwirtschaft. In: Heinen E von (ed) Industriebetriebslehre: Entscheidungen im Industriebetrieb, 9th edn. Gabler, Wiesbaden, pp 731-896

10. Laux H, Liermann F (1987) Grundlagen der Organisation: Die Steuerung von Entscheidungen als Grundproblem der Betriebswirtschaftslehre. Springer, Berlin

11. Polzer M (1995) Einführung neuer Entgeltsysteme: Der Kompromiss über die Leistung!. In: Eckardstein D von, Janes A (edn) Neue Wege der Lohnfindung für die Industrie. Manz, Wien, pp 148-170

12. Probst GJB, Romhardt K (1997) Bausteine des Wissensmanagements: Ein praxisorientierter Ansatz. In: Wieselhuber N (ed) Handbuch Lernende Organisation: Unternehmens- und Mitarbeiterpotentiale erfolgreich erschließen. Gabler, Wiesbaden, pp 129-143

13. Probst G, Raub S, Romhardt K (1999) Wissen managen: Wie Unternehmen ihre wertvollste Ressource optimal nutzen, 3th edn. Gabler, Wiesbaden

14. Rosenstiel L von (1999a) Anerkennung und Kritik als Führungsmittel. In: Rosenstiel L von, Regnet E, Domsch M (edn) Führung von Mitarbeitern: Handbuch für erfolgreiches Personalmanagement, 4th edn. Schäffer-Poeschel, Stuttgart, pp 243-253

15. Thiesse F (2001) Prozessorientiertes Wissensmanagement: Konzepte, Methode, Fallbeispiele. St. Gallen

16. Zaunmüller H (in press), Anreizsysteme für das Wissensmanagement in KMUs: Gestaltung von Anreizsystemen für die Wissensbereitstellung der Mitarbeiter

17. Zeyer U (1996) Implementierungsmanagement: Ein konzeptioneller Ansatz am Beispiel der Implementierung von Lean Management. Hampp, München

18. Zobel JG (2001) Anreizsysteme im Knowledge Management: Ein integrierter Ansatz zur Mitarbeitermotivation. Personal 53 (5): 262-267

19. Zowislo N, Schwab H (2003) Interne Kommunikation im Veränderungsprozess: Mitarbeiter gezielt informieren und erfolgreich einbeziehen. Gabler, Wiesbaden

11 Supporting Knowledge Integration at SMEs – The KINX Portal

Charo Elorrieta [1], Juan Pedro Lopez [2], Fons Wijnhoven [3]

[1]Socintec (Grupo Azertia), Las Arenas, Spain, celorrieta@socintec.es
[2]Socintec (Grupo Azertia), Madrid, Spain, jplopez@socintec.es
[3]University of Twente, Enschede, The Netherlands,
a.b.j.m.wijnhoven@utwente.nl

11.1 Introduction

The knowledge integration process having been clarified in Chap. 2, Chap. 3 described types of problems that high-tech SMEs have with KI in their new product development processes (NPD). Following that, Chap. 4 defined families of solutions related to these problems, and Chaps. 5-10 described the KI problems and solutions matches in practice. In chapter 1, though, we stated that any attempt at being complete with respect to these problems, solutions, and matches will fail, given the almost unlimited list of potential problems and solutions that may exist in reality. Consequently, this chapter describes the development of a portal that will enable the constant submission of new problems and solutions, and the development of the matching of both. The ambitions of the portal are described in the following six points:

- Informing SMEs, consultants, researchers and others about KI problems and solutions for NPD processes of high-tech SMEs.
- Helping SMEs in their process of identifying and defining the problems they encounter with knowledge integration in the NPD context.
- Matching available solutions and problems. By matching their problems with solutions, the KI portal limits the efforts the SMEs have to make searching for an appropriate solution to their problem. The portal will, therefore, (partly) fill in the gap between solution developers and users (SMEs).
- Providing additional information about solutions so that problem owners can make informed decisions on adopting and using the solutions offered.
- Providing a platform to exchange experiences, feelings, ideas and views on KI.
- Improving problem identification and problem classification, developing new solutions and improving existing ones, as well as improving the matching mechanism between problems and solutions.

Thus, the portal is not just another KI tool or solution, but an informative platform on KI. Like most information services [5, 9, 10], the portal links people who have problems and questions on the one hand with resources (including people) that have solutions and answers on the other hand, in either a direct or indirect way. The direct way consists of a forum in which people can discuss problems, solutions, and experiences with regard to KI in the NPD context of high-tech SMEs. This gives many opportunities to exchange latent knowledge. The indirect way consists of the exchange of information, like problem and solution descriptions, and a mechanism that matches both, thereby enabling the exchange of explicit and represented knowledge on KI. The matching mechanism selects and shows the most appropriate solution(s) for a given problem. Additionally, the portal gives meta-information about these solutions, e.g., information on documented experiences and information on suitability and use of the solution(s).

The portal, which can be accessed at kinx.socintec.com, is divided into three different areas (see Fig. 11.1 for the entrance page). The first area is the *public view* with general information that can be accessed by any portal visitor. The main goal of this area is to give the visitor a clear idea of what kind of services and information can be found on the portal. This area was designed, taking into account the characteristics of web users. If the user registers, then she or he can access the *private area*, where specific and more informative sections are available, and more intensive and customised interactions between problem owners and solutions are possible. Finally, the portal has an *administrator area*, which is only accessible to Socintec employees, who maintain and edit the portal. In the administrator area, Socintec decides what to offer to public or private area users.

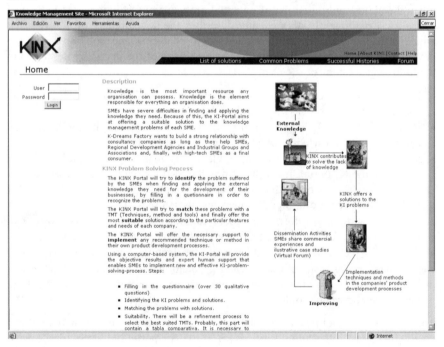

Fig. 11.1. General view of the KINX portal

This chapter will first describe, in a general way, the elements of an information service in Sect. 11.2, to further sharpen what the current KINX portal consists of. Due to the multiplicity of its functions, the portal in its present state has a highly elaborated process model. The elements of this process model are described in Sect. 11.3. Sect. 11.4 describes some of the major challenges that were encountered in the portal development, especially with regard to the matching mechanism. Finally, Sect. 11.5 draws conclusions with regard to the ambitions set forth at the beginning of the project.

11.2 Information Services and Scope of the KINX Portal

A basic problem of the information society is not a lack of information, but rather the opposite: information overload [4, 6], which is further intensified by the Internet through its overabundance of information supply. However, some information goods are scarce, because owners may be unwilling to share them [2] or because they may not be interested in investing highly in presence on the Internet or on intranets (e.g., because of privacy and security reasons). Information services try to bridge these supply and demand gaps in order to increase information value for their clients, who are both information suppliers and information users. An information service can do this by 1) processing, creating and delivering *content* according to specific client needs, so that the data become meaningful information for the services' client, 2) delivering additional *use* features to increase the value experience for information users, and 3) realising a stream of revenues for the information-goods supplier and the information service owners.

These three aspects of an information service (content, use value and revenue) need concrete specifications to make an information service a success. These specifications are mostly done in three design layers. Design layers define different layers of decomposition from abstract notions of a system to its realization in concrete organizational and technical means [7]. Academics in the electronic commerce field distinguish business models, process models, and organizational and technical infrastructures as different layers of abstraction of an e-commerce system [3, 8]. A business model describes the method of doing business in a certain industry or society [3, 8], and answers the question of what is delivered to whom in return for what. The value proposition includes what *content* and *use features* are delivered to whom for what in return. The business *revenue* model explains what revenues can be collected from customers and other actors (e.g., sponsors) involved. These patterns may govern how content is handled, how clients gain use values from them, and how the content providers and information services gain revenues to keep them sufficiently motivated to submit content and services, thus setting the frame for the pertinent process models.

To realize the business and process models, information, organizational structures, and information technology are needed. The technical components consist of the hardware, data communication networks, software platforms, and the system's services infrastructure (comprising items like security, database management, applications development, applications operations and maintenance, disaster and recovery planning).

The information consists of the data available and accessible, the organization of these data and resources, and information needed to update the content. The organizational structure consists of the list of responsibilities, the division of tasks among employees and contractors, and coordination principles. Informational, organisational, and information technological together form the infrastructure [1] of an information service.

The three aspects (content, use facilitation, and revenue) and the three design layers of an information service (business, process, and infrastructure) constitute, in total, nine classes of design constructs for information services (see Fig. 11.2). The KINX consortium has developed most of the insights needed for a successful information service, though the revenue collection is not yet fully developed, as the portal is still sponsored by the EU and cross-subsidized by Socintec's consulting incomes. Thus, because the infrastructure and the business model are mainly a Socintec internal issue, we focus on the business process model in Sect. 11.3. The business model and the remaining infrastructure issues are only shortly discussed in Sect. 11.5 as topics to be developed in the future. Sect. 11.4 discusses a few of the major development challenges that the project group faced.

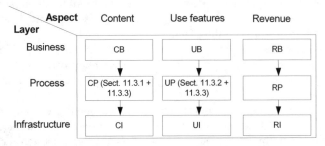

Fig. 11.2. Information service design classes and related sections of this article

11.3 Knowledge Integration Portal Description

Fig. 11.3 gives an overview of the activities that the KINX portal performs to realize matches between KI tools and techniques suppliers and KI problem owners. As described in Sect. 11.1, the KINX portal has three different domains:

- A public area through which external KI problem owners and KI solution providers can browse to find out what the KINX portal is all about. The solution owners can also submit content ((meta-)information on their solutions) via the public area to the portal.

- A private area in which problem owners can interact with the portal to generate a problem diagnosis and potential solution.

- An administrator (Socintec) area that performs activities to increase the value of the portal. These activities consist of the admission of the problem owner to the private area, maintenance and development of the diagnostic questionnaire, maintenance and development of the classification of problems, evaluation of information from solution owners, classification of these solutions in relation to problems areas, development and maintenance of the matching rules, management of the forum, and possibly creating new insights from the forum to improve the matching rules and publish successful experiences from the matching activities and forum to the public area (if the problem owners involved agree).

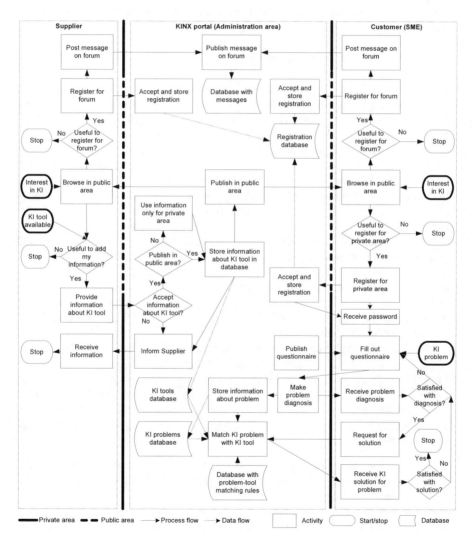

Fig. 11.3. A process model of the KINX information service

11.3.1 The KINX Portal Public Area

The public area of the KINX portal holds information that can be accessed by any portal visitor without registration. The public area is divided into the following subsections:

- General description of the portal
- Common KI problems
- List of KI solutions
- Successful experiences

The main goal of the public area section is to show at a glance the kind of information that the visitor can find on the site. The idea of this section is to get the visitors' attention, and invite them to ask for registration to the private area.

The description or the home page acts as a welcome page to the portal. On this page, there appears a basic explanation of the services and contents that a user can find on the KINX portal. The Home link is always visible on the right upper part of the screen, along with the 'Contact' link, the 'Help' link, and the 'About KINX' link (in the public area only). The 'Contact' page contains localisation data about the company responsible for the KINX portal. It is also stated that the KINX portal is the outcome of a project funded by the European Commission. The 'About KINX' page contains a description of the project's goals and its main contributions. Finally, the Help link opens a pop-up window with a text describing the contents of the portal section visited by the user. This help information is also shown in the right column of the screen, in order to guide the user through the current section.

The 'common KI problems' section presents some aggregated tabular and graphical data obtained by the analysis of the daily data gathered by the portal. This aggregation includes - arranged by companies` economic sector - data about the type of problems found in each sector. The goal of this section is to show general information that can be extracted from the database in order to demonstrate the capabilities and the benefits of the KINX portal beyond the provision of customized solutions for KI problems.

The KINX portal holds detailed information about different tools and/or techniques related to Knowledge Integration. An information template supplies information on more than 40 KI solutions, which are used as suggestions to solve the problems recognised as user problems. This template is structured in two levels, one of which contains basic, the other one detailed information about the given solution. The information fields defined for each solution on the first level are (see Fig. 11.4):

- Name: a short name assigned to the solution, which is used when solutions for a given problem are listed and a text search over all available solutions is performed
- Type: used to distinguish between tools or techniques or both
- Concise Description: a two-line description of the solution, which is returned as a result of a text search over all available solutions

- Basic Description: a detailed description (several paragraphs) of the solution that is shown when the user asks for information about a solution
- Related Solutions: a set of links to related solutions in the database.

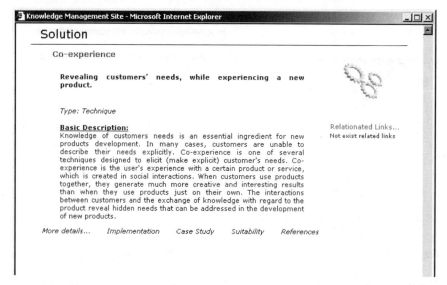

Fig. 11.4. Solutions information window on the KINX portal

The information fields defined for each solution on the second level are (see Fig. 11.5):

- More Details: This section contains more concise information formed by several paragraphs about the solution found in the first level.
- Implementation: This section provides information about the application of the given solution.
- Case Study: A situation where the given solution has been applied is described.
- Suitability: Data about the implementation time, the price and the maturity of the solution is provided
- References: A list with available web links or other information references are provided in this section.

The List of Solutions section also allows for a text search through the text fields defined for the available solutions. To see the details of each of the solutions, the user simply clicks on the corresponding title, and the previously described pop-up windows will be shown. By clicking the links shown in the result list, the pop-up windows with the previously described information for each solution are shown. Furthermore, an Advanced Search section is available, by which more detailed search conditions can be stated. The criteria that can be used to filter the available solutions are the same as the ones defined for the Suitability subsection of the solutions information window.

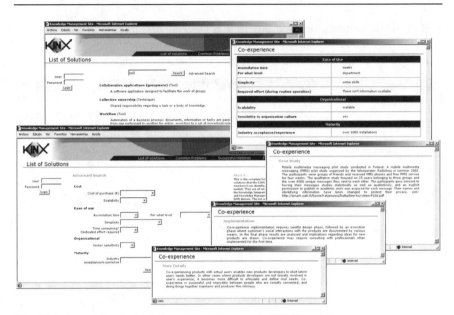

Fig. 11.5. Second level of solutions descriptions on the KINX portal

The section on Successful Histories contains examples of problems detected with the help of the portal including success stories about proposed solutions and characteristics (description and suitability features) of these solutions. These examples are selected by the portal administrator from among the ones made available by portal registered visitors. This means that the user must explicitly permit the use of the problem definitions stated when using the KINX portal. None of the examples presented will show the company name or person that stated the problem, unless the corresponding user has given explicit permission. The main goal of this section is to show casual visitors the capabilities of the KINX portal by presenting some of the real interactions performed by registered users.

11.3.2 The Private Area

A registered visitor of the KINX portal is called a Basic User (to differentiate him or her from the administrator). This registered visitor can interact with the portal to define a specific problem and obtain the most appropriate solution(s) for solving it. The main sections for this kind of user are the 'In progress problem definitions' and the 'Diagnosis' sections. In the first step, the provided questionnaire must be answered to allow the identification of the most relevant problems present in the user's organisation. The next step is to get a diagnostic about potential problems. In a final step, several solutions (techniques and/or tools) (for definitions and distinctions, see Chap. 4) will be provided along with their relevance for the problem at hand. A Basic User can also see a report with information about his or her previously stated problems, solutions offered by the portal or aggregate non-confidential data about the rest of the users, that interact with the system (but only aggregate data). A Basic User can configure the portal so as not to share information about some or every previously executed problem identification process(es) and its/their result(s). Part of this data would then be used to build the Successful experiences public subsection.

The Diagnosis section is designed to assist the user in defining his or her KI problem. This process is divided into the following steps:

- State your problem
- Diagnosis
- Solutions
- Suitability
- Contact

The lateral menu (see Fig. 11.6), appearing on the left-hand side of the browser window when the user visits the Diagnosis section, serves to ease navigation across these different sections. Each step can be accessed at any given moment.

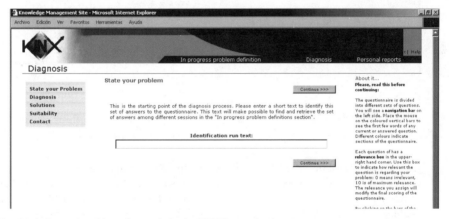

Fig. 11.6. Start of problem diagnosis in the KINX portal private area

State your problem: This is the initial step of the problem definition process. Here, a name is given to provide a unique identifier for the data that is going to be supplied. This name will be used later to return to the process. As mentioned before, each problem definition is called a run or execution.

Questionnaire: The portal has several information resources; one of them is the questionnaire. The questionnaire has been carefully designed to enable detection of the KI problem of the user's organisation. The user has to answer several questions (a variable number depending on the answers given). For each question, he or she can state how important the question is for his or her specific situation. For this purpose, a relevance box is provided on the upper right hand side of the screen. Above each question there are two progress bars: the first bar with the size of the questionnaire and the number of remaining questions, the second bar with the number of answered questions, that can be used to navigate across answered questions (see Fig. 11.7). Answers provided can be modified at any given moment.

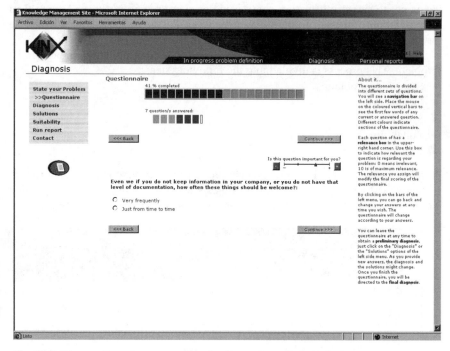

Fig. 11.7. The questionnaire progress bar for diagnosis on the private area

Diagnosis: The submission of information can be interrupted at any point in order to get a problem analysis on the basis of the information supplied so far. The portal analyses the answers given thitherto and provides a description of the problems detected with possible causes. To get a diagnosis, it is not necessary to complete the entire questionnaire - the portal will do its best with the answers provided (see Fig. 11.8).

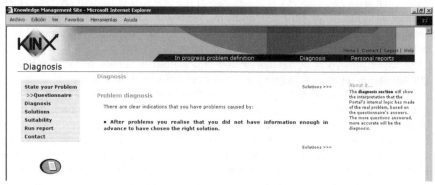

Fig. 11.8. Diagnosis result in the KINX portal private area

Solutions: The answers to the questionnaire are also used by the KINX portal to search for the best available solution (tool and/or technique) in order to solve the recognized problem. Again, it is not necessary to answer the complete questionnaire to get solutions: Solutions are provided on the basis of partial information as well. They are listed with the relevance of the solution concerning its capability to help in solving the identified problem (see Fig. 11.9.).

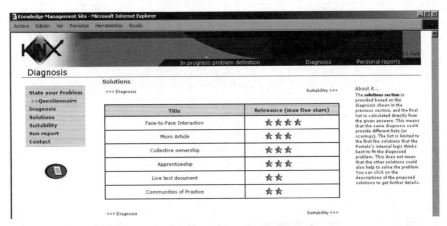

Fig. 11.9. List of solutions proposed after diagnosis on the private area

At present, the KINX portal contains detailed information about more than 40 solutions (tools and/or techniques), that can be proposed as solutions for the previously categorized problems; it is intended to enlarge the set of potential solutions whenever new ones become available. Detailed information about each solution can be accessed from the Solutions list by clicking on the name of the desired element. This information is presented using the same structure as the one described in the List of Solutions section of the public portal area.

Suitability: The last step in the process is the suitability section, where all suggested solutions are compared according to the different parameters. In the first view, solutions are compared according to implementation costs and ease of use. This information is shown in a tabular format (see Fig. 11.10).

A registered user can see here a complete list of previous problem definitions he or she has stated on the KINX site. The Personal Reports section (see Fig. 11.11) includes different reports about previous interactions of the user with the KINX site. These reports include data of the problems detected and the solutions proposed, as well as tables comparing different solutions and problems. The main goal of these reports is to serve as interaction summaries for the user of the KINX portal. The report can be printed or stored in a file for further analysis by the user. These reports can be useful to compare results offered by the portal for different problems. The user will be asked whether a personal report may be used as input to build the content of public sections such as 'Successful experiences' and 'Common problems'.

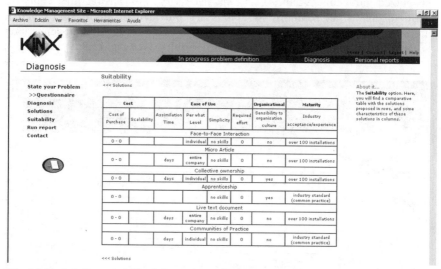

Fig. 11.10. Solution suitability information on the KINX portal private area

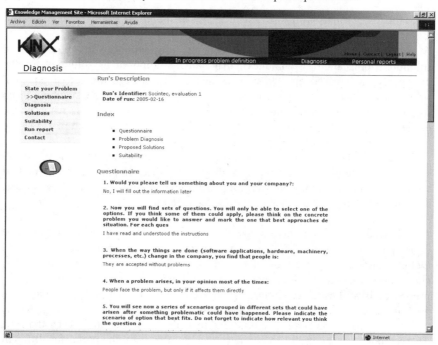

Fig. 11.11. Personal reports generation on the KINX portal private area

One of the most important tools included on the portal is a discussion forum. This forum allows the users of the KINX portal to share experiences, knowledge, comments and feelings regarding KI problems. A forum is formed by one or more discussions, each related to a specific subject selected by the portal administrator. It allows for the posting and reading of messages related to the subject of the respective discussion. To be able to access the forum section, the user must pass through a registration process. This registration is needed to include the identity of the writer with the corresponding messages. Username and password of the forum differ from those necessary for access to the private area of the KINX portal.

11.3.3 The Administration Area

In the administration area, functions for the daily maintenance and operation of the portal are provided. The various functions include:

- Portal Content Snapshot: This option facilitates storage of (parts of) the data contained on the database portal. This file contains the questions and answers for the questionnaire, and the data for all the runs performed by the users.
- Load a new questionnaire for the portal. Using a predefined format in an MS Excel file, it is possible to change the set of questions (the order in which they are presented and the associated weights to state their importance) presented by the portal. Questions and problems are characterized by a set of features or variables (for example, the way in which information is codified) previously defined and identified.
- Load new problem definitions. New problem descriptions, and the way they are characterized by a set of predefined features, can be loaded into the portal to be used in the problem identification stage. For this purpose, a preformatted MS Excel file must be used.
- Load new solution descriptions. New solution descriptions can be loaded using an MS Access file. If the content of this database is stored as text files, this subsection allows the loading of these text files onto the portal database. In this way, the process of updating the content related to the information regarding solutions is automatic, without the need of specialised staff intervention.

An overview of the questionnaire, of the problem descriptions, and of the KI solutions as of March 2005, is given in Chap. 4 of this book. The matching of problems and solutions proceeds as follows: First of all, using the questionnaire, the internal logic of the portal will score the problem for each of the KI activities. This conforms to what we call the vector in the problem space. This information representation structure is termed the Vector Space Model, commonly used to represent content for information retrieval purposes (see Chap. 7). Once the problem vector has been constructed, the portal will use a set of rules to transform it into two different spaces:

- the diagnosis space, used to communicate the interpretation of the problem to the user, and

- the solution space, used to construct the list of suitable solutions

This means, that - starting from the set of problems identified - a matrix is constructed to obtain a universe of vectors. The coordinates of these vectors in a multidimensional space indicate how well each solution and each diagnosis option fit to a specific problem. Using a mathematical standard function for measuring the distances between the needs and the possible solutions, the best set(s) of solutions and the most suitable diagnoses are identified.

11.4 Portal Development Process

The portal's implementation started with the design of a zero level demonstrator in order to understand the product and clarify some specific issues regarding user-interfaces for problem description/self-diagnosis. The experts discussed and developed a reference model of Knowledge Integration for SMEs departing from the conclusions of Chap. 2. The purpose was to develop a preliminary tool in Microsoft Access 2000 to understand the complexity of the product and to test the ideas of the portal with some Spanish companies.

Taking into account the discussions regarding the diagnosis implementation, a non-functional prototype was designed. This first prototype consisted of a set of Microsoft PowerPoint slides, that were built according to the portal's future appearance. After approval of the non-functional prototype, real web implementation began. To realize the final version of the portal, three preliminary prototypes were released. Every release of the portal was thoroughly tested, both by internal members of the KINX project, and by external people specifically contacted for the task of testing the prototypes. The testing process was structured around the following aspects:

- User reaction
- Need for explanations and content
- What more details will be needed
- Needs for navigation and structure (including questionnaire)
- Design
- Other comments

One of the key findings of the testing process was that the portal cannot replace "human contact". In accordance with the modularity philosophy of the portal's design, for each prototype all the sections were revisited, in order to improve them in the next releases of the portal. One of the sections that was changed most was the internal logic of the portal, thus attempting to come close to the best possible solution for scoring a questionnaire of variable length. The main problems faced in the development of the matching algorithm were two:

- First of all, the questionnaire is not of a fixed length, and the user may leave it at any time, or even change answers to questions previously answered.

- Secondly, the scoring system had to cope with balancing weighted scores of the individual KI activities to compute a correct score for the whole questionnaire.

The latter problem was solved through simulation in Excel and through a scoring system based on average scores and independent weights assigned to each question. The calculation process self-balances the scores into a canonical form that is used to transfer the problem vector into the diagnosis and solutions spaces.

11.5 Conclusions and Discussion

In summary, the KINX portal - being developed as an information service - delivers a compendium of KI problems and solutions to improve the NPD process of SMEs, and facilitates the matching of KI solutions with problems and vice versa. With respect to the ambitions of the portal defined in the beginning of this chapter, the following conclusions can be drawn:

- Informing SMEs, consultants, researchers and others about KI problems and solutions for NPD processes of high-tech SMEs: This is realized by the browsing opportunities in the public area of the portal. Socintec acts as editor and reviewer for what is submitted by solution owners.
- Helping SMEs in their process of identifying and defining the problems they encounter with knowledge integration in the NPD context: This is realized in the private area of the portal through the problem articulation that the questionnaire offers and the KI diagnostic reports that are delivered to the users.
- Matching available solutions and problems: By matching their problems with solutions, the KI portal limits the efforts the SMEs have to make searching for an appropriate solution to their problem. The portal will, therefore, (partly) fill in the gap between solution developers and users (SMEs). A problem-solution matching mechanism is offered and maintained by Socintec.
- Providing additional information about solutions so that problem owners can make informed decisions on adopting and using solutions offered: An important part of this is the SME suitability of KI solutions that is indicated by the portal. Furthermore, extensive descriptions of the solutions offered and detailed case studies of their application guarantee that users are able to judge the solutions' adequacy.
- Providing a platform to exchange experiences, feelings, ideas and views on KI: The portal offers a forum for problems owners, solutions owners, and others with experiences and expertise in KI for SMEs. Socintec acts as a facilitator for this forum.

These results have been discussed with a representative group of users. In these discussions, the following points for future directions have been mentioned:

- a global collection, evaluation and improvement of KI problems and solutions;
- a framework and context for coherent KI diagnosis and solution finding;

- a way of integrating different KI initiatives in an organization;
- a practical method to measure KI progress in time;
- a tool for communicating about KI with organization members and increasing their motivation and propensity to change when needed;
- the facilitating of benchmarking and transferring of best practices of KI in new process development processes;
- a way for establishing external and internal KI reference points.

An information service in its best shape develops on the basis of its interactions with its environment. For the Kinx portal, this involves constant monitoring of what problem owners do and what they want, and what new opportunities are offered by solution suppliers. Additionally, currently only investments by the EU and Socintec itself are implemented as part of the revenue model of the portal. After the completion of the KINX project, the EU sponsorship will terminate, and other options for sponsorships or payments will have to be considered to give the KINX portal the longer term resources needed to make it as important as it should be. Such a revenue model should be based on a consideration of the stakeholders around this portal and their ability and willingness to invest or pay. These stakeholders may be basic users who need external aid, advanced users (like consultants) who may be interested in using the portal and in submitting solution (meta-)information, and KI researchers. An appropriate business model will lay the foundations for a good organizational and information technological infrastructure.

References

1. Broadbent M, Weill P (1997) Management by maxim: How business and IT managers can create IT infrastructures. Sloan Management Review 38 (3): 77-92
2. Davenport TH, Prusak L (1997) Information ecology: Mastering the information and knowledge environment. Oxford University Press, Oxford
3. Gordijn J. (2002) Value-based requirements engineering: Exploring innovative e-commerce ideas. Ph.D. dissertation Free University Amsterdam, Amsterdam
4. Landau M. (1969) Redundancy, rationality, and the problem of duplication and overlap. Public Administration Review 29 (4): 346-356
5. Shapiro C, Varian H (1999) Information Rules: A Strategic Guide to the Network Economy. Harvard Business School Press, Boston , MA
6. Simon H (1976) Administrative behavior. Free Press 3, New York
7. Sowa J, Zachman J (1992) Extending and formalizaing the framwork for information systems architecture. IBM systems journal 31 (3): 590-616
8. Timmers P (1998) Electronic Commerce: Strategies and Models for Business-to-Business Trading. Wiley, Chichester (UK)
9. Wijnhoven F (2002) Design components for information market services: A framework for research and practice. Monteiro J, Swatman P, Valadares Tavares L (eds) Towards the knowledge society: eCommerce, eBusiness and eGovernment. Kluwer Academic Publishers, Boston , MA, pp 49-65

10. Wijnhoven F, Kraaijenbrink J (2005) Design theory for digital information services: Product-oriented analysis and design constructs for information services. Research memo University of Twente, Department of Business Information Systems, Enschede

12 Supporting Knowledge Integration at SMEs – Policies

Yoel Raban

Interdisciplinary Center for Technology Analysis and Forecasting (ICTAF) at Tel-Aviv University, Israel, raban@post.tau.ac.il

12.1 Introduction

SMEs are widely recognized as an important source of GNP growth in many countries. Yet, SMEs are largely dependent on external competencies in order to successfully carry out innovation processes. In a recent OECD report [14], networking and clusters were described to be a key enabler for the success of SMEs. The report calls for increasing the participation of SMEs in research networks and supporting the emergence and maintenance of innovative clusters.

European governments and the European Commission operate a varied mix of innovation support measures for SMEs. Most of these measures were not designed to specifically support Knowledge Integration (KI). However, some of these measures are more tuned to the special needs of SMEs in the area of KI.

As shown in Chap. 3, KI is not utilised to the maximum potential in SMEs due to lack of awareness and skills. KI is an important enabler of NPD processes in SMEs. Therefore, it deserves more governmental policy development efforts.

This chapter characterises KI support measures that are available to SMEs in Europe. We start with explaining why it is important to support KI in SMEs (Sect. 12.2). We then describe profiles of representative KI support measures in European countries (Sect. 12.3), evaluate their effectiveness (Sects. 12.4 and 12.5) and conclude with some recommendations (Sect. 12.6).

12.2 Reasons for Supporting KI in SMEs

Why should governments support knowledge integration activities? In general, governmental industrial policy is said to be justified when there are market failures that prevent certain desirable economic activities from materializing. In economics theory, market failure can take the form of externalities, market power, information problems and public goods. The most widely accepted rationale for public action is externalities in R&D and knowledge creation. The social return on investment in R&D and knowledge creation is larger than the private return since new knowledge is added to a global (or national) pool that is publicly available [9]. This argument is valid for explicit knowledge. An important enabler for industrial innovation, however, is tacit and latent knowledge, hands-on knowledge that is not being codified in innovation processes.

More recent studies take into account "stickiness" of knowledge and stress the importance of encouraging networking and collaborations between firms (Chap. 9).The importance of networks to SMEs and their public support has been shown in many studies [7]. Some authors, furthermore, distinguish between networks and clusters where the former are defined as "relationships connecting actors that are cooperating in order to acquire resources they may not themselves possess" and the latter as a "geographic concentration of interconnected companies and institutions in a particular field" [6]. These authors also note that spatial proximity facilitates knowledge transfer and spillovers, including knowledge that is tacit. A recent summary paper [5] on innovation policy reaches the following conclusions:

- Technological co-operation and collaboration among firms is essential. One of the reasons for that is that a large part of the knowledge needed in innovation processes is tacit, and can be transferred only through social interactions. Collaborations should be supported in order to capture the social return on R&D.
- Innovative firms draw largely on the science system. Public authorities, therefore, should foster the links between industrial R&D and the science system. The tacit knowledge argument is applicable here, too; an important mechanism through which technology is transferred from science to industries is knowledge integration.

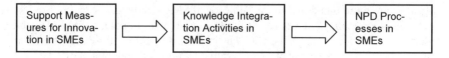

Fig. 12.1. Possible links between support measures, KI and NPD processes in SMEs

The above diagram shows the linkage between support measures and NPD processes in SMEs: Support measures have an impact on the performance of KI activities inside SMEs which, in turn, impacts on the NPD processes in SMEs (for a more detailed discussion of this relationship, see Chap. 2). Thus, policy support measures can be evaluated by their possible impact on the various KI activities. The following section will therefore categorize existing support measures and will discuss how they support specific KI activities, such as detection, codification, elicitation, and assessment.

12.3   Profiles of KI Support Measures for SMEs

There are several distinct groups of support measures for knowledge-intensive SMEs:

- Technology transfer from science to SMEs. These are programs that are aimed at encouraging the unilateral transfer of knowledge from universities and science institutions to SMEs. These programmes sometimes include a subsidy element intended to advance the academic research to a point where SMEs can exploit and commercialize it.

- Competence development. These programmes aim at improving the competence and knowledge of SMEs, including unilateral transfer of knowledge through training, consultancy and mentoring.
- Mobility. These are programmes designed to improve personnel exchange between industry and universities or research institutions..
- Regional clustering. These programmes include various support elements intended to foster collaborations between different types of organizations in a certain geographic region. Generally, SMEs are an important part of such clusters. In some cases, these programmes also subsidize collaborative R&D.
- Collaborative R&D. These programmes support R&D cooperations between SMEs and RTD performers. The idea is to harness the research power of larger RTD performers (large companies, universities) to the benefit of SMEs.
- Knowledge sharing networks. These programmes enable cost sharing of knowledge, which is - such as knowledge from extensive market research - not accessible for individual SMEs.
- Knowledge brokers. These are intermediaries assisting SMEs in finding technology that suits their needs.

The legitimacy of supporting knowledge integration as part of the innovation process was already mentioned in the first section. The question is which of the varied KI activities should be supported. Are all KI activities equally important? Do they have similar impact on the NPD process? These are difficult questions, since there is very little research evidence with respect to tying KI activities to the NPD process and to their scientific and commercial results.

Indeed, we cannot say with certainty which KI activities should be supported by specific measures, and which activities may be left unsupported. There is a growing awareness that tacit and latent knowledge are important to R&D (or NPD), and that codification of latent knowledge is a cost-benefit issue [3]. The importance of knowledge elicitation in developing new products is also well documented. Ethnographic techniques are gaining popularity among marketing professionals as a way of eliciting latent customer's knowledge [8]. All KI activities could be important to SMEs in different phases in their NPD processes. It is therefore important to classify existing support measures for innovation processes in SMEs according to their contribution to the KI activities.

In Table 12.1, we develop a mapping mechanism of innovation support measures to KI activities (described in Chap. 4). For each KI activity, we suggest a possible function of supportive policy measure, and then add representative support measures from different European countries[1]. It should be noted, however, that

---

[1] The information has been taken from TrendChart Innovation Policy in Europe (http://trendchart.cordis.lu/index.cfm) that provides policy makers and managers of innovation support schemes with summarized information and statistics on innovation poli-

some support measures may be mapped into several KI activities, but only the most important one is depicted in Table 12.1.

Table 12.1. Mapping KI activities to innovation support measures

KI activity	Main functions of support measures	Representative support measures
Detection	Assistance in locating external knowledge	Knowledge brokers (Syntens – the Netherlands, Patent Information Centres – Germany, TUFF - Sweden)
Codification	Promoting the codification of external knowledge	Technology codification and transfer from universities (GTS – Denmark, Technology Clinic - Finland)
Transfer	Assisting in transfer of external knowledge, such as subsidizing market research	Training (KeBB – the Netherlands), knowledge sharing (ILTAM – Israel, Techinform – Austria, TOP - Germany)
Assessment	Assisting the assessment of external knowledge	Consultants (SKO - the Netherlands), knowledge brokers (Export Institute – Israel)
Elicitation	Assisting in elicitation of external latent knowledge	Clustering (VINNVAXT – Sweden, CoEs - Finland), collaborative R&D (Tekes Technology Programmes – Finland)
Nurturing	Promoting nurturing of tacit external knowledge	Mentoring (PLATO - Belgium)
Transfer owner	Assistance in recruiting or outsourcing external knowledge owners	Recruitment and mobility mechanisms (CORTECHS – France, Knowledge Transfer Partnerships - UK)

Support measures that encourage SMEs in detection or location of external knowledge are manifold and usually provided by knowledge brokers. The knowledge-brokers' main asset is "knowledge about knowledge". They close the gap between knowledge needs of SMEs and knowledge owners in research institutions and large companies. Representative examples of knowledge brokers are Syntens[2] (the Netherlands), Patent Information Centres[3] (Germany), and TUFF[4] (Sweden). Syntens is a network of regional centres which provide support and advice to SMEs on technology and innovation. The Patent Information Centres provide access to scientific and technological information that is contained within patents,

---

cies, performances and trends in member states, and supports the exchange of good practice in this area.

[2] www.syntens.nl

[3] www.patentinformation.de

[4] Operated by VINNOVA - http://publiceng.vinnova.se

registered designs and trademarks for firms and private inventors. The TUFF programme encourages trade in technological services between public R&D technology providers and groups of SMEs. It stimulates SME demand by supporting feasibility studies, inter-firm networking, and co-operative projects.

There are many instances where external knowledge has to be codified prior to
its use in SMEs. In such cases, external knowledge owners (such as universities
and research centres) and SME personnel have to codify the knowledge, and they
can be assisted by specific support measures. Representative support measures
that promote the *codification* of external knowledge are GTS[5] (Denmark) and
Technology Clinics[6] (Finland). The 11 institutes making up the GTS network develop and communicate technologically-based knowledge to SMEs and other organizations. By selling consultancy services and acting as co-operation partner,
GTS helps companies to gain access to research. The Technology Clinics carry
out technology transfer from research institutes and universities to SMEs. The
main goal of the initiative is to promote adaptation of specified technologies for
problem solving in SMEs in order to exploit new technological opportunities and
to raise awareness of external R&D resources.

Governments assist SMEs' *transfer* of explicit external knowledge by various
support measures, such as KeBB[7] (the Netherlands), ILTAM[8] (Israel), Techinform[9] (Austria) and TOP (Germany). KeBB promotes knowledge transfer between
vocational training organizations and SMEs. Its objective is to initiate a continuous process of knowledge transfer. ILTAM's (Israeli Users' Association of Advanced Technologies in Electronics) aim is to support and encourage knowledge
sharing on the latest technological breakthroughs developed in Israel and abroad
among its members. This is achieved by establishing working groups of experts of
the same discipline from different companies, who meet and exchange information, discuss common problems and ideas, and share knowledge between the participants. Techinform offers access to thousands of databases on diverse topics,
such as state-of-the-art technologies, patent and industrial design surveys, industrial design, trade-mark rights, information on legal status and activities of firms
and information on suppliers. The TOP programme provides support for knowledge exchange, learning and co-operation among companies. Managers from
SMEs are invited to leading firms in a certain field of technology to learn how
these organize their innovation processes. They can discuss different approaches
and learn from the experience of the leaders in the field.

Support measures promoting the *assessment* of external knowledge usually involve consultants (SKO[10] – the Netherlands) or knowledge brokers (Export Insti-

---

[5] www.teknologiportalen.dk/EN/
[6] www.tekes.fi/eng
[7] Operated by Senter – www.senter.nl
[8] www.iltam.org
[9] www.techinform.at
[10] Operated by Senter – www.senter.nl

tute[11] – Israel). Assessment includes activities to determine the credibility of knowledge sources, and activities to assess the value of knowledge. Knowledge brokers can help SMEs in determining the credibility of external knowledge sources. The Export Institute provides SMEs with competitive intelligence services, including assessment of external knowledge sources by experts. The SKO measure subsidizes the employment of external knowledge carriers (graduates from universities or technical colleges) for the elaboration of innovation plans comprising organization, market, product and/or process.

In the *latent and tacit* knowledge domains, support measures have to help SMEs in making external knowledge more accessible. This can be achieved through different types of collaborative R&D schemes, in particular networks, partnerships and clusters, as a recent OECD study stated [13]. Collaborative R&D schemes particularly assist SMEs in the elicitation of external knowledge. Measures to support collaborative R&D encourage SMEs, large companies and science institutions to share innovative resources for the development of new products. Sharing resources with large companies and science institutions enables SMEs to extract knowledge from external experts and engage in cross fertilization activities. Resource sharing is also part of clustering support measures, although clustering requires some extent of geographical proximity, which is an important enabler for nurturing external tacit knowledge by SMEs, as some scholars note [6].

Tekes Technology Programmess[12] are a representative example of collaborative R&D support measures. They are used to promote development in specific sectors of technology or industry, and to pass on the research results to the business community. The technology programmes are planned in cooperation with companies, research institutes, and Tekes. The duration of the programmes ranges from three to five years. Tekes usually finances about half of the costs of programmes, and about 50 of the total funds go to SMEs.

An example of clustering support measures is Sweden's VINNVAXT[13] (Regional growth through dynamic innovation systems). The concept behind the programme is the promotion of effective cooperation between companies, research and development organizations and the political system within each region, with the aim of developing dynamic and globally competitive regional innovation systems. VINNOVA (Swedish Agency for Innovation Systems) offers support for process management and competence development in that specific area. The Centre of Expertise Programme[14] (CoEs, Finland) aims at increasing co-operation between research centres and local companies. There are 14 regional Centres of Expertise and two nation-wide networks carrying out the programme. The programme focuses on selected fields of expertise which are considered to be internationally competitive. One aim is to convey the latest information and know-how to SMEs. The Centres usually base their activities on the services provided by

---

[11] http://www.export.gov.il/eng/
[12] www.tekes.fi/eng
[13] Operated by VINNOVA - http://publiceng.vinnova.se
[14] www.oske.net/in_english

Technology Centres, including project management, marketing, technology transfer, business incubators, patenting, etc.

Another type of support measure that promotes *nurturing* of external tacit knowledge is mentoring. PLATO[15] is a programme of parenthood or mentoring for SMEs, where large enterprises assist, both collectively and individually, smaller firms in the latter's innovation processes.

A different approach of exploiting external tacit knowledge comprises *transferring external knowledge owners* to SMEs, assistance in recruiting external knowledge owners or outsourcing. There are numerous support measures for mobility and recruitment of personnel by SMEs, such as CORTECHS (France) and Knowledge Transfer Partnerships (UK). CORTECHS contributes to the mobility of researchers by supporting the recruitment of a technician, for one year, for the initiation of an innovation project. Knowledge Transfer Partnerships increase interactions between universities and companies. Graduates are recruited to work in a company for two years on a strategically important project in close cooperation with a university. They enjoy enhanced career development benefits, while the SME and the university learn to collaborate. France has similar support measures for young PhDs (CIFRE) from which, over its lifetime, more than 6,000 PhD candidates have benefitted. Both CORTECHS and CIFRE are operated by Anvar[16].

12.4 Usage of Selected KI Support Measures

The usage of support measures by innovative SMEs in the EU is very limited, as the findings of Innobarometer 2004 [4], presented in Table 12.1, show: 15% of smaller (20-500 employees) EU companies received public assistance or subsidies for R&D, 17% obtained public support for training their staff, and only 7 % were supported for collaborative R&D.

Table 12.2. Support measures utilization rate in the EU according to Innobarometer 2004

Support measure	EU25 average utilization rate	Users rating measure as "crucial"
Training	17%	9.6%
R&D	15%	23%
Market research	14%	4.5%
Knowledge networks	13%	12.4%
External advice	10%	11.7%
Collaborative R&D	7%	40.1%

When asked whether a particular programme was crucial to the development of at least one of their innovations, 40% of the companies stated that collaborative

---

[15] www.plato.be
[16] www.anvar.fr

R&D support was crucial to their innovative activities. Thus, collaborative R&D is regarded as crucial to innovation by more companies than traditional support for R&D (40% and 23%) is.

The KINX empirical study (see Chap. 3) consisted of 33 in-depth interviews with NPD managers in 19 SMEs, followed by a large scale questionnaire-based survey with actual participation of 317 SMEs in Germany, the Netherlands, Spain and Israel. Policy-related questions are described in Fig. 12.2.

It may be concluded that - although awareness of support measures is generally high - usage is limited: Only 13% of SMEs use subsidization measures for hiring personnel. Twenty-nine per cent use subsidization schemes for collaborative R&D, and 18% use measures for subsidized knowledge acquisition.

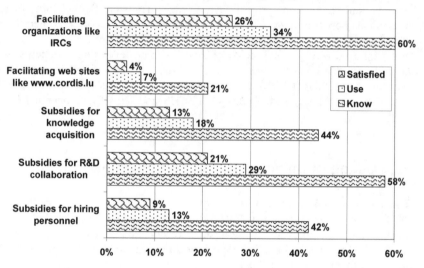

Fig. 12.2. Knowledge of, use of and satisfaction with governmental KI measures

Utilization rate of KI policy measures in SMEs is contingent on many factors. In larger companies, utilization rates are generally higher: Only 21% of smaller SMEs (2-9 employees) in the total sample use measures for R&D collaborations, compared to 38% in larger SMEs. The type of production processes employed is another significant factor determining usage of KI policy measures. Among SMEs with make-to-stock production, the utilization rate of R&D collaboration schemes is 42%, compared with only 22% in SMEs with make-to-order production.

12.5 The Effectiveness of KI Support Measures

The effectiveness of KI support measures may be defined as the overall contribution to the success of innovation processes of SMEs. An objective evaluation of effectiveness is impossible due to limited empirical studies on the topic. We will therefore have to resort to a subjective evaluation of effectiveness. In assessing effectiveness, we shall consider several factors, such as utilization rate by SMEs, satisfaction levels of users, and experts' opinions, provided that such data exists.

There are several groups of support measures, such as cluster programmes, collaborative R&D, mobility programmes, etc., which we have mapped in Sect. 12.3 to knowledge activities (Table 12.1). We shall compare support measures within groups, because they serve similar needs of SMEs, but not between groups. For each group, we present one or more support measures that are effective according to our judgment. Short descriptions of the support measures can be found in Sect. 12.3.

Detection supported by knowledge brokers: Knowledge brokers play an important role in catering to the knowledge needs of SMEs. There are several forms of knowledge brokering support measures, but not many can claim such a widespread acceptance as Syntens: This network of support centers assists some 20,000 SMEs by matching technology needs with technology suppliers. Furthermore, Syntens promotes the creation and development of industrial micro-clusters of SMEs that are jointly developing new products.

Codification supported by technology transfer: Industry Science Relationships (ISRs) in several countries were recently benchmarked by the OECD [12]. A comparison of ISR indicators for 10 countries showed that some countries outperformed others. Finland, for example, leads in several indicators, including the share of innovative manufacturing companies cooperating with universities (47%). From the numerous support measures for ISR, GTS (Denmark) certainly is one of the more successful ones: About a quarter of Danish small companies (with less than 50 employees) used the service, according to a survey held in 1998, and 55% of them were very satisfied. The mission of the GTS institutes is to convert knowledge to value. They accomplish this by working in the borderland between business, science, education and public authorities. The GTS institutes are close to the customers and base their services on their customers´ requirements. Customer-driven services make the GTS unique and distinguish them from other ISRs. An evaluation of the 14 GTS institutes states that "GTS institutes have managed effectively to convert their government grants into technological service at a high level of competence to the benefit of trade and industry and of society in general"[17].

Knowledge transfer supported by education & training: Training support measures tailored specifically to SMEs are rather scarce in Europe. KeBB (the Netherlands) assists SMEs in acquiring knowledge from vocational training organizations. KeBB aims at developing and implementing innovative educational tools, including ICT, for knowledge transfer between companies and vocational training institutions. This programme finances defined knowledge transfer projects that improve education and harmonize it with developments at companies. The fo-

---

[17] Combined performance accounts for 14 GTS institutes -
www.videnskabsministeriet.dk/fsk/publ/2000/performance1999/all_eng.html#usefullness

cus of such projects is to initiate a continuous process of knowledge exchange, not a one-off effort. Projects must be carried out in partnerships that include at least one regional training centre and a company with a direct interest in the availability of well-educated workers with intermediate vocational qualifications. KeBB is differentiated from other education & training programmes in that it encourages vocational training centers to tailor their services to the needs of groups of SMEs. All regional educational centers have taken part in the programme and, in most of the projects, the results were successfully implemented.

Knowledge transfer supported by knowledge sharing networks: There are several benefits arising from cooperation between SMEs, such as economies of scale and economies of scope, sharing of costs and risks, improved ability to deal with complexity and flexibility and efficiency in knowledge management [11]. ILTAM is a good example of knowledge sharing support measures: It supports knowledge sharing among its members, about 85 high-tech companies in the field of electronics, which own the association and pay membership fees in addition to governmental financial support. ILTAM organizes about 40 meetings a year with top experts in electronics from Israel and abroad, and has an advanced information centre. The association also functions as a community of practice with forums in several areas.

Knowledge elicitation supported by collaborative R&D: In general, collaborative R&D programmes involve players from universities and industry, including SMEs. Tekes Technology Programmes (Finland) include 2000-3000 companies and 800 research units. SMEs are getting almost half of the total funds of Tekes. Internationalization is an important factor of the programmes' success, since it is believed to have a positive impact on competitiveness. Thirty-seven per cent of the projects involve international cooperation [16]. Other important success factors of the programme are the bottom-up and top-down planning process, cooperation with all stakeholders in the planning and implementation phases, high motivation and trust among participants, and the willingness to share experience and open dialogue and emphasis on networking and cooperation in R&D projects[18].

Knowledge nurturing supported by cluster programmes: There are cluster programmes in almost every European country, with a large variety of support mechanisms. Finland's Centre of Expertise (CoEs) programme has contributed to the creation of 290 new high-tech firms in 1994-1998 [10]; it is probably one of the most productive programmes. Another effective cluster programme is Clusterland Upper Austria. The programme provides funding for innovative projects performed in specific clusters, thus upgrading local SMEs to? suppliers of larger firms. At present 1,646 companies (85% of which are SMEs), R&D bodies and educational institutes participate in the eight inter-branch clusters. An evaluation of the programme, carried out in 2001 [15], states that "The initiatives have proved to be effective and the results have been persistent and noticeable. They

---

[18] Taken from a presentation by Dr. K. Tilli in a workshop on benchmarking national and regional policies in support of the competitiveness of the ICT sector; 12 November 2004, Brussels

have produced a marked integrative effect on the economy of Upper Austria and have also contributed greatly towards increased self-confidence". Three ingredients are believed to be the key to the programme's success; generous financial provision, predictability and political restraint.

Transfer of knowledge owners supported by mobility schemes: Schemes for encouraging mobility of researchers and experts between universities, large companies and SMEs are prevalent in most countries. According to a recent survey of the OECD [12], such schemes seem to work well for a relatively long time, particularly in France and the UK. CORTECHS (France), for example, has grown from 190 technicians mobilized in 1990 to 370 technicians mobilized in 1999. CIFRE (France) has placed more than 6,000 PhD candidates over its entire lifetime. Furthermore, a comparative analysis of mobility schemes [1] found that 80% of participating enterprises claimed to have benefited from the CIFRE scheme, in particular in terms of increased expertise in conducting in-house research projects. Retention of PhDs after termination of the contract is relatively high at around 75%. Table 12.3 summarizes the main findings about the effectiveness of KI support measures:

Table 12.3. Characterization of effective KI support measures

KI activity and programme	Examples of programme	Indicator for success of programme	Focus of the programme
Detection supported by knowledge brokers	Syntens, the Netherlands, http://www.syntens.nl	Assistance of 20,000 SMEs, creation of clusters	Regional centres providing support to SMEs on technology and innovation
Codification supported by technology transfer from research institutes	GTS, Denmark www.gts.dk	A quarter of Danish small companies used the service, 55% of them were very satisfied.	GTS is the technology transfer office of a network of 11 research institutes involved in knowledge transfer to SMEs
Knowledge transfer supported by education & training	KeBB, the Netherlands, www.senter.nl	KeBB encourages vocational training centers to tailor their services to the needs of groups of SMEs.	The programme finances defined knowledge transfer through education in SMEs
Knowledge elicitation supported by collaborative R&D	Tekes Technology Programmes, http://www.tekes.fi/eng/	The programme includes 2000-3000 companies and 800 research units. SMEs get 50% of the funding	Promotion of the development in specific sectors of technology or industry, and transfer of the research work to the business community=

Table 12.3. Characterization of effective KI support measures (continued)

KI activity and programme	Examples of programme	Indicator for success of programme	Focus of the programme
Knowledge nurturing supported by clusters programmes	Clusterland Upper Austria, http://www.clusterland.at/index_eng.php	1,646 companies (85% are SMEs), R&D bodies and educational institutes are partners, with a distinct contribution to the economy of the region	The programme provides funding for innovative projects performed in 8 specific clusters, upgrading local SMEs as suppliers of larger firms
Transfer of knowledge owners supported by mobility schemes	CIFRE, France, http://www.anvar.fr	80% of participating enterprises benefited from the scheme in terms of increased expertise in conducting in-house research projects.	Grants to PhD students researching applied topics in SMEs under the supervision of a university or public laboratory

12.6 Summary and Recommendations

The utilization rate of innovation KI support measures in Europe is still limited to 7%-15% of the total population of innovative SMEs. The utilization rate of some support measures, in particular those that are crucial for innovation success, such as collaborative R&D, needs improvement.

We have demonstrated that, for each KI activity, groups of existing available support measure can be identified that promote its utilization in SMEs. We have also demonstrated the feasibility of subjectively evaluating the KI effectiveness of innovation support measures for SMEs. Presently employed support measures can provide a good basis for closing the gap between desirable and actual utilization of KI activities for NPD in high-tech SMEs, but offer ample opportunities for improvements with regard to specific KI needs and for the development of new and improved KI policies. When designing measures to support KI for NPD in high-tech SMEs, it should be noted, however, that current research on effective KI support measures is still at an early stage, and more research will be needed in order to be able to develop a scientifically sound comprehensive KI policy for innovative SMEs.

With this limitation in mind, we recommend SMEs to look for KI support measures that best promote their NPD processes. NPD problems regarding explicit, latent or tacit knowledge (see Table 2.4 in Chap. 2) may require the use of different KI activities. When the problem is well defined, one may look for appropriate support measures available from national, regional, and local governments or from the EU. Some very rough guidelines are given below in conclusion.

In the case of explicit knowledge, there are several support measures that can assist SMEs in detection, assessment, codification and transfer of knowledge. For knowledge detection there are knowledge brokers that can help SMEs in locating essential external knowledge (Syntens, the Netherlands). For assessment of external knowledge, there are consultants and organizations that can be of assistance (SKO, the Netherlands). For codification of external knowledge, there are mechanisms of technology transfer from universities to SMEs (GTS, Denmark). Support measures for transfer of external knowledge are more varied, including training & education (KeBB, the Netherlands), and knowledge sharing mechanisms (ILTAM, Israel).

In cases where knowledge is less accessible (latent or tacit), there are support measures that promote knowledge elicitation, knowledge nurturing and transfer of knowledge owners. Support measures for geographic cluster formation and maintenance, such as Clusterland Upper Austria, encourage elicitation and nurturing of external knowledge by SMEs. Collaborative R&D support measures, e.g., Tekes Technology Programmes (Finland), encourage elicitation, codification and transfer of knowledge. For transfer of knowledge owners, SMEs may use mobility mechanisms, such as CIFRE and CORTECHS (France).

References

1. Arnold E, Teather S (2001) People as Vectors of Technological Capability in Technology, Knowledge and Skills Transfer Schemes. Technopolis Group
2. COM (2004) 64 final Report from the Commission to the Council and the European Parliament on the Implementation of the European Charter for Small Enterprises
3. Cowan R, David PA, Foray D (2000) The Explicit Economics of Knowledge Codification and Tacitness. Industrial and Corporate Change 9 (2): 211-253
4. EOS Gallup Europe (2004) FLASH EUROBAROMETER 164: Innobarometer 2004
5. European Commission (2003) Industrial policy in the economic literature: Recent theoretical developments and implications for EU policy. Enterprise Papers No 12, Enterprise Directorate
6. Forsman M, Solitander N (2003) Knowledge Transfer in Clusters and Networks – An Interdisciplinary Conceptual Analysis. Journal of International Business Studies
7. Kingsely G, Malecki EJ (2004) Networking for Competitiveness. Small Business Economics 23: 71-84
8. Leonard D, Rayport JF (1997) Spark Innovation through Emphatic Design. Harvard Business Review 6: 102-113
9. Machlup, F. (1980) Knowledge: Its Creation, Distribution and Economic Significance, Vol. 1, Knowledge and Knowledge Production. Princeton University Press
10. Observatory of European SMEs (2002) Regional Clusters in Europe, No. 3
11. OECD (2001) Innovative Networks: Co-operation in National Innovation Systems
12. OECD (2002) Benchmarking Industry Science Relationships
13. OECD (2004) Networks, Partnerships, Clusters and Intellectual Property Rights: Opportunities and Challenges for Innovative SMEs in a Global Economy. 2nd OECD Conference of Ministers Responsible for SMEs

14. OECD (2004) Promoting Entrepreneurship and Innovative SMEs in a Global Economy, Second OECD Conference of Ministers Responsible For SMEs
15. Ohler F (2001). Evaluation of the Upper Austrian Cluster Initiatives. Abstract, Technopolis Group
16. TEKES (2004) Competitiveness through Internationalization: Evaluation of Means and Mechanisms in Technology Programmes. Technology Programme Report 10, TEKES, Finland

13 Wrapping It All Up - Past, Present and Future of Knowledge Integration

Hans-Horst Schröder

Chair for Business Administration with focus on Technology and Innovation Management, RWTH Aachen University, Germany, schroeder@tim.rwth-aachen.de

13.1 Introduction

Small and medium sized enterprises (SMEs) play a vital role for the competitiveness of the European economy: 99.8 % of the almost 20.5 million enterprises in the European Economic Area (EEA) and Switzerland are SMEs. They employ more than 80 million people, thus providing about two thirds of all jobs in the EEA. SMEs are characterized by their dynamics: Whereas employment in large enterprises has decreased in the past 15 years, SMEs, on balance, have created new jobs [7].

These statements in particular hold true for high-tech SMEs that operate in industries with R&D expenditures well above industry average and develop, produce and market new and improved products and processes based on their R&D activities. Whereas their number is relatively small - about 750,000, i.e., less than 4 % of all EEA enterprises [8] -, their importance for the competitiveness of the European economy can hardly be overrated: Due to their agility and flexibility, they are able to respond very fast to new opportunities, in particular new technological trends. In addition, they contribute to the technological development by further developing new technologies to applicability. Though their growth rates vary considerably due to the high risks involved, on average they outperform low-tech enterprises with respect to both output and employment growth rates [8]. Many economists believe that the wealth of nations and the growth of their economies strongly depend upon their SMEs' performance.

High-tech SMEs are often referred to as knowledge-intensive or knowledge-based firms, indicating that their most important resource - and often their principal product, too - is knowledge. Therefore, an effective and efficient knowledge management on an operational as well as on a tactical and strategic level in these enterprises is crucial.

Whereas the scope of the knowledge management processes and activities in high-tech SMEs, as well as the external environments in which these processes and activities are performed, are much the same as in their larger counterparts, the relative importance of these activities differs. While for large high-tech enterprises the main problem is "to know what they know" and to ensure that the knowledge available in the heads of their employees and in their extensive collections of documents reaches all points of need, identification of available knowledge and its internal distribution is usually not the core problem in high-tech SMEs, especially not in very small ("micros") and small ones. Since employees in these organizations usually know each other personally, they tend to be well informed about each other. Furthermore, there is ample opportunity for face-to-face communication and sometimes even for observing each other's activities and behaviour, thus facilitating the acquisition of other employees´ latent and tacit knowledge. Also, personal knowledge of each other tends to increase mutual trust, thereby improving the conditions for knowledge sharing. Finally, cognitive distance tends to be lower for employees in SMEs, thus increasing the likelihood of successful knowledge transfer, as shown in Chap. 9.

While high-tech SMEs tend to encounter less problems in identifying and distributing the knowledge available, they are usually confronted with serious problems in acquiring the knowledge they need: Due to their limited resources and their low degree of job specialization and professionalism, they tend to have much less internal knowledge than their larger competitors. Furthermore, their scarce resources prevent them from generating the knowledge required in-house. Therefore, *acquisition of external* knowledge, e.g., from customers, suppliers and research institutions, is of utmost importance for them. This explains why this book is not concerned with knowledge management in general, but focuses upon external knowledge acquisition.

Acquisition of external knowledge presupposes the identification of knowledge requirements that cannot be met by internal knowledge, and is triggered by the intention to utilize the knowledge acquired. Thus, identification, acquisition, and utilization of external knowledge form a unity - termed *Knowledge Integration (KI)* throughout this book that deals with knowledge integration theory and practice. The development of the concept of KI has been the main concern of this book. Equally important, it aimed at providing a structured *toolbox* to solve KI problems that occur in the core process in high-tech SMEs: new product development (NPD).

This final chapter serves to determine whether and to what extent these aims have been achieved. Based on this evaluation, which will be carried out in Sect. 13.2, some future requirements and opportunities for improving the KI concept and toolbox presented will be outlined in Sect. 13.3. The chapter - and the book - will close with a short outlook on the future development of KI in Sect. 13.4.

13.2 Evaluation of KI - What Does It Promise and Does It Keep What It Promises?

KI is a *theoretical* concept based on a comprehensive *empirical* investigation of more than 300 SMEs in Germany, Israel, the Netherlands and Spain. It serves as a basis for the development of tools to solve problems that occur during the identification, acquisition and utilization of external knowledge for NPD processes in high-tech SMEs. Thus, three perspectives - a theoretical, an empirical and a tool perspective - may be distinguished for its evaluation. While the first two are mainly reflected in the concept's promises, the last one rather affects its ability to live up to the expectations.

13.2.1 The Theoretical Perspective

KI is a subset of knowledge management (KM) that comprises all activities concerned with transforming and manipulating external knowledge; it includes all processes acting upon knowledge as an input, but excludes all activities where knowledge is the result, as well as activities that merely use knowledge. Within these boundaries, it is extremely broad both with respect to its object - knowledge - as well as to the activities included: As a subset of KM, it has inherited all the features of the concept of knowledge management presented in Chap. 1.

With respect to its objects, KI is not confined to scientific or "true" knowledge, as proposed by Schreyögg & Geiger [19], but encompasses all types of knowledge discussed in Chaps. 1 and 2. In particular, in line with Nonaka & Takeuchi [16], KI includes activities acting upon both explicit knowledge, i.e., knowledge that can and is articulated, and tacit knowledge, i.e., knowledge that neither can be nor is articulated. In addition to this dichotomy, going back to the work of Polanyi [17], KI distinguishes latent knowledge, i.e., knowledge that can be articulated in principle but only with attenuation because it does not come easily to the forefront of one's consciousness (see Chaps. 1, 2 and 4). This distinction is important because the identification, acquisition and utilization of latent knowledge require other tools than the identification, acquisition and utilization of tacit and explicit knowledge do, as shown particularly in Chaps. 4, 6 and 9.

With respect to the activities involved, KI encompasses all pertinent activities on a strategic, as well as on a tactical and operational level (for details, see Chap. 1), and is not restricted to knowledge policymaking, planning, valuation, control and process management, but includes context analysis and knowledge facilitation as well. The broad concept of knowledge used implies that all types of sources differentiated in Chap. 2 may be relevant when external knowledge is identified and acquired.

Also, KI comprises all knowledge media and all utilization contexts with respect to task and industry specificity identified in Chap. 1. Thus, knowledge from human media is included in the concept, such as semiotic and episodic knowledge (c.f. Chap. 5), professional skills, personal ethics and beliefs or knowledge about individual and cultural routines and organizational procedures and decision criteria. Also, knowledge from information technological media, for instance, electronic storage media and architectural elements of knowledge management software systems is covered by KI (see Chap. 1).

The all-encompassing character of KI is intensified by the demand that KI is not confined to its own, internal processes, but also considers the links to regular business processes. Identification and acquisition of external knowledge are no goals of their own, and are only justified when the knowledge acquired is used in business processes, such as NPD. It is therefore indispensable to turn KI into an integral part of all regular business functions.

This very broad approach enabled the inclusion of the manifold manifestations of the multifaceted term "knowledge", ranging from faint inklings to scientifically proven laws of nature. It also raised, however, serious problems, in particular the *arbitrariness problem* and the *problem of methodological support.* The former problem may be circumscribed by the title of Schreyögg & Geiger's paper "If knowledge is everything, maybe in the end, knowledge is nothing?!" [19]; it can be coped with by appropriate assessment and selection procedures. The latter problem arises from the observation that identification, acquisition and utilization of the numerous types of knowledge may require different techniques and tools. It is met by determining the appropriateness of the available tools and techniques for different knowledge types and by developing new ones if required. Meeting this latter demand was the motivation for writing this book, as well as for the KINX project - the results of which are reflected herein.

An important aspect within KI is the distinction between the various *KI activities* superseding the KI phases, which, in turn, support the NPD process of high-tech SMEs. This distinction proved to be indispensable because the problems occurring in KI are not phase-specific, but linked to the various KI activities (for details, see Chap. 2). Furthermore, since KI tools and techniques are, again, not directly related to KI-specific KI problems, but to KI activities, the identification of KI activities facilitates the matching of KI problems (in NPD) with solutions. Finally, the identification of various KI activities is closely related to the distinction between tacit, latent and explicit knowledge as shown in Chap. 4 and modeled in the watermill metaphor described in Chap. 2 and depicted in Fig. 2.3. This way, it contributes to meeting the demand for situation-specific tools and techniques arising from the breadth of the KI concept developed. Fig. 13.1. (next page) visualizes these considerations.

The KI activities - depicted in the watermill model introduced in Chap. 2 - form a solid basis for the identification and solution of problems that high-tech SMEs encounter when they attempt to identify, acquire and utilize knowledge from external sources, from customers, suppliers, research institutions, as well as from public databanks, e.g., patent banks. Thus, the theoretical aim of this book has been attained.

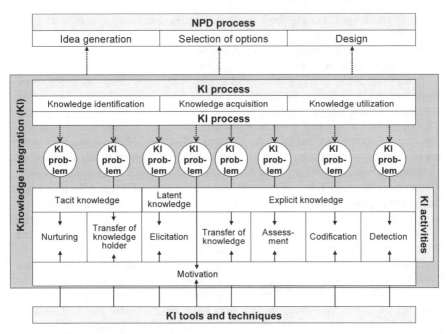

Fig. 13.1. NPD process, KI process and KI activities

13.2.2 The Empirical Perspective

As evidenced by the results of the questionnaire survey of more than 300 European high-tech SMEs presented in Chap. 3, dependence on external knowledge usually is perceived to be low: Whereas almost half of the respondents indicated that they were not - or even not at all - dependent upon external knowledge, only one fifth of them reported that they were strongly or even fully dependent upon external knowledge. These shares did not change significantly between the different phases of the KI process. Interviews conducted with more than 30 NPD managers in 4 European countries (Germany, Israel, Spain and the Netherlands) suggest that the dependence on external knowledge is influenced by the development strategies employed: In push projects, where underused potentials of new technologies trigger the NPD process, more external knowledge is integrated than in pull projects, where market demands set off the development efforts. This conforms to expectations because push strategies usually involve higher degrees of (technical) novelty and therefore require more knowledge.

The interviews furthermore showed that, as a rule, KI is not perceived as a separate process with tools and techniques of its own but as a set of activities that are inextricably interwoven with the NPD process. Though KI activities, in practice, tend to be loosely structured at best, respondents tended to be satisfied with their NPD processes. Yet almost all of them reported problems of varying importance and urgency with their KI processes. There was a slight tendency towards fewer problems with finding the knowledge needed and, in particular, with gaining ownership. However, no clear predominance of certain problems associated with critical KI activities, such as identification of knowledge needs or dissemination and application of externally acquired knowledge, occurred.

Except for some very general techniques and tools, such as brainstorming/informal discussions, documentation procedures, regular meetings, quality systems, e-mail/chatting software, search engines and catalogues (e.g., yellow pages), each of which was used by more than half of the respondents, the utilization rates of techniques and tools for KI were rather low. When respondents were asked why they did not use KI-specific tools and techniques more often, almost 90 % of them answered that they were not aware of any specific techniques and tools that support the acquisition of external technological knowledge; only about two thirds gave this reason for customer/market knowledge. These observations in conjunction with the fact that about 50 respondents indicated that they did not use specific techniques and tools because there were too many of them, suggest that there is little transparency with respect to KI techniques and tools.

This is all the more deplorable since the findings also suggest that those companies that do use specific KI methods and techniques tend, as a rule, to be satisfied with them. More than 95 % of the respondents reporting that they were using mapping software, e.g., indicated that they were satisfied with this tool, and almost 95 % of the users of extranets reported satisfaction. The fraction of satisfied users varied, however, considerably: Only 58 %, respectively 64 %, of the users reported satisfaction with utilizing intelligent agents, respectively external benchmarks. For none of the techniques and tools included, however, were there more users dissatisfied with their use than were satisfied.

Though specific public measures to support KI for NPD in European high-tech SMEs are rare, there is no lack of public programmes that support KI in SMEs, as shown in Chap. 12. Among the measures that promote the acquisition of explicit external knowledge, funding knowledge brokerage services (for discovery of external knowledge), assistance in transferring technology from public research institutions to private companies (for acquisition of external knowledge) and public support of knowledge sharing arrangements (for utilization of external knowledge), for example, deserve mentioning. Among the measures intended to foster the integration of external latent and tacit knowledge, programmes that support the formation of networks and clusters between SMEs and mobility support schemes seem to be particularly effective. The utilization rates of these measures in general are low: Only 7 - 15 % of the members of the respective target groups make use of the programmes. Therefore, and because of the low specificity of the programmes, there is still ample room for improvements.

Summarizing the findings from the empirical perspective, it may be concluded that KI in high-tech SMEs at present is covert. It is not considered to be an activity of its own and, therefore, does not get the attention it deserves. As a result, KI processes in high-tech SMEs tend to be ill-structured. The low degree of KI awareness also leads to an underutilization of KI tools and techniques, which is intensified by the low transparency of the tools and techniques market. Thus, the empirical perspective evidences that KI in SMEs needs improvement.

13.2.3 The Tools Perspective

According to the two basic hypotheses visualized in Fig. 13.1, a) that KI tools and techniques may be distinguished by the KI activities they support, and b) that KI activities are linked to a certain type of knowledge (content) that they operate on, the KI tools and techniques presented in Chaps. 5 to 10 are (indirectly) characterized by the type of knowledge (content) they manipulate and/or transform.

Furthermore, with respect to their prevalent medium, the tools and techniques for KI may be classified as to whether they operate predominantly on human or on information technological *media*, where the latter is taken to include all formal representations of knowledge. This classification also reflects two of the three roots of knowledge management described in Chap. 1 - computer technology/artificial intelligence and human relations/organizational learning. The third root, strategic management, is reflected in the third dimension of the analysis, the management level, that is addressed by the respective management tool or technique. Employing this perspective, techniques and tools are characterized as to whether they are designed to support (primarily) operational or strategic management. Thus, the following analysis of the tools (and techniques) perspective is structured along three dimensions - type of knowledge (content), prevailing medium and management level.

Elicitation, i.e., the articulation of latent knowledge, is the only KI activity that operates on latent knowledge. It serves to transform latent into explicit knowledge and thus enables detachment of knowledge from its individual human carrier. This way, individual knowledge may become organizational knowledge, as well. Since latent knowledge resides solely in human carriers, elicitation is primarily concerned with human media and strongly resorts to psychological processes. It is, however, not limited to human media, because it also involves knowledge interpretation and documentation, as shown in Chap. 5. It may be employed on all management levels, and is particularly applicable for the acquisition of strategic knowledge, as shown in Chap. 8.

Activation of knowledge is the core sub-activity of elicitation and may be supported by a variety of techniques, such as thinking aloud, sorting and probing. In particular, free word association and episodic interviews proved to be effective techniques for knowledge activation, as evidenced by the case study presented in Chap. 5. In addition to activation of knowledge, experts have to be identified, whose knowledge is elicited, and the knowledge articulated has to be captured, interpreted and documented. Expert identification may be achieved by systematically questioning those people, who frequently need a certain type of knowledge, about their preferred knowledge source(s). Interpretation and documentation can be supported by ontology building (for details, see Chaps. 5 and 7). The case study presented in Chap. 5 demonstrates that the utilization of these techniques in high-tech SMEs is possible and effective, though not free of problems.

The KI activities discussed in Chaps. 6 to 9 and their associated tools and techniques are all concerned with explicit knowledge. While the tools and techniques presented in Chaps. 6, 7 and 9 for knowledge codification, knowledge detection and knowledge transfer in networks respectively analyzed KI activities from an operational or tactical level, Chap. 8, knowledge assessment, addressed KI from a strategic view. With respect to the medium considered, Chaps. 6 and 7 are strongly IT-orientated, whereas Chaps. 8 and 9 are human-orientated.

Like knowledge elicitation, *knowledge codification* aims at detaching knowledge from a human source and making it available to others. Unlike knowledge elicitation, however, it is concerned with explicit knowledge only. Rather than specifying the large number of codification styles and targets, distinguished in Chap. 4, Chap. 5 describes a specific variant of structuring - *knowledge mapping,* which so far has been widely neglected in KM. It is shown that knowledge mapping serves two closely related, but distinct functions, structuring knowledge and helping to find knowledge. Maps for knowledge detections aim at the efficient use of knowledge from well-known domains. Maps for knowledge structuring in contrast help to provide a common view and vocabulary and to maintain meta-knowledge about a certain domain. Thus, they enable the codification of mental models and facilitate knowledge assessment. The descriptions of the different types of knowledge maps – concept and mind maps, causal maps, knowledge source maps and knowledge flow maps – clearly give evidence of the wide application area of knowledge mapping. Finally, taking knowledge flow maps as an example, the applicability and usefulness of knowledge mapping for NPD processes in high-tech SMEs is demonstrated. Thus, it is not only shown that knowledge codification goes far beyond alphanumerical data coding for EDP, but also that SME-apt techniques are available to codify fuzzy knowledge that is difficult to articulate.

Knowledge detection, i.e., the intended or accidental identification of potentially useful explicit knowledge, may happen in either of two ways: Whereas knowledge retrieval and knowledge search are employed in order to satisfy given knowledge needs, in the case of knowledge discovery the order is reversed: potentially useful knowledge is detected before a specific need is defined (for details, see Chap. 4). Chap. 7 discusses means to increase the efficiency of knowledge detection the World Wide Web (WWW), thus addressing one of the most challenging KM and KI fields at present. It suggests the use of semantic networks to increase the precision of knowledge detection on the WWW employing search engines. Using ontologies as a specific variant of semantic networks, it shows that utilization of semantic networks may have positive effects both on the effectiveness of queries, i.e., the number of "hits", as well as on their efficiency, i.e., the fraction of hits in the set of responses supplied by the search engine. The fact that the respective case study was conducted in a German high-tech SME evidences the technique's SME-suitability.

Knowledge assessment attaches credibility, value, significance or meaning to explicit knowledge. Chap. 4 argues that this KI activity may be broken down into two sub-activities – identifying the credibility of its source and ascertaining its value for the specific company or; more specifically, for the respective problem solution. Chap. 8 analyses the latter problem, but – driven by the conviction that a specific assessment is strongly influenced by its framework – it does not consider assessment in itself, but rather its framework. Similar to the concept of double-loop learning proposed by Argyris/Schön [1] it scrutinizes the validity of the mental model on the basis of which the meaning, significance and value of knowledge are determined. The decision-validity-tracking (DVT) method developed to this end in Chap. 8 thus is directed towards strategic decision-making which, in turn, implies human (media)-orientation. Implementation of the DVT four-step process – elicitation of the (mostly latent) existing mental model, scenario development, definition of crisp indirect measures (indicators) for each scenario, and model validation by regular monitoring of each scenario's indicators – in an Israeli high-tech SME not only brought the prevailing mental model of the company to the surface, but also provided insight into the model's rigidity and restrictions. This way, it helped to correct misperceptions of relations which were fundamental to the company's operations, and to adapt to changes in its environment. In addition to putting strategic management on a realistic basis, it also indirectly contributed to proper knowledge assessment on an operational level.

The term knowledge transfer has been used throughout this book to mean transit of explicit knowledge from one human source directly to (an) other human(s) (for details, see Chap. 4). It is therefore, by definition, human- (media-) oriented. While it is predominantly used for KI on an operational or tactical level, it may also be employed for strategic KI, depending on the transfer contents and arrangements. Chap. 9 has discussed knowledge transfer in networks, a specific institutional arrangement for the integration of external knowledge, that not only supports mutual knowledge exchange, but also exchange of "sticky" information [23] and even latent and tacit knowledge. Using the WAP project of the University of Twente as an example, it is shown that the appropriateness of knowledge transfer mechanisms strongly depends on the cognitive distance between the partners, also referred to as "downward slope" or "noise" in the information theoretical model of technology transfer [12]. Chap. 9, furthermore, provides evidence of the importance of "maieutics", i.e., close interactioning between the partners involved, for the success of knowledge transfer, particularly if the cognitive distance is high.

Disclosing and sharing knowledge may change power structures and threaten an individual's position within them. Hence, barriers may arise in the KI process, and people have to be *motivated* by being offered incentives in order to overcome those barriers. A specific aspect of this problem, which is at the bottom of KI and crucially affects its effectiveness, is the design and implementation of incentive systems for provision of knowledge about customers, which was investigated in Chap. 10. Based on theoretical arguments and empirical research it was shown that intrinsic and immaterial or non-monetary material extrinsic incentives are crucial for stimulating knowledge provision. In addition, appreciation/awards may be used for remuneration of extraordinary achievements. Furthermore, the definition of KI goals was shown to be an indispensable prerequisite for the design of appropriate incentive mechanisms. Experiences from the implementation of an incentive system for knowledge provision in a German high-tech SME demonstrated the crucial role of top management attitude and behaviour for implementation success.

Fig. 13.2 summarizes the preceding analysis of the tools (and techniques) perspective with respect to type of knowledge (content) and dominating medium:

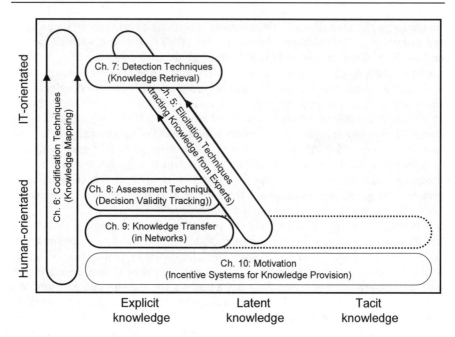

Fig. 13.2. KI tools and techniques for different knowledge types and media

It shows that the techniques and tools presented in this book cover all dimensions employed, with only one exception - the identification, acquisition and utilization of external tacit knowledge. This void has been considered acceptable because there are numerous tools and techniques for knowledge nurturing and transfer of knowledge holders - the KI activities appropriate for tacit knowledge. Since several of these techniques, such as head-hunting for knowledgeable team members and the formation of interdisciplinary project teams with different and complementary qualifications, are well-known and accepted in practice, they have only been touched upon in this book.

Thus, Fig. 13.2 can be interpreted as indicating that scarcity of tools and techniques does not (any longer) hamper effective KI for NPD in high-tech SMEs. Rather, the hypothesis may be stated that the *crucial problem* of KI for NPD in SMEs is lacking knowledge about existing tools and techniques, due to the large number of available KI solutions and the intransparency of the respective KI solutions market. This hypothesis is corroborated by the results of the preceding analyses from an empirical perspective.

The *KINX portal* introduced in Chap. 11 tackles this intransparency problem. It matches the problems SMEs have in KI with the tools and techniques available, and offers SMEs appropriate solutions for their KI problems. By providing information about the adequacy of the proposed solutions for the respective SME and its KI problem, the KINX portal enables enquiring SMEs to make informed decisions about the potential solutions. Furthermore, the KINX portal helps SMEs to identify and define their specific KI problem(s) and offers a platform for the exchange of KI problems and solutions. Finally, it may also be used as an information pool about KI problems of high-tech SMEs in NPD and their solutions.

The KINX portal responds to the major problems that high-tech SMEs encounter in their KI activities, as evidenced by the empirical investigation described in Chap. 3 and summarized in Sect. 13.2.2: By providing information about available tools and techniques, it counteracts the problem of scarcity of information about tools and techniques for KI ("... not aware of any..."), by using the matching mechanism it tackles the problem of overabundance of specific techniques and tools ("... too many of them ..."). Since it is based on the KI theory developed in Chap. 2 and summarized in Sect. 13.2.1, in particular on the definition and distinction of KI activities that represent the reference for both KI problems (see Chap. 2) and KI tools and techniques (see Chap. 4), it rests on solid theoretical grounds.

Summarizing the preceding evaluation of KI from various perspectives, it is concluded that KI

a) rests on a sound theoretical basis,
b) responds to clearly expressed and thoroughly captured needs of high-tech SMEs, and
c) is equipped with a comprehensive arsenal of tools and techniques appropriate for NPD in high-tech SMEs.

Nevertheless, there is ample room for further development and improvement, as will be shown in the next section.

13.3 The Further Development of KI Requirements and Opportunities for Improvement

The future development of knowledge integration can be approached from two perspectives – a conceptual and an instrumental one. Whereas the conceptual perspective is concerned with requirements and opportunities to improve the KI theory, the instrumental perspective views the further development of KI from a tool perspective.

13.3.1 Conceptual Improvements

With respect to its object – knowledge – KI is an extremely broad concept, encompassing such diverse phenomena as knowledge contained in encyclopedias and textbooks, (partly subconscious) knowledge about cultural routines and values, professional skills and personal ethics and beliefs (see Chap. 1). The extremely broad interpretation of the term knowledge, however, implies a *selection problem*, i.e., the necessity to identify true, reliable and useful knowledge and to distinguish it from merely alleged, non-proven "wisdom". This selection problem has gained outstanding importance, in particular against the background of the knowledge explosion within the past two decades.

As well as any other KM concept developed so far, KI cannot offer a ready-made solution for the selection problem. Whereas it offers a framework for the assessment of knowledge - the DVT method - it neither provides a concept or technique for evaluating the credibility of the knowledge source nor a method or technique for assessing the significance, reliability and value of a piece of information. It should be kept in mind, however, that this deficiency is not specific to KI but extends to many concepts dealing with knowledge. There are some suggestions for knowledge assessment methods both on the conceptual level, e.g., the adherence to scientific knowledge or the confinement to knowledge that has been scrutinized by applying widely acknowledge test procedures [19], and on the instrumental level, e.g., the application of balanced scorecards [11], the "Skandia Navigator" [14, 18, 22] and the "Intangible Asset Monitor" [2, 22]. None of them, however, meets the requirements for evaluation methods or has only found wide acceptance so far (see [10]). Thus, further research in this area is urgently needed.

An important distinction for KM is the distinction between individual and organizational knowledge because the transformation of individual into organizational knowledge is at the core of knowledge management in practice. KI does not give this distinction the prominence it deserves but addresses it rather implicitly by the elicitation activity. Explicit consideration of this distinction in all KI activities, therefore, is required.

13.3.2 Instrumental Improvements

Instrumental improvements are required and possible, both with respect to individual tools and techniques and with respect to the KINX portal that assembles them and matches them with KI problems. Focusing upon the former aspect first, two alternatives – improvements to available tools and techniques, in particular to those which have been presented in the preceding chapters of this book, and development of new ones – can be distinguished.

Since most of the techniques described in Chaps. 5 to 10 have only recently been developed, experience with their use so far is still limited. Therefore, little information is available about their effectiveness and efficiency, the conditions which have to be satisfied for their effective application, and the determinants of their impact, for example. Further research is required to support their target-oriented application. Further research is also necessary for the techniques themselves, e.g., research on principles guiding the construction of semantic networks for knowledge detection purposes or research on scenario development and on selection of appropriate indicators to evaluate them for the DVT method.

With respect to the development of new tools, techniques and methods, two types of methods deserve specific attention: methods to transform the plethora of data, stored in public as well as private databases and (almost) universally available via the WWW, into useful knowledge, and methods to support the acquisition of external knowledge within a network arrangement. While the former are directed towards acquisition of explicit knowledge by knowledge detection, the latter facilitate acquisition of latent and sometimes even tacit (in addition to explicit) knowledge. Thus, they are complementary to each other.

Concerning methods and techniques for converting data from databases into knowledge, mining techniques, in particular data and text mining techniques, may offer promising potentials. *Data mining* is a phase within KDD (Knowledge Discovery in Databases), the latter being defined by Fayyad/Piatetsky-Shapiro [9] as "… non trivial process of identifying valid novel, potentially useful, and ultimately understandable patterns in data" (p. 6). It differs from the traditional knowledge retrieval and search activities discussed in Chap. 7 insofar as it does not retrieve/search for specific knowledge (patterns) known to exist and determined beforehand, but for new knowledge (patterns) implicit to the database explored. It may be regarded as a specific variant of discovering codified knowledge that is characterized by its systematic approach based on quantitative techniques. Whereas data mining may offer considerable potentials for KM in general, its potentials for the identification, acquisition and utilization of external knowledge, however, are much lower: Due to its preoccupation with in-house databases, it is a concept for the internal generation of knowledge rather than for its external acquisition.

More recently, the concept of data mining has been augmented to also cover knowledge contained in text documents. This extension, which has been termed *text mining*, offers much more potentialities for KI because – in addition to encompassing the large number of internal documents – it opens up the avenue to the abundance of textual information available on the WWW. First attempts to exploit the opportunities of the WWW by text mining techniques have been undertaken, in particular for technology intelligence purposes (e.g., [13, 15, 20, 21, 24, 26, 27]). As promising as they are, these attempts still suffer from the difficulties involved in translating the results of the analyses from a *syntactic* level (where the analyses are performed) to a *semantic* level (where knowledge resides).

As stated on theoretical grounds in Chap. 1 and substantiated by the case study in Chap. 9, *networking* is an important mechanism for KI. KI by network arrangements, however, also encounters specific problems, above all, the risk of unwanted knowledge drain [25]. Therefore, specific tools and techniques are needed for KI in networks that differ from those required for in-house knowledge provision and knowledge sharing in internal distributed knowledge systems [5], such as intranet-based knowledge platforms [4]. While there are some tools for explicit knowledge, in particular CSCW (Computer Supported Cooperative Work) systems, e.g., Brain Space [3] and eProduct Manager [6], tools and techniques that support the acquisition of external latent and tacit knowledge are rare. Since it is exactly this type of knowledge that might be acquired in networks, but not in other institutional arrangements for knowledge acquisition, further research is required.

Turning to the second aspect of requirements and opportunities for instrumental improvements, two trends may be anticipated for the KINX portal: enhancement by several additional features that increase the users' benefits and transformation into an adaptive system by adding a learning component:

- The solutions offered by the KINX portal are usually on the level of techniques rather than on the level of tools, as distinguished in chap. 4. The utility of the system for the user might be increased by further disaggregating the methods to the tools level wherever possible. Furthermore, links to vendors of appropriate software packages and programs might increase the portal's value for the user. With the same objective in mind, links to consultants and experts in KM and KI might be provided.

- With respect to problem identification and matching the problems identified with the solutions stored, the KINX portal at present is a static system: The algorithms developed for abstracting problems from the users' case descriptions and for matching them with the set of solutions do not respond to the users' degree of satisfaction with the solutions supplied. Since a sound theory for the matching process supported by rigorous empirical tests lacks at present, and the matching rules therefore are essentially heuristic, an adaptive system is needed. Such an adaptive system should be able to learn from the users' reactions to the problem descriptions provided by the portal and, above all, to the solutions offered. To this end, the KINX portal would have to be augmented by a feedback component and a mechanism that links the users' feedback to appropriate modifications of the algorithms employed.

Realization of these further development opportunities will improve both the validity of the KINX matching process and the portal's utility for the user.

13.4 Outlook - The Future of KI

When the KINX project was started, almost four years before publication of this book, KI in high-tech SMEs was impeded by several barriers. As evidenced by the empirical investigations conducted within the KINX project, two barriers stood out: the *awareness barrier*, i.e. the lacking awareness of KI and its peculiarities, and the *methodical barrier*, i.e., the low utilization rate of tools and techniques to support the KI process. The latter was the result of both a technology gap, i.e., a lack of tools and techniques tailored to the needs of high-tech SMEs, and a knowledge gap, i.e., a lack of knowledge about the available tools and techniques due to the low transparency of the market for problem solutions. The KINX project tackled both of these barriers:

- By developing the KI concept, a cohesive concept for the identification, acquisition and utilization of external knowledge, it sets the stage for activities aiming to raise the level of awareness of the importance of integrating external knowledge - an activity that is of crucial importance for high-tech SMEs operating in complex, highly dynamic environments and - far beyond - for the competitiveness of nations. This book may be considered to be a first activity in this direction.
- By developing several new tools and techniques for KI in high-tech SMEs and in particular by developing the KINX-portal, it lays the foundations for overcoming the methodical barrier. The development of new tools and techniques contributes to closing the "technology gap". The KINX portal serves to provide

both knowledge and transparency about the availability of KI tools and techniques. In addition, it helps high-tech SMEs to identify and solve their KI problems, thereby compensating for their lacking expertise in the area of KI.

Thus, the way is paved for the unhampered diffusion of KI among high-tech SMEs, in particular for NPD processes. For the time being, this path is still a cumbersome one to go down, because the KINX portal primarily operates on the technique level and the solutions offered mostly describe general approaches and methods far apart from recipes that can be put to immediate use. The *concept*, however, is attractive and powerful, and well suited to smoothing the way:

- Whenever high-tech SMEs encounter problems in their attempts to acquire external knowledge, they may consult the KINX portal which helps them to identify and to specify their KI problem(s) and which recommends suitable solutions with descriptions of their characteristics and ratings of their suitability, as well as with guidelines for their implementation. Assuming that the portal has been further developed to an adaptive system, as outlined in the preceding section, the solutions recommended are highly responsive to the specific problem situation; furthermore, they are "practice proven", since they are based on the feedback of former portal users. The quality of the solutions recommended, in addition, is increased, due to the further development of present and new tools and techniques.
- Assuming again that the opportunities for instrumental improvement have been exploited, the portal, upon request, also provides information on pertinent tools and their suppliers, experts in the respective problem areas and potentially available public support programs. Furthermore, it offers links to the persons and institutions which might be of use for implementing the recommended solution(s). The selection of these links is geared to the specific situation of the enquirer.

The user interface of the KINX portal employs the language of its users. Therefore, it may be utilized by each employee coming upon a KI problem. Since KI problems occur in any functional area and within any type of activity, it is realistic to expect that KI will not become the domain of specialists but an integral part of each activity of a company. The portal, with the augmented functionality outlined, will enable each employee to find and implement appropriate solutions even if they are highly sophisticated. This way, KI will be an activity inextricably interwoven with regular business activities. It ceases to be a concept of its own and is re-integrated as a cross-sectional function into the regular business activities and processes.

While this vision of the future position of KI may appear to be a simple extrapolation of the situation observed in the empirical investigations described in Chap. 3 it is fundamentally different from the present situation:

- It is based on the awareness of the critical role of KI for (NPD in) high-tech SMEs.
- It fully utilizes the techniques and tools available for KI.

- It uses selection principles fitting to the user's needs and possibilities. Brave New World? Yes, indeed - but a Brave New World that is possible and worth striving for. Thus, it may serve to direct future KI activities. Without doubt, the way to implementation is a long one. The KINX project has been a first step in that direction.

References

1. Argyris C, Schön DA (1978) Organizational Learning: A Theory of Action Perspective. Addison-Wesley Publishing Co., Reading (Mass.)
2. Barchan M (1999) The means of measurement, Conference Proceedings "Wissen managen. Im Fokus: Wissensträger Mensch", Cologne, September 20-22
3. Buesser M, Ninck A (2004) BrainSpace: a virtual environment for collaboration and innovation. International Journal of Technology Management 28 (7/8): 702-713
4. Buniyamin N, Barber KD (2004) The intranet: a platform for knowledge management system based on knowledge mapping. International Journal of Technology Management 28 (7/8): 729-746
5. Chai KH, Gregory M, Shi Y (2003) Bridging islands of knowledge: a framework of knowledge sharing mechanisms. International Journal of Technology Management 25 (8): 703-727
6. Cormican K, O'Sullivan D (2003) A collaborative knowledge management tool for product innovation management. International Journal of Technology Management 26 (1): 53-67
7. European Commission (ed.) (2002a) SMEs in focus. Main results from the 2002 Observatory of European SMEs, ISBN 92-894-4878-4, European Communities: Luxembourg
8. European Commission (ed.) (2002b) High-tech SMEs in Europe. Observatory of European SMEs 2002, No. 6, ISBN 92-894-3583-6, European Communities: Luxembourg
9. Fayyad UM, Piatetsky-Shapiro G, Smyth P (1996) From Data Mining to Knowledge Discovery: An Overview. In: Fayyad UM, Piatetsky-Shapiro G, Smyth P, Uthurusamy R (eds) Advances in Knowledge Discovery and Data Mining, Menlo Park Cal., AAAI Press/The MIT Press Cambridge, Mass., London, pp 1 - 34
10. Gehle M (2005) Internationales Wissensmanagement. Steigerung der Flexibilität und Schlagkraft wissensintensiver Unternehmen im internationalen Wettbewerb. Ph.D. thesis, RWTH Aachen
11. Kaplan RS, Norton DP (1996) Translating Strategy into Action: The Balanced Scorecard, Harvard Business School Press, Boston
12. Kern W (1973) Zur Analyse des internationalen Transfers von Technologien: Ein Erfahrungsbericht. Zeitschrift für betriebswirtschaftliche Forschung 25 (2): 85-98
13. Kostoff RN, Eberhart HJ, Toothman DR (1997) Database tomography for information retrieval. Journal of Information Science 23 (4): 301-311
14. Leithoff T (1999) Anreize für geteiltes Wissen bei Skandia Deutschland, Conference Proceedings „Wissen managen. Im Fokus: Wissensträger Mensch", Cologne, September, pp 20-22

15. Losiewicz P, Oard DW, Kostoff RN (2000) Textual Data Mining to Support Science and Technology Management. Journal of Intelligent Information Systems 15: 99-119
16. Nonaka I, Takeuchi H (1995) The Knowledge-Creating Company. Oxford University Press, New York, Oxford
17. Polanyi M (1966) The Tacit Dimension. Anchor Books, Garden City (NY)
18. Probst G, Raub S, Romhardt K (1999) Wissen managen: Wie Unternehmen ihre wertvollste Ressource optimal nutzen. Frankfurter Allgemeine Zeitung/ Betriebswirtschaftlicher Verlag Dr. Th. Gabler, Wiesbaden
19. Schreyögg G, Geiger D (2003) Wenn alles Wissen ist, ist Wissen am Ende nichts?! Die Betriebswirtschaft 63 (1): 7-22
20. Schröder HH (2004a) Early Information (EI) Based on Knowledge Discovery in Databases (KDD). In: Albers S. (ed) Cross-functional Innovation Management. Perspectives from Different Disciplines. Gabler, Wiesbaden, pp 121-138
21. Schröder HH (2004b) Marrying Knowledge Discovery in Databases (KDD) with Technology Intelligence (TI) - Avenue to Paradise or Blind Alley?. In: Xie M, Durrani TS, Tang HK (eds) Innovation and Entrepreneurship for Sustainable Development, 2004 IEEE International Engineering Management Conference, 18-21 October 2004, Singapore, Proceedings, Vol. 1, pp 276-282
22. Sveiby KE (1998) Wissenskapital - das unentdeckte Vermögen: Immaterielle Vermögenswerte aufspüren, messen und steigern. Verlag Moderne Industrie, Landsberg a. Lech
23. von Hippel E (1994) "Sticky Information" and the Locus of Problem Solving. Management Science 40 (4): 429-439
24. Watts RJ, Porter AL (2003) R&D cluster quality measures and technology maturity. Technological Forecasting & Social Change 70: 735-758
25. Weisenberger-Eibl MA (2003) Interaktionsorientiertes Agentensystem. Zeitschrift für Betriebswirtschaft 71 (2): 203-220
26. Zeller A (2003) Technologiefrühaufklärung mit Data Mining. Deutscher Universitäts-Verlag, Wiesbaden
27. Zhu D, Porter AL (2002) Automated extraction and visualization of information for technology intelligence and forecasting. Technological Forecasting & Social Change 69: 495-506

Biographical Information about the Authors

Charo Elorrieta M.Sc., is a manager and consultant with SOCINTEC (Grupo Azertia). She has worked for over ten years in the field of business and ICT and has substantial experience in helping small and medium sized companies to establish practical KM solutions that range from overcoming organizational and cultural barriers for knowledge sharing to implementing enterprise content management tools. In her work, Charo focuses on improving organizational performance from a business perspective, using ICT as an important enabler.

Doron Faran is a co-partner at Net Knowledge, a KM consulting firm, and a lecturer at Ort Braude Academic College (Department of Industrial Engineering and Management), both in Karmiel, Israel. Formerly a senior IDF Intelligence Officer, he is vastly experienced in information and knowledge management. His interests cover knowledge management, organizational learning and competitive intelligence. Doron gained his Master's degree in Social Studies from Tel-Aviv University.

Dina Franzen graduated in business administration in 2002. She is a scientific employee with the Chair of Technology and Innovation Management at RWTH Aachen University and is currently working on a Ph.D. dissertation on ontology-based knowledge acquisition. Her research interests include cognitive psychology, knowledge representation, knowledge management and Internet-based knowledge acquisition.

Aard Groen is the institute director of NIKOS, the Dutch Institute for Knowledge Intensive Entrepreneurship at the University of Twente. Aard holds a Ph.D. in Business Administration from the University of Groningen and an M.Sc. in Public Administration from the University of Twente. His research interests include high-tech entrepreneurship in networks, development of social system theory and business development support systems in a university-industry context.

Aharon Hauptman holds a Ph.D. degree and M.Sc. in Engineering from Tel-Aviv University (1986) and a B.Sc. from the Technion (Israel Institute of Technology). Since 1988, he has been a senior researcher at the Interdisciplinary Center for Technology Analysis and Forecasting (ICTAF) at Tel-Aviv University, specializing in technology foresight, technology assessment, knowledge management and evaluation of trends in emerging technologies.

Antonie Jetter worked for a high-tech entrepreneurial company before she graduated in business administration from RWTH Aachen University. She joined the Chair of Technology and Innovation Management at RWTH Aachen University in 1998 and has since been involved in various research projects. She completed her doctoral dissertation on the "fuzzy front end of innovation" in 2004. In line with her work with KINX, her research interests also include knowledge management and small and medium sized enterprises

Jeroen Kraaijenbrink is a Ph.D. candidate at the MIS Department at the University of Twente, the Netherlands. He holds an M.Sc. in Industrial Engineering and Management, and an M.A. in Public Administration from the University of Twente. His research interests include knowledge integration, inter-organizational knowledge management, and innovation, in particular in small and medium sized enterprises.

Juan Pedro Lopez gained a degree in industrial engineering from ICAI in 1995. Since 2000, he has been a Senior Consultant at SOCINTEC (Grupo Azertia). and has been working on various projects on IT planning and implementation and on studies regarding the information society and regional strategies for innovation and technology transfer. Before joining SOCINTEC, he worked for the CEMEX Group as a project engineer, as an IT specialist for systems for plant automation and control, and as an assessor in the operational area.

Yoel Raban, Senior Research Fellow, ICTAF.
Dr. Raban has a Ph.D. in Marketing from the Leon Recanatti Graduate School of Business Administration, and an M.A. in Economics from the Eitan Berglas School of Economics, Tel Aviv University. He has extensive research and consulting experience in the area of socio-economic impacts of technology. His research interests include social networking, economics of collaborative innovations, knowledge management and foresight management.

Hans-Horst Schröder studied business administration at the universities of Hamburg, Cologne and at Northwestern University (Evanston, Ill.). In 1973, he obtained a Ph.D. from the University of Cologne. He worked with the University of Cologne until 1992, when he became head of the Chair of Technology and Innovation Management at RWTH Aachen University. He has written more than 50 books and articles in the fields of business administration, industrial engineering and technology and innovation management. His current research focuses upon decision support systems in R&D, business and technology intelligence systems, knowledge management, and innovation climate and culture.

Fons Wijnhoven has an M.Sc. in Research Methodology and a Ph.D. in Management. He is an associate professor of knowledge management and information systems at the Faculty of Business, Public Administration and Technology of the University of Twente, and an associate of the national research school BETA. In the last decade, over thirty of his articles have appeared in international academic journals and books. His current research focuses on the support of knowledge sharing among firms, the creation of information markets, and the development of information services.

Hannah Zaunmüller has recently received a doctoral degree from the Faculty of Economics and Business Administration, Chair of Technology and Innovation Management at RWTH Aachen University. Her dissertation on incentive systems in knowledge management was based on research work carried out with KINX. Hannah holds an M.Ec. from Maastricht University in the Netherlands.

List of Authors' Addresses

Elorrieta, Charo
  SOCINTEC
  Mayor, 10-5° plta., 48930 Las Arenas
  Spain
  +34 9 44 80 02 11
  Celorrieta@socintec.es

Faran, Doron
  Net Knowledge Ltd.
  PO Box 1036, 36 Haharohet St., 20100 Carmiel
  Israel
  +972 49 52 24 99
  dfaran@net-knowledge.co.il

Franzen, Dina
  RWTH – Aachen University of Technology
  Lehrstuhl für Betriebswirtschaftslehre mit Schwerpunkt
  Technologie- und Innovationsmanagement (TIM)
  Templergraben 64, 52056 Aachen
  Germany
  +49-241-80 96659
  franzen@tim.rwth-aachen.de

Groen, Aard, Prof.
  Nikos (Dutch Institute for Knowledge Intensive Entrepreneurship)
  University of Twente
  Postbus 217, 7500 AE Enschede
  Netherlands
  +31-53-489 2885
  a.j.groen@utwente.nl

Hauptman, Aharon, Dr.
  Interdisciplinary Center for Technological Analysis and Forecasting (ICTAF)
  Tel-Aviv University, 69978 Tel Aviv
  Israel
  +972 3 6 40 75 80
  haupt@post.tau.ac.il

Jetter, Antonie, Dr.
RWTH – Aachen University of Technology
Lehrstuhl für Betriebswirtschaftslehre mit Schwerpunkt
Technologie- und Innovationsmanagement (TIM)
Templergraben 64, 52056 Aachen
Germany
+49-241-80 93541
jetter@tim.rwth-aachen.de

Kraaijenbrink, Jeroen
University of Twente
School of Business, Public Administration and Technology
P.O. Box 217, 7500 AE Enschede
Netherlands
+31-53-489 5367
j.kraaijenbrink@utwente.nl

López, Juan Pedro
SOCINTEC
C/ Hermanos Pinzón, 4. 1º., 28036 Madrid
Spain
+34 15622524
jplopez@socintec.es

Raban, Yoel, Dr.
Interdisciplinary Center for Technological Analysis and Forecasting (ICTAF)
Tel-Aviv University, 69978 Tel Aviv
Israel
+972 3 640 75 72
raban@post.tau.ac.il

Schröder, Hans-Horst, Prof.
RWTH – Aachen University of Technology
Lehrstuhl für Betriebswirtschaftslehre mit Schwerpunkt
Technologie- und Innovationsmanagement (TIM)
Templergraben 64, 52056 Aachen
Germany
+49-241-80 93577
schroeder@tim.rwth-aachen.de

Wijnhoven, Fons, Prof.
  University of Twente
  School of Business, Public Administration & Technology
  P.O. Box 217, 7500 AE Enschede
  Netherlands
  +31-53-489 3853
  a.b.j.m.wijnhoven@utwente.nl

Zaunmüller, Hannah, Dr.
  RWTH – Aachen University of Technology
  Lehrstuhl für Betriebswirtschaftslehre mit Schwerpunkt
  Technologie- und Innovationsmanagement (TIM)
  Templergraben 64, 52056 Aachen
  Germany
  +49-241-80 96659
  zaunmueller@tim.rwth-aachen.de

Index

Printing: Krips bv, Meppel
Binding: Stürtz, Würzburg